The Author

David Thornton is one of the most-respec
works include the authoritative book Le
comprehensive history of the city. The holder of a doctorate from
the University of Leeds for a thesis on Leeds history, he lectured on
the subject for many years. Born and bred in Leeds he was head
teacher of both Royal Park and Holt Park Middle Schools during
his teaching career in the city. He was a contributor to the *Yorkshire
Evening Post* for ten years. Dr Thornton is also a leading member of
the Thoresby Society, the oldest historical society in the city.

GREAT LEEDS STORIES

David Thornton MPhil, PhD

FORT PUBLISHING LTD

First published in 2005 by Fort Publishing Ltd,
12 Robsland Avenue, Ayr, KA7 2RW

Printed by Bell and Bain Ltd, Glasgow

Cover photograph: 'Meeting Place' by Haywood Magee, from the
magazine *Picture Post*, 5 February 1949. The happy couple are Sheila
Young and Terry Duffy, meeting at the stone circle on the pavement of
the Victoria Arcade outside Schofields. The *Picture Post* caption was:
'You meet everyone in the Arcades'. Schofields was a leading
department store in Leeds, known for its exclusivity. It has been closed
for many years. (Photograph courtesy of Getty Images.)

Graphic design by Mark Blackadder

Typeset by Senga Fairgrieve (0131-658-1763)

ISBN 0-9544461-9-4

For

Lorna Walker,

Ellen Fahey

and

Brian Chippendale

CONTENTS

PREFACE

Some years ago, when I was writing *Leeds: the Story of a City*, I set out to tell the history of the town as a continuous narrative and place its individual story against the unfolding drama of British history. I wrote then that I hoped people would see it as a 'guidebook of a journey that points out certain places to visit, certain sights to see'. Here in *Great Leeds Stories* I have looked again at some of those sights but examined them now in greater detail. For example, how did the people of Leeds react to that awful tragedy at a Wortley Sunday school when eleven children were burnt to death on the night of New Year's Day, 1891; how did Leeds folk face the devastating influenza epidemic of 1918 which wreaked such havoc in the town; how did people cope when the bitter winter of 1947 brought the city to a standstill?

But history is not simply what happened in the long-gone past. Yesterday's news is tomorrow's history and so events that happened only twenty-five years ago are included because they reflect aspects of life in late twentieth-century Leeds and are subjects with which historians of the future need to be familiar. How traumatic was it for its citizens when the horrific episode of the Yorkshire Ripper spread fear across the city? What lay behind the race riots of the 1970s and 1980s in the city? Just how damaging to the image of the town was the football hooliganism associated with Leeds United supporters?

No subject should be too insignificant if we are truly to understand the lives of the people of this city and the issues that occupied their minds. They asked what has Boar Lane and Swinegate to do with pigs? Why is Cardigan Road named after a woolly jumper? The answer in each case is nothing whatsoever! Why

Leeds streets have the names they have may be trivia but it is trivia that fascinates people. And other trivial issues – the humble parcel of fish and chips wrapped up in an old newspaper or carrying a bucket of water down the street to flush the privy when the cistern froze in winter – were looked upon in their time as mere trivialities and yet today give an intriguing insight into the everyday experiences of so many Leeds people.

Some of these stories are tinged with a certain nostalgia for me. Life in the back-to-backs brings back memories of living in Tadcaster Street off Tong Road, the place where I was born. In writing of fish and chips I recollected my aunt and uncle who owned the Addingham fish and chip shop in West Leeds. Researching the Home Guard evoked fond memories of my father who served in Number 4 platoon based on Whingate Road. In the chapter on Leeds authors, I quoted Alan Bennett's *Writing Home* where he remarked, 'Mr Chamberlain's broadcast found us on a tram going down Tong Road into Leeds'. I vividly remember that Sunday, 3 September 1939 and being taken on a similar tram going down Tong Road – perhaps the same tram – though I was more reluctant to be there than Alan Bennett. I was being taken to Mason's, the local dentist, for emergency treatment.

The winter of 1947 is etched on my mind not so much because schools had to close for lack of fuel but because it was the only winter I can ever remember when the snow was deep enough for us to build igloos in the streets and, like Barbara Taylor Bradford, I too queued up in Armley at our local cinema, the Pictodrome – though to us it was simply the Drome.

For those readers who wish to pursue the subjects in this book further, Leeds City Libraries and Leeds City Local and Family History Library are excellent sources of information, as is the Thoresby Society. The most informative books on the history of the city are: *A History of Modern Leeds* edited by D. Fraser (Manchester 1980); S. Burt and K. Grady: *The Illustrated History of Leeds* (Derby 1994); A. Heap and P. Brears, *Leeds Describ'd; Eyewitness Accounts of Leeds 1534–1905*; and *Leeds: the Story of a City* (Ayr, 2002). Other more specialist books the reader may find useful are; J. Thompson, *Leeds*

Born and Bred (Clapham, 1982); G. Priestland, *Frying Tonight – the Saga of Fish and Chips* (1972); M. Wright, *Armley Gaol 1864 to 1961, the Execution Era* (Leeds, 2003); and B. Nelson, *The Woollen Industry of Leeds* (Leeds 1980).

The first draft of history appears in our newspapers and Leeds is fortunate in that historians have many local ones available to help us. These include: *Armley and Wortley News, Chapeltown News, Leeds Daily News, Leeds Evening Express, Leeds Intelligencer, Leeds Mercury, Leeds Other Paper, Leeds Weekly Citizen, Yorkshire Evening News, Yorkshire Evening Post* and *Yorkshire Post.* They are all available in the Local and Family History Library.

I have been fortunate that once again friends, acquaintances and professional organisations have helped me. Those individuals include; Nellie Atha, Peter Bardon, Pam Boyd, Mabel Buckle, Anna Burke, Bob Carrington, Dorothy Chippendale, Jack Carter, Al Clark, Etta Cohen, David Durkin, Dennis Edmondson, Margaret Elphick, Brenda Gill, Lawrence Gosney, Hilda Hampshire, Martin Harrison, Andrew Houseman, Stuart Ivinson, Charles H. Jackson, Sam Kendrick, Winnie Kendrick, Ann Kirk, Mahendrakumar Mistry, Howard Martell, Guy Missett, Mick Rainford, Simon Reid, Duncan Semmens, Bill Shackleton, John Spencer, Maureen Stansfield, Victor Teasdale, Andrew Thornton, Jack Thornton, Ethel Vine and David Wanless. There is also the institutions; the *Birmingham Post & Mail* Ltd, Bournemouth Reference Library, *Bournemouth Evening Echo*, the Duke of Wellington's Regimental Museum, Hancocks jewellers, Harry Ramsden's (Restaurant) Ltd, the King's Own Yorkshire Light Infantry Museum, Leeds Local and Family History Library, Leeds Trades Union Council, Leeds United AFC, the National Fish Fryers' Federation, the Prince of Wales's Own Regiment of Yorkshire Museum; the Royal Armouries, the Second World War Experience Centre, the Thoresby Society, Town Centre Securities, the University of Leeds, West Yorkshire Archive Service, West Yorkshire Police, and Yorkshire Television.

I am also indebted to my publisher, James McCarroll, for his advice and suggestions, and particularly to Lorna Walker, Ellen

Fahey, Brian Chippendale and my wife, June, for all their help and encouragement. Like any author, I must acknowledge that any mistakes in the book are mine and mine alone; in doing so I take consolation in G. B. Shaw's comforting words, 'A life spent in making mistakes is . . . more useful than a life spent doing nothing.'

David Thornton
Leeds 2005

1

WHAT'S IN A NAME?

Where can we find out about the history of Leeds? The city boasts one of the finest and most accessible local-history libraries in the country. It also has the Thoresby Society and numerous local history groups that offer lectures and produce publications, while authors over the years have produced a mountain of books on the subject. Plaques on the walls and memorials in churches all make their contribution. Yet so often the most valuable source about Leeds and its past is ignored. People walk around, their eyes firmly fixed on shop windows, and never look up to see the magnificent buildings above them. Each of these buildings has a tale to tell; each of its streets tells a story.

Kirkgate is the oldest of those streets. It was here that the original village of Leeds was established and the church there became the focal point of the community sometime during the sixth or seventh centuries. From here, the settlement, no more than a straggle of wooden huts, sprawled north-east. The old Viking words *kirkja* meant church and *gat* meant a passage or way to. The street was simply the way to the church, the kirkgate, though Leeds people always refer to it simply as *kergit*. At the top of this street is Vicar Lane. The vicarage stood here from about the fifteenth century until two covered markets were built on the site; one in 1857, and the present one between 1903 and 1904. It was also in a house in Vicar Lane that Alice Musgrave developed bubonic plague in 1645 and heralded one of the worst disasters the town has ever faced.

Running down to the river from Kirkgate is Call Lane where this street meets the Calls. The Calls runs parallel to the river and was at one time a pathway flanked by orchards and open fields where tenter frames were built to dry the locally made cloth. It may well be that *Calls* comes from the Latin *callis* meaning a footpath. The origin of a word, however, is sometimes uncertain and the unwary can often draw the wrong conclusion. That frequently happens regarding both Boar Lane and Swinegate. Neither has anything to do with pigs!

Swinegate probably originates from the word *swein* meaning someone living in the countryside as opposed to a town or borough. Certainly that area was outside the newly established borough of Leeds, which Maurice Paynel had created in 1207. The new Leeds stood in Briggate some distance from the old village that ran down Kirkgate. Boar Lane led to that new settlement but had a variety of spellings. It was originally Bore Layne in 1575, then Boar Lane in 1591 and Bowre Lane in 1594. This last name is said by some experts to reflect the Norse word *bor* meaning a farmstead. Others, however, believe that as peasants were referred to in medieval times as *bore-men*, men of the borough, Boar Lane was the lane that led to the new borough. Thus it was that the parcels of farming land known as tofts, which these men of the borough acquired some way from the new development, were known as the borough men's tofts, the area around what is now Burmantofts Street.

Paynel, then, developed his new town on Briggate, the street that led down to the river. As this new street was the way to the bridge it was known as the *brig-gat*. It was here that the famous cloth market Daniel Defoe described in about 1720 was held each week and where, in 1643 during the Civil War, Briggate echoed to the sound of muskets and cannon-fire as Roundheads and Cavaliers fought to gain possession of the town.

In medieval times, Paynel built himself a fortified manor house roughly where today Bishopgate Street and Boar Lane meet. Beyond his manor house, stretching to the north-west, was his huge hunting park. Park Row, Park Square, Park Place and Park Lane – the original road to Bradford – each act as reminders of it. Park Row became the great banking centre in Leeds. When it was originally built in the 1770s it was intended to make it part of a residential square for middle-class occupants incorporating both South Parade and East Parade. But the plan was never realised. Park Square, however, begun in 1788, was completed as a square in 1810. The most fashionable and desirable of all addresses was Park Place, also laid out in 1788 but offering extensive views of the open fields down to the river Aire.

Running south from Boar Lane lies Mill Hill, without doubt one of the most descriptive streets in the city. It is certainly on a hill, sloping down towards the river and there on the water's edge the town's great corn mill stood. It was significant enough in 1086 for the commissioners compiling the Domesday Book to mention it. But it did not remain the only mill in the area. In about 1560 Thomas Falkingham decided to build a mill by Sheepscar Beck. It led to a legal dispute with the miller of the original mill in Leeds. As a result the first map of the borough was drawn up to show the location to the judge. The incident left behind a memento in the area, the name Millgarth Street.

There are other echoes of medieval Leeds still to be seen. Basinghall Street was originally known as Butts Lane, the site of the archery butts of the town. In 1826 its name was changed but Butts Court remains to remind us of the activities that went on nearby. Less-innocent antics occurred in Mabgate. A *mab* was a woman of loose morals, so in all probability that area was the red-light district of Leeds in the Middle Ages. Lady Lane, however, was much more respectable. Here in medieval times stood the chantry chapel of Our Lady. Later the town's workhouse was built on the north end of the lane and it was also here in 1790 that Roman Catholics established their first church in Leeds after the Reformation.

From Lady Lane and running westwards is the Headrow, which marked the northern end of the old township. Until 1924 it was no more than a narrow lane but then the council decided to widen it and create an impressive east-to-west thoroughfare. Sir Reginald Blomfeld was employed to design a single style for all the buildings on the newly replaced north side. The road had originally been known as the Upper and Lower Headrows. Some councillors wanted the new highway's name to be changed to Kingsway but, in 1929, it was decided to retain a link with the past and it became known as the Headrows. Only a few years later, however, the final s was dropped. This impressive street runs in front of the equally impressive Leeds town hall, opened by Queen Victoria in September 1858. The area immediately in front of the building is known as Victoria Square and from 1906 until 1937 a statue of the Queen stood there until it was moved to Woodhouse Moor.

At the junction of Woodhouse Lane and the Headrow are found Fountaine Street and Wormald Row. Here the clothing magnates, Joseph Fountaine and Thomas Wormald, had their warehouse and employed a young Benjamin Gott in their counting house. He eventually became the firm's owner, built the massive Park Mills where he brought together all the processes of woollen cloth manufacture and became one of Europe's largest employers. Gott, however, is not commemorated in central Leeds. Gotts Park Avenue is found in Armley near where his once-palatial home and extensive estate stood. It is now enjoyed by the Leeds public as Gott's Park.

Another Leeds luminary who well deserved to have a street named after him was John Harrison. He was one of the greatest benefactors the town has known providing it with a new market cross, the magnificent St John's church in 1634 and, ten years earlier, a new grammar school which he built near the site of the present Grand Theatre. Harrison Street there, like his statue in City Square, is a daily reminder of this great Leeds man. One of Harrison's legendary acts of charity, it is said, was to no less a person than Charles I. In 1647, Parliamentarian troops brought Charles as a prisoner to Leeds en route for London. They kept him overnight in John Metcalfe's newly built Red Hall on the Upper Headrow. Harrison called on the King and, ostensibly, offered him a tankard of Leeds ale; the tankard was in fact, filled with gold coins. Red Hall has long since disappeared but King Charles Street, approximately where Red Hall stood, is a twenty-first century reminder of an act of kindness made some 350 years before. Wade Lane, however, though frequently linked with field marshal Wade – who commanded the army that stayed in Leeds during the 1745 Jacobite rebellion – has nothing to do with the great soldier. Though his army was encamped between Sheepscar and Woodhouse, the thoroughfare had borne that name as early as 1677.

Running westwards from City Square is Infirmary Street where the original Leeds General Infirmary stood. It was opened there in 1771 but moved to its present site on Great George Street in 1868. The council then used the old building by locating the first central and reference libraries there. Just above Infirmary Street is found South Parade. In 1826 the Baptists opened a fine new church with a school-room on the street. However, by the end of the nineteenth century the population drift from the town centre to the northern suburbs had begun. The Baptists built themselves a new church in North Lane at Headingley. They retained the name of their church and so the road adjoining it became known as South Parade some two to three miles from its original location. Another place of worship giving its name to a street was St Philip's Roman Catholic church at Middleton. Originally the Catholics there had no building in which to hold services. When the Anglicans decided to close St Philip's – their church on Wellington Street – the Catholics bought the complete edifice and re-erected it at Middleton. Stone by stone the building was carried up the steep incline to Middleton and reconstructed there in 1934. The street where it was built became St Philip's Avenue.

Travelling north from Middleton is Belle Isle Road leading down to Leeds city centre. The whole of this area was rich in coal deposits and the medieval miners of Leeds and district used the simple technique of digging small bell-pits in order to extract it. According to some authorities, it was these bell pits that gave the district the name of Belle Isle. Intersecting Belle Isle Road is Windmill Road and nearby Windmill Approach, routes that reflect the siting of the old windmill which operated there in the past. Windmill Court and Windmill Rise at the junction of Silver Royd Hill and Blue Hill Lane in West Leeds again reflect the fact that the local windmill stood in the vicinity on a prominent hill overlooking the old townships of Armley and Wortley.

Holbeck, another of the ancient townships of Leeds, is rich in street names. The place was famous for its pure water. Sellers transported it to supply customers in Leeds while visitors to the township in the 1820s enjoyed the hot and cold baths it offered. Bath Street reflects this and runs parallel to Marshall Street. Here John Marshall set up his linen factory in 1792 and established what would become the centre of the British flax industry. The later mill he built between 1838 and 1840 is based on the ancient Egyptian temple of Horus at Edfu. It was reputed to contain the largest room in the world and had a flock of sheep grazing on its roof. Parallel to Marshall Street runs Foundry Street. This was the site of Matthew Murray's famous Round Foundry which saw the great engineer build the world's first commercially viable steam locomotives for Middleton colliery. Thousands turned out to see the test run across Hunslet Moor in 1812 and, in 1816, the Grand Duke Nicholas, the future Czar of Russia, paid a visit to the factory.

He may well have been familiar with the products of nearby Leeds Pottery, established in 1770 in Jack Lane, Hunslet. Its famous and distinctive creamware was exported to Russia as well as to Germany, France, Spain, the Netherlands and the growing colonies of the British Empire. Pottery Road off Jack Lane evokes memories of the works. If Leeds Pottery had an international reputation so too had Hugh Gaitskell, who was the Labour MP for South Leeds and also the leader of the opposition at Westminster. His name appears in the area in both Gaitskell Court and Gaitskell Walk. He was one of Britain's most respected politicians and his unexpected death in 1963, which some historians believe was brought about by the KGB, deprived the nation of a potentially great prime minister.

There were other famous historical figures associated with the town who gave their names to several streets and roads. By the close of the eighteenth century the wealthy and powerful Brudenell family held vast estates across the country including land in south Headingley. Brudenell Road – and a series of other streets bearing the name – identifies these early owners. But since 1661 the Brudenells had also been earls of Cardigan. In 1888 the Cardigan estate in Leeds came up for sale and lot 17a achieved international fame. The Leeds Cricket, Football and Athletic Company bought the land and built a sports ground that catered for cricket, rugby, association football, bowls, athletics, tennis and cycling. The Headingley ground opened in 1890. The new road built outside became Cardigan Road, perpetuating forever the family of the man who led the infamous Charge of the Light Brigade at Balaclava and gave us the knitted woollen waistcoat known as the cardigan.

Before Cardigan Road was built a large part of the area through which it later ran was the site of the Leeds Zoological and Botanical Gardens, which opened in 1840. The only visible sign of the place today is the Bear Pit. The owner, Thomas Clapham, eventually sold the grounds and opened another pleasure garden near Woodhouse Moor. The Royal Park, as it was known, offered various attractions such as a skating rink, bandstand and greenhouses. Its name lives on in Royal Park Road, Royal Park View and Royal Park Mount.

Across Woodhouse Moor runs Rampart Road. At the time of the Roman invasion the Iron Age tribe, the Brigantes, built themselves defensive works in the area at Gipton, Temple Newsam, Chapel Allerton and very probably on Woodhouse Moor. The first three are still visible but it appears that the large rectangular earthwork that stood on the Moor was obliterated during the nineteenth century. However, Rampart Road, which still runs across it, may well indicate the ramparts of that long-lost fortification. Beyond Woodhouse Moor eastwards is Scott Hall Road. In medieval times the Scott family lived in Scott Hall at Potternewton. They were well-known benefactors in the Leeds area during the Middle Ages. In 1453, William Scott gave the house and garden which eventually became the vicarage for Leeds parish church.

The earls of Cardigan were not the only aristocratic landowners in Leeds. Two others, the earls Mexborough and Cowper, each held substantial estates in the parish. Their property covered lands at Potternewton and Chapel Allerton, which were then merely rural villages while their land at Chapeltown was nothing more than rolling farmland. As the burgeoning town of Leeds began to expand

and the successful middle classes sought relief from the pollution and congestion of the town, a drift to the northern suburbs began. The lords Mexborough and Cowper eagerly seized the opportunity to exploit the value of their properties by offering to sell their land for building.

To ensure that the new housing development – which became Chapeltown – retained a residential aspect the fifth Earl Cowper, Louis Francis, insisted that no mills or factories should be built there. Cowper Street, Louis Street and Francis Street were named after him. Similarly, Mexborough Street, Mexborough Grove and Mexborough Avenue each bear the name of the earls of Mexborough, the Irish title borne by the Savile family of Yorkshire. The Mexboroughs had been active politicians for several centuries with their estates based in Yorkshire at Methley Park, Arden Hall, Helmsley and Leeds. It was another branch of the Savile family that provided the first alderman of Leeds in 1626.

Just south of Chapeltown is Barrack Road. Following the Peterloo massacre in Manchester in 1819, the government was concerned about civil disorder, perhaps even revolution, breaking out across the country. To combat this threat a cavalry barracks on an eleven-acre site was established at Buslingthorpe. Barrack Road runs through its old parade ground. The continuation of Barrack Road is Round-hay Road. A hay was a hedge. In medieval times a circular hedge had been established to cut off an area stretching from Oakwood to Shadwell and Seacroft in order to form a royal hunting-enclosure. It was a round hay.

North of Roundhay lies the district of Allerton. The series of roads and streets – including Allerton Grange Rise, Allerton Grange Way and Allerton Grange Walk – record the fact that the Cistercian monks from Kirkstall Abbey had located there one of the many sheep granges, or farms, that they ran in the Leeds area. One of these granges lay to the east at Seacroft where Seacroft Avenue and Seacroft Crescent are to be found. The original name was Saecroft where a *sae* meant a pool or lake and *croft* was an enclosure farm.

Travelling farther east from Seacroft lies Whitkirk where

Whitkirk Lane leads towards St Mary's, the fourteenth-century church that gave its name to the area. Inside is a memorial to John Smeaton, the local engineer, whose most famous work was the construction of the Eddystone lighthouse. Smeaton Approach in nearby Manston commemorates this distinguished Fellow of the Royal Society.

At times running parallel to Smeaton Approach is Penda's Way. Penda was the pagan king of Mercia who successfully defeated and killed King Edwin of Northumbria. But Penda himself was killed, probably at the Battle of Winwaed fought in AD 655. The site of the battle is uncertain but it is believed to be in the Stanks and Seacroft area about where Penda's Way is sited today. Farther south is Temple Newsam Road.

When the Domesday commissioners visited the area in 1086 they found a village perched on the hill high above the river Aire. The settlement was made up of new houses and was appropriately named Neuhusu or new houses, a name that eventually changed to Newsam. About 1155 the Knights Templar acquired the manor and so the name of the village was modified again, this time to reflect its new owners. It became Temple Newsam. Although most of the knights' land later became the manor of Whitkirk, they also held some small plots of property in Leeds itself around where Templar Street and Templar Lane now stand.

Some streets indicate the day-to-day affairs of the community. Pinfold Lane at Halton was the site of the common pound, or pinfold, where stray animals were kept locked up until they were reclaimed by their owner and a fine was paid to the local pinder. Similarly at Cookridge the pound was on Pinfold Lane. The key to it was held by the local smith who doubled as the township's pinder and whose smithy stood on what is now Smithy Lane. Catching birds as opposed to stray animals took place on the borders of Armley and Bramley where Cockshott Lane climbs up the hill from the Aire valley to Stanningley Road. Cockshott is simply a corruption of *cockshoot*. This was a glade in a wood through which woodcocks or other birds might dart or *shoot* and where they were caught in nets stretched across the entrance. One of the best-known places in Bramley, however, is Stocks Hill off Town Street where stocks were built to accommodate local miscreants.

Cookridge, Armley and Bramley were all areas where the monks of Kirkstall were involved. The Cistercians established their abbey at Kirkstall in 1152 and its great basilica, or church, is still one of Europe's finest ruins. It would be reasonable then to assume that the district of Kirkstall, along with Kirkstall Road and Kirkstall Lane, owe their name to the abbey and its fine church. However, the monks' own account of the founding of the abbey describes how a devout hermit called Seleth had a vision of the Virgin Mary which instructed him to go to 'Kirkestall' or 'Kirkstall' in Yorkshire and found a religious settlement there. The Cistercians, when they came, simply took over the site. Thus the name kirk may suggest that a church of some kind was there in the Aire valley before either the hermits or the monks arrived. However, Edward Parsons, the Leeds historian, argues that, as regards Kirkstall, the 'name was unknown until after the foundation of the Abbey'.

But there can be no dispute about certain streets that run off Kirkstall Road. Vesper Lane, reflecting vespers – the evening service the monks held – actually runs through what was once one of the side gates to the abbey. The remains of it, though now no more than a pile of stones, can still be seen. Norman View and Norman Row record the fact that it was during the Norman period that the abbey was established. De Lacy Mount even records the name of the Norman lord who granted the land to the Cistercians and laid the foundation stone of the great church. Henry de Lacy was the Earl of Lincoln and grandson of Ilbert de Lacy, the Norman baron who had accompanied William I on his 1066 conquest. Henry fell seriously ill in his castle at Pontefract. He vowed he would atone for his sins if he recovered by building a Cistercian abbey in honour of 'the glorious Virgin and Mother of God, Mary' and in May 1152 his promise began to be fulfilled.

Not all street names go back so far in the history of the city. Many people still fondly recall the bumpy bus rides to Otley along

Kirkstall Road in Sammy Ledgard's buses. Sammy Ledgard came to Armley in 1890 when his father became landlord of the Nelson public house. Sammy took over from his father but went on to develop a haulage business, eventually using steam wagons. In 1912 he set up Ledgard's Luxury Tours, charabanc trips to Bridlington and Scarborough and, in 1920, he began his bus service to Otley. Ledgard Way, leading up from Canal Road to Stanningley Road, was where his old bus depot was sited.

Some evocative names have now sadly long since disappeared. Bramley offered Longbrush Row, so named because the sweep needed an extra-long brush to sweep the chimneys there. Another was Reservoir Ginnel. Ginnel was the common name used in Leeds for a passageway, or snicket, and Bramley had a whole system running off Town Street offering shortcuts for pedestrians.

Leeds street names offer a rich source of evidence for people interested in its history and we should thank those who used their imagination in naming them and preserving for us a glimpse of the city's past. And we should be equally grateful that the system of street naming that was used along Tong Road was not repeated elsewhere. Here First Avenue was followed by Second Avenue, Second Avenue by Third Avenue and so forth to Eighteenth Avenue. It may have been useful for the postman but it offered nothing to the local historian.

2

LIVING BACK-TO-BACK

They were called the barracks of industry. And like barracks, the endless rows of redbrick back-to-back houses sprawled over the working-class areas of Leeds for nigh on two hundred years. They were born in the town some time after 1787 as the demand for cheap labour grew and grew during the Industrial Revolution. But the first cheap houses were not strictly back-to-backs and were usually built around insanitary yards in the east of the town where outbreaks of diseases such as typhus and cholera were regular occurrences. Every so often, a tunnel – known in Leeds as a ginnel – led through the row to the yard behind.

One such street was High Street which stood roughly on the site of the West Yorkshire Playhouse. It was here during the 1880s that Jane Lacey, herself a foundling child, and her husband Tom, brought up their family of eight. With only two bedrooms, Jane thought up an imaginative solution to their overcrowding problem. She knew their neighbour, a single man, slept downstairs. She came to an agreement with him, had her husband knock a door in the bedroom wall and used the neighbour's two bedrooms for her own family. He was happy to receive sixpence a week as rent, and the real landlord raised no objection. They never told him!

Such solutions to overcrowding, however, were rarely available for the larger families in the cramped accommodation of the newer back-to-backs. These homes were butted up against each other, backside to backside, so that each house was in fact half a house, each with only one doorway facing onto the cobbled street. Between every four houses a lavatory yard and midden broke up the row and streets might contain two or three dozen houses. Building back-to-backs reached a peak between 1886 and 1914 when more than 38,000 such homes were put up in the town.

The smallest of these homes had a living room combined with a scullery (hardly ever referred to as a kitchen), a cellar, one bedroom and an attic. They were known as an 'up and a down'. Most houses, however, had two bedrooms and an attic, which could also be utilised as a bedroom. These homes also had a living-room but the scullery was separate and beneath were a coal cellar and an all-purpose cellar. Such houses were known as 'two up and two downs'. Many were overcrowded as large families were common. It was sometimes necessary for small children to sleep in drawers taken out of the sideboard each night or for bigger children to sleep top-to-toe like sardines in a bed. Alternatively a child might spend the night at a nearby aunt's or grandparent's house.

Occasionally more opulent houses were built with double fronts, larger rooms and a front and back door. These 'through houses' had a living-room, kitchen, cellars and an attic but most importantly, a front room. This, however, was sacrosanct, opened only for very special occasions; when visitors came to tea on Sunday, for a family get-together at Christmas or for a funeral.

As these homes were obviously superior, their rents were inevitably higher. In Harehills, in 1909, a back-to-back cost 5s. 3d. a week, compared to a through house which cost up to 8s. Government experts argued that by having a draught of air flowing through them they were far healthier. So, in that year, it proposed legislation that forbade the building of any more back-to-backs. Leeds City Council, however, sent a delegation to London to argue that most working-class people in the town could not afford the more expensive properties. A loophole was found in the law and the last back-to-backs in the city were built as late as 1937. At the beginning of the twenty-first century some thirty thousand of them were still providing homes for Leeds people.

The people in these areas formed tight-knit communities, often facing economic deprivation and limited opportunities. Their lives were hard. Pupils left elementary school at thirteen, though in 1918 this was extended to fourteen. Most found work in the local mills, tailoring factories and engineering works. A few, if their family could afford to support them, became apprentices while some would be recommended to local firms by a head teacher as suitable for clerical work.

Their broad Yorkshire accent would seem a foreign tongue to most Leeds inhabitants of the twenty-first century. Expressions like, 'Sithee, tha's nobbut a bairn. Gi' ower tha' chelpin' and fratchin' or tha's off t' bobby 'oil.' [See here you are only a child. Stop your arguing and fighting or you will be taken to the police station] would be meaningless to later generations. Equally, for many people today, it is difficult to understand the phlegmatic manner most people adopted in dealing with the grim realities of their existence. Some showed considerable enterprise in trying to improve their lot by raising pigs and hens in smallholdings, hiring allotments and doing additional jobs in the evening, such as acting as projectionists or usherettes at local cinemas or helping out at night chopping chips in local fish-and-chip shops.

Jane Lacey was one such enterprising individual. She turned part of her living room into a shop. Others in the town did the same thing, often partitioning off their living room with a curtain from the public. But it was the purpose-built corner shops that provided the bedrock of these communities and a vital amenity in the lives of the people living there.

It is true that other important amenities were provided in these areas. By the end of the nineteenth century, local schools, swimming baths, public libraries and parks had been established. A considerable number of churches and chapels, particularly Methodist chapels, provided for those with spiritual needs. For many, religion had little relevance and they sought an escape from the pressures of their day-to-day existence in local pubs and clubs. In just half a mile on Wellington Road, for example, there were eight public houses and three working men's clubs.

But the corner shops were the mainstay. There were bakers selling white and brown bread, teacakes and parkin; butchers selling beef, pork, veal and mutton (it was never lamb); pork shops, like Walkers at Bramley, selling sausages, polony and black pudding; fish-and-chip shops; pea-and-pie shops; wet-fish shops; and specialist tripe shops like Amy Mitchell's in New Wortley, which sold white honeycomb and dark shag tripe and pig's trotters.

Some women's hairdressers were opened advertising permanent waving but most working-class women up to the 1950s would curl their own hair using tongs heated up in the coal fire. Similarly some men mended the family shoes, but there was an obvious need for cobblers. Many men used the local barber's shop at least once a week. Such was the demand for shaving at weekends that in the early part of the twentieth century barbers often refused to cut hair on a Saturday and remained open until 10 or 11 o'clock at night. Some barbers, often in dilapidated premises, took on the most grandiose names; Tomlinson's Tonsorial Emporium was a wooden hut on Dewsbury Road while Michael Angelo's in Marsh Lane offered one style; the basin cut!

Carters' off-licence at Woodhouse, like most off-licences, sold far more than hand-pulled beer, spirits and cordials (wine was never a working-class drink). They acted as a general store selling such food items as cheese, butter, sugar, bacon and corned beef and, in addition, sold flypapers, firelighters, carbolic soap and babies' dummies. Many shops doubled up as newsagents, sweet shops and tobacconists and also carried a wide range of goods including bundles of sticks for lighting the fire and known locally as 'chips'. A few stocked small libraries of romantic fiction, detective novels and cowboy adventures, available for a few pence a week.

Street sellers were also commonplace selling kippers, skinned rabbits, Selby 'taties' and pints of cockles and mussels. The milkman with his float or trap, the coal man, the tingalary man with his barrel-organ, the rag-and-bone man and the essential chimney sweep were all characters regularly targeting the back-to-backs.

For many people, big local stores such as Maypole, Gallons, Thrift and the Co-op offered the widest range of goods. The managers of these stores, like the smaller shopkeepers, were happy to allow people to buy things on credit and settle up at the end of the week. The 'tick list' was common to most local shops with the vast majority of customers paying up on time. Small shops were prepared to sell a single light-bulb, or a single razor-blade, and some shops even sold things in penn'orths; local historian Sam Wood recalled being sent with a cup to a local shop to buy a penn'orth of jam.

Inevitably, the shop which answered the most pressing financial needs of the community was the pawnshop. Many were individually owned although Archie Broadbent Beetham owned a chain. A common practice was to take something of value to the local pawn-broker, usually on a Monday morning. It was often the man's best suit or even a wedding ring. The pledge would be redeemed on Friday when the weekly wage was received but be back in hock again the following Monday. Most accepted this as a normal feature of everyday life. Those who felt shame would pay someone else to make the visit to the 'pop shop' for them.

Unemployment brought with it the dreaded means test. The state decided which possessions were essential and forced families to sell the rest. After the Second World War many people were paid a social security benefit, known in Leeds as the 'Pancrac'. But the greater poverty experienced before 1939 saw charities offer some help. Unfortunately, clothing given to poor children was often pawned by irresponsible parents. So it was that the *Yorkshire Evening Post* and the Leeds Education Committee established Boots for the Bairns, a charity that gave needy children footwear. Three small holes were punched in the top of the boots and a promise was given by local pawnbrokers not to take the footwear as a pledge. Many children were described as being 'Sunday and weekday alike' which meant they had only one set of clothes for school and best. New clothes, when they could be afforded, were bought for Whit Sunday.

Sometimes new clothes were bought, like furniture or pots and pans, on the 'never-never', a series of weekly payments made over a certain period of time. Aker's in Armley Town Street offered a wide range of bedding, clothing, crockery and hardware goods and the weekly payment would be collected by one of the Aker family on a Friday night. Others who made weekly visits included insurance collectors, coal men, rent collectors, men collecting money for doctors' bills and collectors of various 'diddle-em' clubs. In these clubs people saved to buy anything from scent to Christmas gifts and holidays. When enough money had been accumulated they were given a token to spend at the participating shop or to book their holiday.

Most men never told their wives how much they earned but preferred to give them what they considered was a suitable amount on which to run the house. It was considered the manly thing to do and to act otherwise was seen, by some men, as a sign of weakness. Thus if a husband was parsimonious or selfish it meant an even greater struggle for his wife to cope. Some women were forced to supplement the family income by taking in washing, going out cleaning or borrowing from a neighbour who was slightly better off and paying back interest at the rate of three halfpence for every shilling borrowed. Occasionally the situation was temporarily remedied when the gas man came, emptied the meter and left behind a refund or when the twice yearly Co-op divi was paid out at Albion Street. Another source of income during the Second World War was the selling of clothing coupons for which a black market was always available in Leeds.

But limited financial resources, inadequate living conditions and a lack of education often led to poor health, particularly in the early years of the twentieth century. The death rate in the poorer areas was twice that in the more salubrious district of Chapeltown. Food was limited to cheap meat, vegetables, fish and chips, tripe and onions cooked in milk, and bread spread with jam but quite often with Nestlés condensed milk, tomato sauce, or just sprinkled with sugar. The most popular spread, however, was dripping; 'mucky fat' being its popular name.

At the beginning of the twentieth century adulterated and badly kept food added to the poor health of many working-class people. In 1906 Thomas Fairley, the city analyst, claimed that 25 per cent of all food in the town was adulterated. He recorded that sugar was mixed with sand, dyed and sold as Demerara; tinned peas were given colouring by adding copper; coffee contained some 30 per cent chicory; and 21 per cent of milk was diluted with water.

To improve things the Leeds Pure Milk Supply Movement was launched in 1906. In a relatively short space of time its milk depot in Kirkgate and other suppliers, subsidised by the movement, were supplying unadulterated milk from a farm at Potternewton. It was sold within twenty-four hours of milking with the result that an enormous improvement in children's health was observed. Then, from September 1929, the local authority provided a third of a pint of milk daily to Leeds schoolchildren for just 5*d*. a week.

The health of working-class children was a major concern and steps had been taken as early as May 1909 to set up the first Babies' Welcome where mothers could get advice. Many parents were delighted at the idea, others objected to this meddling in their private affairs. Nevertheless, the first one, financed by Henry Barran, opened in Ellerby Lane in South Leeds where infant mortality was higher than in the rest of the city. That same month Leeds Education Committee began carrying out medical inspections of children in schools and, in 1916, dental inspections began.

Medical and dental treatment had to be paid for and visits to dentists were particularly rare. In the early part of the century Leeds chemists would carry out extractions in their shops, offering a cheaper rate than dentists. Teeth were cleaned once a week at best and the lack of dental hygiene meant the condition of many people's teeth was extremely poor. By the 1920s, it had become the fashion among a good number of people to have their teeth extracted and dentures provided as a twenty-first birthday present.

Personal hygiene was not easy with traditional back-to-backs having just one cold-water tap. Hot water had to be boiled on the fire where cooking was also carried out. Eventually, by the middle of the twentieth century, many families had managed to have hot water geysers and gas cookers installed. Bathing took place in the scullery where sometimes a curtain was erected to give some privacy, and often on Friday nights a tin bath was filled with water and placed in front of the fire. Then family members took it in turn to bathe in the same water. Some people, however, were able to use slipper baths attached to local swimming pools such as those at Meanwood and Armley. These were normal baths like the ones found in a modern bathroom.

Hygiene for many was not a top priority. Body odours were commonplace, clothes were often worn for days if not weeks, the washing of hands after visiting the lavatory ignored and many children were infected with head lice. It is a tribute to many families, however, that despite limited facilities, they took a great pride in their personal cleanliness. Such mothers dragged nit combs through their children's hair to ensure that heads were clean, washed ears until they shone red and insisted on necks being scrubbed until they hurt.

Most people took a pride in their homes. The stone-slab floors were usually covered with linoleum, and rugs were made by pricking clippings of old coats onto a backing usually made from a sack. These were regularly shaken and the floor mopped and swept. The fireplace was black-leaded weekly and the ashes from the coal fires emptied every day. Constant pollution meant that dusting was sometimes a twice-daily affair. Net curtaining needed regular washing; people with grubby-looking curtains were frowned upon as being 'mucky folk'.

Every week pavements – they were always referred to as 'flags' – were swilled, and steps and windowsills scoured or donkey-stoned. Where families shared a lavatory they took it in turns to clean the privy and sweep out the midden where the dustbins were kept (Originally rubbish was thrown into the midden and refuse collectors had to dig it out and take it away in a cart. This continued in some streets off Wellington Road until the 1950s.) Refuse in the house was stored in a slop bucket and ash bucket, usually kept under the sink. With the midden several yards away down the street it was not convenient to dispose of everything immediately. During the night people used chamber pots and slop buckets rather than face a cold trip to the lavatory. In winter, when the cistern froze, it was necessary to carry a bucket of water down the street to the privy to flush it. Torn-up newspapers were used as toilet paper.

Those unable to wash clothes used local laundries but, for most, Monday was wash day. It was a heavy physical activity that involved agitating the clothes in a peggy tub with a peggy stick, or posser, scrubbing them on a rubbing board and then ringing them in a mangle. To dry off on wet days, clothes were hung over the fireplace and spread out on wooden-framed clothes-horses but on dry days they were hung from one side of the street to the other. However, clothes were never hung out on the day of a funeral.

When a person died a local woman who specialised in laying-out bodies was summoned to prepare the deceased for the undertaker. Many people had already prepared their shrouds and most belonged to burial clubs or had insurance to cover the cost of the funeral. 'Don't forget, when I die, I want a boiled ham tea' was a common instruction. There were no funeral parlours at the time and so the dead were placed in their coffins, usually under the window in the living room, where the fire was kept low. Most people were buried. Although Lawnswood's first cremation took place in January 1905, suspicion of the process was still strongly felt until the 1950s. Neighbours came to pay their last respects, and on the day of the funeral all the curtains in the street would be drawn. Those not attending formally would stand on the street corner. To show respect, women would roll up their pinnies round their arms and the men remove their flat caps.

The mourners would wear their darkest clothes or sew on a black patch. Dyers and cleaners sometimes offered a service to dye garments black and mourning would be worn, in the early years of the century, for up to six months. Men would often sport a bowler hat, known usually as a 'billycock', and women always had their heads covered with a scarf or hat. After the service they would be invited back to the house or to a local schoolroom for a boiled-ham tea.

In the first quarter of the century premature death was common but life expectancy did improve, thanks in no small part to the efforts of Dr J. Johnston Jervis, the Leeds Medical Officer of Health. Speaking to Leeds Rotary Club in 1927 he pointed out that one of the main causes of death in the city, by then, was cancer although organic heart disease was the greatest killer. Tuberculosis – normally referred to as consumption – was feared in a way that cancer is today. Infant mortality continued to be serious. Jervis claimed that it was 'ignorance and indifference' which was the major cause. Although scarlet fever and diphtheria were better controlled, measles and whooping cough were still regarded by many working-class parents as inevitable. Some even argued that unless a child had 'whooped and measled' it had no prospect of adulthood.

One of the main causes of ill health was poor housing. From the beginning of the century a slow start had been made sweeping away some of the worst property but these slum-clearance schemes themselves created problems. The *Yorkshire Evening News* exposed the practice of landlords whose property was due for demolition flatly refusing to carry out further repairs even though people were still living in their condemned homes. Rats were another problem. In 1906 the *Yorkshire Evening Post* reported the case of an old Chapeltown couple who called the rat catcher in. His dog found a nest with nine young rats; the nest was hidden inside the mattress where the old couple slept.

One of the problems of slum clearance was that people were often rehoused far from their place of work. Most of them, indeed most working people in Leeds, were employed in manufacturing or service industries with tailoring, the distributive trades, engineering, woollen and worsted manufacture and printing accounting for two thirds of the industrial population. Local government and office work also provided employment for some. 'Collar-and-tie' workers were considered a little higher up the social scale.

The middle classes, living in their semis and detached houses, were viewed with some suspicion as were employers. There was also a deep mistrust among many working-class people of the so-called 'bosses'. Management had an equally deep suspicion of trade union 'bother causers' and crusading Communists. Humour often reflected those differing attitudes. The *Bramley Almanac*, bought annually by some ten thousand in Leeds, summed up the feeling of many workers' attitudes in its 1881 edition: 'It's hard what poor fowk mun put up wi! What insults an' snubs they've to tack! What bowin' and scrapins expected, if a chap's a black coit on his back!' Similarly a pithy response by a member of management occurred at Ingham's brickyard in the 1940s when a worker, reacting to the speed expected to complete one particular job, complained: 'Rome wasn't built in a day.' Jim Stringer, the foreman, made a quick riposte: 'I wasn't foreman then!'

Discipline at work was generally strict. Even when paid holidays were introduced, people late for work the day after could lose their whole holiday pay. Schools, too, exercised strict regimes where the cane was liberally used and rote learning was the mainstay. But a good grounding in arithmetic and English was invariably achieved. Opportunities were created for schools to compete with others at various sports culminating in Children's Day at Roundhay Park. The high schools or grammar schools, however, tended not to compete with the elementary schools and remained somewhat aloof, opting to play rugby union whereas council schools opted for rugby league or soccer.

With the car a rarity, and horse-drawn traffic slow enough to avoid, the street was an ideal playground. The occasional tarmac road was ideal for whip and top, and roller skating. Lavatory yards provided good hiding places for those playing hide and seek and kick-out-ball. Cricket was played with wickets chalked on a wall or sometimes, like football, played on any spare piece of wasteland often referred to as 't' moor'. It was here, too, that piggy, a game involving knocking a piece of shaped wood a certain distance, was also played.

Girls joined boys in some games but excelled in skipping and higher-and-higher, where a rope was raised in turns and the compet-itors had to jump over it. Skipping ropes were bought as presents but often pieces of old clothesline were utilised and greengrocers sometimes gave the straw that bound-up orange boxes and which made an excellent substitute. On 24 May, Empire Day, one girl took centre stage. Dressed up in an old net curtain she led a procession of other children in an assortment of fancy-dress outfits made from odds and ends round the streets. Singing as they went, pennies were collected from generous neighbours and then often spent in the local pea-and-pie shop.

For many the local Boys' Brigade, Scouts, Guides and other youth organisations gave young people the chance to take part in well-organised activities and offered an escape from the drabness of the streets. Often camps were organised in a country location giving some children the only chance they ever got to witness the richness of nature. Generally, these organisations were associated with local churches and chapels.

Sunday schools were also well attended. For the first half of the twentieth century, Sunday was viewed by both church regulars and non-attenders as special. No-one would dream of hanging washing out; ball games for many children were strictly prohibited and Florrie Greenhalgh recalled how, in the early years of the century, even singing ragtime songs at home was forbidden; only hymns were allowed. Public houses operated restricted hours, neither football nor cricket was played at Headingley and theatres and cinemas were closed. However, things began to change when a referendum voted for picture palaces to open on Sundays in the autumn of 1946. The annual feasts, too, remained silent on the sabbath but on Friday, Saturday and Monday they became focal points.

These annual feasts – they were never known as fairs in Leeds – were always eagerly anticipated by adults as well as children. Each year they brought to the various districts, Armley, Holbeck, Hunslet, Woodhouse and the rest, the excitement of the chairo' planes, the huge steam swings Shamrock and Columbia, coconut shies, regulars such as Chicken Joe, freaks like the largest rat in the world – it was in reality a coypu – and boxing booths where the resident boxer would take on all comers for three rounds and pay up if beaten.

Boxing on a larger scale was organised in Leeds by Barber Green, a Jewish entrepreneur just off North Street, and unusually for the period, the matches were held every Sunday afternoon and evening. Professional wrestling matches took place in the town hall and professional sport in general commanded huge support from the end of the nineteenth century. Leeds City, which became Leeds United, the rugby league teams Leeds, Hunslet and Bramley, the Yorkshire cricket team at Headingley and the amateur Headingly and Roundhay rugby union teams (they merged as Leeds in 1991, and became Leeds Tykes in 1998) all attracted large followings.

Cinemas became the mainstay of entertainment right across the city with each back-to-back community boasting at least one. By the end of the twentieth century, however, the Hillcrest at Harehills, the Regent at Burmantofts, the Lyric in Tong Road, the Star on York Road, the Strand at Hunslet and the rest had disappeared. The Theatre Royal, Empire and Grand Theatre offered live entertainment with the City Varieties renowned for its risqué nude shows such as 'Hi Diddle Diddle' starring the *Daily Mirror's* Jane, and revues such as *My Bare Lady*.

It was illegal for the nudes to move on stage as it was illegal for gambling to take place anywhere other than at a racecourse. Nevertheless, local bookmakers flourished and employed runners to collect bets from local pubs and street corners. Police would occasionally raid a bookmaker's shop, often sited in some dilapidated building, but it was a token gesture. With gambling illegal, few pubs in Leeds allowed cards to be played in the taproom though dominoes, fives and threes and darts (using a Yorkshire board without either trebles or a twenty-five) were popular. The taproom was a strictly male preserve with no women allowed.

Some women did go in the singing room or smoke room on Friday and Saturday nights and though most public houses were orderly, certain working-class pubs, like the Spotted Cow on Wellington Road, gained an unsavoury reputation for drunkenness and violence. The drinking culture that had long pervaded working-class life was gradually reduced with the introduction of licensing hours. Leeds pubs closed at 10 p.m. until well after the Second World War. However, many working-class people were bitterly resentful of the social damage drink could inflict and joined Methodist chapels and temperance societies. Often young men and women were encouraged to sign the Band of Hope pledge.

Just as drinking attracted large numbers, so too did dancing in several large dancehalls across the city. Local churches and chapels also offered socials on a Saturday evening where couples danced to a gramophone and soft drinks were served. Smoking concerts were popular; on arrival the men were given tobacco or cigarettes and the women chocolates. Smoking was widely enjoyed with Woodbines, often bought in fives, by the far the most popular cheap cigarette among the Leeds working classes. Some older people still viewed women who smoked as beyond the pale.

But whatever entertainment was pursued, young women in particular were usually expected to be home no later than half past ten. Such prudery was simply characteristic of the age, and was typified by the window dressers at Marshall and Snelgroves on Bond Street. When changing the clothes on the dummies in the windows, they covered the naked mannequins with brown paper. It was somewhat ironic that Bond Street was a red-light area. Many of the men and women living in the back-to-back communities exhibited a degree of sexual naivety, for sex was a taboo subject. Boys received no sex education and for girls it consisted of being shown pictures of a bowel and how to bathe a toy doll. The majority were virgins on their wedding day. Many women went into childbirth with no idea what was to happen to them other than to bear in mind the advice that they had been given. The only advice given to one woman was that she would feel as if she had been kicked by a horse. When menstruation started a girl would be told it was simply nature taking its course, shown how to use torn-up rags as sanitary towels and warned to be careful with men – but not told what to be careful of!

Education was regarded by many with suspicion. Others saw it as the way to a better life. Few could afford their children to take up scholarships to local high schools, such as Cockburn or West Leeds. Many, however, sought self-improvement by attending Education Committee night schools and Workers' Educational

Association classes. Some studied correspondence classes, avidly used public libraries and bought the Thinker's Library series and various Odham's publications when they could afford it.

Bigotry was not confined to education. Conversations about sex were by nods and whispers. Women of supposedly loose morals, or unmarried couples living together, were frowned upon. Illegitimate births did occur and some pregnant girls were rejected by their families. Little reference was made to the New Penny in The Calls, the meeting place for lesbians, or the Mitre in Briggate, where homosexuals met. They were strictly unmentionable topics though homosexuals were considered fair game for beatings by some young working-class men.

It was not the only aspect of intolerance demonstrated by certain members of working-class society up to the Second World War. Suspicion existed between different religious groups. Many Anglicans and Nonconformists viewed each other warily. Even Nonconformists at times resented those of different persuasions, as Methodists eyed Wesleyans with misgivings; Catholics and Jews were viewed suspiciously by many but, in most cases, it was a product of ignorance. In due course, ecumenicalism fostered better relations and the bitterness of the pre-war years became a distant memory.

Unlike the Southern states of the United States of America, where racial hatred was rampant during the 1920s and 1930s, working-class people in Leeds never used the word 'nigger' pejoratively. They did use it regularly to describe a person of Negroid extraction or the colour of an object that was dark brown. But the expression was used in a purely objective sense without any offensive intent. It was only with the arrival of New Commonwealth immigrants in the 1960s that racism began to grow among some working people in Leeds and much of that was born of a misunderstanding of their culture, the fear that the new arrivals might cause unemployment and a failure by some immigrants to integrate.

By the end of the twentieth century, the city council and community groups had made enormous efforts to generate a sense of harmony. Nevertheless, some racial bigotry could still be detected. Although the law had suppressed more extreme sentiments, an undercurrent of racism was still evident. At the same time, however, many accepted the changing nature of the city and saw diversity as a virtue. They became less concerned with the ethnic origin of people and more with their worth as individuals. It was that same belief in the fundamental goodness and value of their neighbours that enabled past generations who grew up in the back-to-backs not only to survive, but also to prosper.

3

MILLS AND MILLFOLK

At the dawn of the twenty-first century the mills of Leeds, once the bulwark of the city, were no more. Some were empty relics awaiting the developers' bulldozers. Some had been converted into luxury apartments. Others had been sublet to small businesses: motor mechanics, double glaziers, joiners, bookbinders and engineers. The dinnertime hooters that summoned the millhands back to work were silent; a whole industry had virtually disappeared. The towering chimneys and faceless mill frontages gazed blankly down, testaments to a way of life long gone. It was a way of life that had dominated the city and its people for a century or more.

Whole families were often employed; the mothers were weavers, the daughters started as menders and the husbands and sons were involved in the scouring or finishing departments or worked as tuners. A camaraderie existed in the communities in which those mills were based. It existed in the mills themselves. Those men and women cared: when workers fell on hard times, a collection would be taken to help them out; when a young couple announced their engagement there would be a collection to buy a present. For many, the mill was the only place they had ever worked, the only life they had ever known.

It would have been hard to envisage a hundred years ago that the woollen industry would disappear, that a whole way of life would be swept away. It had been the major industry of the town for centuries. Its history went back to the Middle Ages so that when John Leland, the historian, visited Leeds in 1534 he commented that,

'The Toun stondith most by Clothing'. It was a prophetic observation. To protect that industry the Leeds merchants persuaded Charles I to grant the town a charter in 1626 and thus formed its own corporation. Through this, it was hoped, the industry could be effectively regulated. And it is no coincidence that a fleece was chosen to be the focal point of the new Leeds coat-of-arms.

By the twentieth century ready-made clothing was the principal industry of Leeds – along with engineering – and employed thousands of people. But what was life like for them? Sarah Ellen Calvert was born in Leeds during the summer of 1862. By the time she was nine, like many other children of her age, she was working in the local mill. Her job was simple enough. She spent most of her day running from the factory to the local public house with a jug, fetching and carrying beer for the millhands. But then the employment of children was not unusual. In 1832 Joseph Isherwood's mill down Stonebridge Lane employed five boys and two girls under ten years of age. They worked from 6.00 a.m. to 7.00 p.m. daily.

Nor should we be surprised by the consumption of alcohol at work; beer drinking was a well established tradition in the mills of Leeds. When the Factories Inquiry Commission reported in 1834 it drew attention to the problem: 'It is our opinion that, if you can stop the process of drinking, the poor man will be more enabled to send his children to where they work regular hours, or keep more of them at home', it commented.

Mills were dangerous places. Limb deformities were common and unfenced machinery regularly caused accidents. When 13-year-old George Dyson arrived at Armley Mills (now the Industrial Museum) in February 1822, he was set to work on the carding machine. A moment's lapse of concentration saw him caught up in the mechanism. His thigh was severed and his body so mangled that he died shortly afterwards.

Fire was an ever-present hazard. Wooden floors, impregnated with oil over the years, easily caught hold. When Armley Mills, at the time the largest fulling mill in the world, burnt down in 1805 it was rebuilt as a fireproof building, the first such woollen mill in Yorkshire. And even that did not prevent a fire from breaking out there in August 1825. The same thing happened in April 1882 at Hiley's Springfield Mill in Armley, while in 1883 Bramley's Victoria Mill was totally destroyed. To offset such dangers Yates's Mill in Bramley, in the early twentieth century, even had its own fire engine and held regular fire drills every month.

But traditions, like the employment of children and drinking at work, died hard in the industry. Resistance to change – whether over the fencing of machines or the introduction of new production techniques – was commonplace. Why change, the manufacturers asked, when their industry had been the mainstay of the British economy. It was not just the manufacturers who resented change. When a delivery of slubbings – wool made ready for spinning – reached Bramley from Copley's Mill in Hunslet, the women in the village attacked the waggon. They had heard that the slubbings had been prepared on a new-fangled machine, so dragged them from the cart and trampled them underfoot to show their disgust. In 1797 rioters in South Leeds attacked Johnson's Mill in Holbeck over the use of machinery there, fifteen years before Luddism reared its head in the town. It was understandable; the textile industry had long provided the main employment for the people of Leeds and its out-townships. Their very livelihood seemed threatened.

When Benjamin Gott wanted to introduce a hydraulic press for finishing the cloth in his factory, it stood idle for fifteen years because his workers refused to use it. When he did introduce gig-mills for raising the nap of the cloth he got threatening letters and the windows of his home at Armley were smashed. Gott, however, was the most successful and imaginative wool manufacturer. In 1790, at the age of only twenty-eight, he became head of a firm of Leeds woollen merchants and a year later decided to become a cloth manufacturer. In 1792 he bought land by the river Aire – where the *Yorkshire Post* offices stand today – and opened what became one of the largest factories in Europe. It was probably the first to concentrate all the production processes under one roof and, by 1800, was employing over 1,000 workers and turning out 4,000 broadcloths a year. He expanded by taking over Armley Mills and the impetus he gave to the industry saw other merchants open similar establishments, usually within easy reach of the Leeds and Liverpool Canal.

In the early years of the twentieth century many Leeds people started work in the local mill when they left school at twelve to work part-time, or to work full-time at thirteen; only after 1918 was the age raised to fourteen. A 14-year-old would probably have started on about ten shillings a week. Some 18-year-old female workers earlier in the century, however, earned only nine shillings and sixpence a week. Their days began at six in the morning and finished at half past five in the evening.

The mills employed both males and females and there was a wide range of skills to be learned. Some jobs, like weaving and warping, were performed by both men and women; others, such as burling and mending, were carried out solely by women while scouring and finishing were tasks for men.

Few working-class families could afford to send their children to a grammar school and so the prospect of continuing their education at university or college was denied them. Working in the mills was an obvious choice and some parents took the view that if the mill was good enough for them it was good enough for their children. Office staff in mills were considered a cut above the workers and enjoyed better working conditions. Doreen Wilson started work in the offices of Fred Lodge in 1948. Her job was to prepare invoices, operate the telephone switchboard, take dictation for letters and keep stock records up to date. In the Wortley Local History Group book, *Stonebridge Mills*, she also recounted how she had the job of ordering hay. Lodges also owned Winker Green Mills on Stanningley Road. In 1948 they still transported the finished cloth to their warehouse by horse and dray. She tells how Ernest Wade, the horse man, would appear at her office and announce, 'I want some hay for me 'oss, and if it's not 'ere tomorrow, I'll come for t'blankets off th' bed!'

Office staff and mill workers rarely mixed although office staff did have to visit the working areas at times. Doreen went to the weaving shed at Winker Green every week. She climbed the greasy and worn steps and then noted the number of pieces woven each week, and commented on their quality, length and weight. 'It took a few years to get used to the smell of the oil and noise of the looms,' she reflected.

Office workers enjoyed holidays with pay long before the mill workers ever did, and their hours also varied from those of the millhands. Office staff got two weeks' holiday a year and could choose when to take them; mill workers had one week and were forced to take them when the mills were closed down, usually the first week in August, which in those days was bank-holiday week. Christmas Day and Boxing Day were holidays everyone enjoyed and in some mills at Christmas workers were known to decorate the various departments, and sing carols. Work in the mill often came to a halt at lunchtime on Christmas Eve when fuddles took place. New Year's Day and May Day, however, were normal working days, as was Good Friday. In the mills of Leeds, Easter Tuesday was taken as a holiday instead. Yates's millhands and office workers did get together at least once a year for a game of cricket. It was a 'needle match', one retired worker grinned.

In the 1920s and 1930s office hours were usually 8.30 a.m. to noon; and 1.00 p.m. to 5.00 p.m. Mill workers began work at 7.00 a.m. At 8.30, half an hour was allowed for breakfast. Work continued until noon, or 12.30 p.m., depending upon the mill. Either half an hour or an hour was allowed for dinner, again depending upon the mill, and work ended usually at 5.00 p.m. or 5.15 p.m. Every mill worked from seven in the morning until noon on Saturdays.

Workers had to clock in each morning and out in the evening. At Yates's anyone three minutes late was docked one penny and a penny for every three minutes thereafter. The clocking-in area, not surprisingly, was known there as the 'penny 'ole'. At Arthur Harrison's, workers were allowed to be three minutes late twice a week but after that they were 'quartered', a quarter of an hour's pay being deducted. Using financial penalties for lateness was standard practice throughout the industry.

Working conditions were both noisy and dirty and left much to be desired. In the smaller mills it was not uncommon for workers to take it in turns to clean the outside lavatory. In the weaving sheds the smell of the oil and the noise of the looms hung in the air. As one old weaver recalled in *The Armley Album*: 'You get a hell of a lot of cracking and banging with worsteds, the shuttle moves across much quicker – [it's] finer cloth you see. . . . They were automatic looms, and you imagine, two shuttles banging and clashing across, and the machinery with belts going round. . . . [In some places the] floor was real thick with old grease, it was shocking, dusty, dust flying about.' Attempts were made to keep the dust under control by using watering cans to sprinkle water on the floor but it was ineffective. So noisy was the environment that weavers had to communicate with each other by lip reading. Inevitably, the constant noise meant that deafness was a serious industrial hazard.

Many mills had no canteen. Those workers who were able went home for their dinners; a warning hooter would resound from the mill when it was time to return. Others would eat their food by their looms or try to find a suitable place somewhere in the building. In the mill's dirty environment the wind frequently blew dust and debris onto their food. Some covered their plates with paper as they ate; others never bothered. Children sometimes took their father's dinner to the mill each day while other millhands brought sandwiches or bowls of potatoes and vegetables to be warmed up. A small gas ring was sometimes available for heating food and a geyser for hot water enabled pots of tea to be mashed. (In Leeds tea was always *mashed*, as opposed to *brewed* in Lancashire.) Every Wednesday and Friday fish and chips would be brought in from the local 'fish 'ole', or 'fish 'oil', as the fish-and-chip shops in Leeds were known. A millhand errand boy would be despatched with the bulk order. On other days he would be sent to the local butchers to buy steak or pork chops, which again could then be heated on the gas ring.

Other mills, like Yates's, Joshua Wilson's and Elmfield, did have canteens. And workers appreciated those considerate employers. Harrison's was looked on by its workers as being particularly fair because it made sure that difficult jobs and easier ones were distributed even-handedly. Yates's, in particular, was well thought of. At the beginning of the twentieth century they built two rows of cottages for workers and when someone retired they could continue living in the property. In the 1930s the firm ran a pension fund; women received seven shillings and sixpence a week and men ten shillings. They also ran a friendly society to which people could make weekly contributions, so that when they were sick they got some pay at a time when sick pay was virtually non-existent. Most firms were prepared to make deductions from wages for a fund in which employees could save towards an annual holiday. Few working-class people in those days had bank accounts. In other mills the employees operated unofficial holiday clubs known as 'diddlum clubs'.

Yates's also ran hockey, cricket and football teams, provided tennis courts and, at weekends, social evenings and dances. Every year a day trip was organised for the whole mill and each December a Christmas box was given. Other firms also ran outings. Lodge's Mill organised annual day trips to venues such as Scarborough or the Lake District. Most people went; the alternative was work! Mill sports' clubs were also popular, with some even organising swimming clubs. Those in Bramley, for example, hired the local public baths for their meetings. And many mills in Bramley also entered floats in the annual Bramley carnival.

The cloths these mills produced ranged from expensive high quality worsteds to a lesser quality material known generally as *woollens*, though all these fabrics were actually made from wool. Some firms, like the one in Milford Place, produced harding, a coarse material used for making labourers' aprons and backing for rugs. Slater's, of Providence Mills at Stanningley, specialised in producing venetians, a closely woven cloth used for making suits or dresses; covert coatings, used for making shooting coats; and meltons used for overcoats. Bentley and Tempest at Armley Mills also manufactured meltons and, in addition, beavers, a heavy woollen cloth; serges, a durable twilled worsted; vicuñas, made from the fine silky wool of the South American llama-like animal; and unions, a fabric produced by weaving together two materials such as wool and cotton.

Most people, however, preferred to work in the worsted mills where a genuine pride was taken in the quality of the cloth being produced and the pay was also better. Arthur Harrison's firm produced worsted, but they also turned out other fabrics: plain twills; serges; birds' eye, often two shades of grey or dark and light blue; and coffin cloths. Some mills, like Smith Renton's, produced double plains, a high-quality worsted which was a double-sided cloth and extremely expensive. After the Second World War others, like L. J. Booth's of Rawdon, began weaving synthetic fibres such as acrilan but care had to be taken with it. If packed when wet internal combustion could cause the bale to burst into flames.

The success of a mill depended upon its ability to meet the demands of its customers. Occasionally, specialist orders, such as those for khaki were received. Lodge's on Stonebridge Lane produced this for the Boer War in 1899 and Yates's on Broad Lane began its production in 1939 to provide for the Second World War. Success also depended upon astute management. In consequence, nothing in the mill was ever wasted. Even the dust under the looms was carefully swept up and bagged by boys. It contained pieces of knotted wool known as thrums. This waste was then sent to be made into shoddy, an inferior material made by recycling old woollen cloth.

Each mill was divided into a series of departments where various processes turned the raw wool into the finished product. In the Leigh Mills at Stanningley the wool was taken to the top floor and from there it was brought down floor by floor through the various processes. In any mill the raw material was first taken into what was commonly known as the 'willy 'ole' where it was tossed on the floor, thickened with a noxious smelling oil and blended to aid the weaving. Wool arrived in three states. Some was the natural white wool which was spun, woven into cloth and then finally dyed. Other wool was dyed as soon as it arrived and the coloured yarn then woven. A third kind was actually brought in as dyed wool.

Whichever wool was ordered, when it arrived it was then thrown into a scribbling machine where teazels pulled it into yarn. This was followed by the spinning mule which wound the yarn onto spools and from there it was transported to the winding-room. Here it was twined onto either cheeses or cones for warping. Finally it was wound onto bobbins. The warper then attached it to a beam and sent this on to the twisting department. It was here the twister set the gear which created the pattern which had already been designed. At Wilson's the designer was, appropriately, a Mr Tweed! It was the tuner's job then to set it up on the loom ready for weaving. Tuners, however, were the one set of workers the supervisors were happy to see idle at times. Their other responsibility was to keep the looms running. An idle tuner meant that every loom was working to capacity. The only times the looms were stopped was on a Friday afternoon at about three o'clock in order to allow weavers to clean under them.

Each weaver had his, or her, own loom and, though most were automatic, a few handlooms were retained for producing smaller pieces of cloth. Mechanisation continued to be introduced. At Yates's at the beginning of the 1930s one weaver operated one loom, by the end of the decade a single weaver was running eight. Generally a piece of cloth would be between sixty-five and seventy-five yards long and be fifty-four, sixty or seventy-two inches wide. Depending upon the complexity of the pattern it would take a weaver between one-and-a-half and two-and-a-half days to complete. Should a thread break on the machine it was tied with a special weaver's knot. When the weaving was completed the cloth was said to be *felled.* Then the weaver was sent home for three or four hours while the loom was prepared for the next job. While they waited they received no pay and so were always pleased when a messenger arrived to summon them back to work.

The woven cloth was taken to the burling and mending department. The female workers here needed a well-lit room to work in as their job was rectifying any faults in the newly woven material. Burling was the lifting of any knots that had been tied in the cloth or removing faulty yarns from it. Carefully and skilfully, the menders then had to repair the newly woven material. To check seventy-five yards of cloth could take anything from four hours to a week.

It was particularly difficult if the cloth had not been dyed. One mender recalled her mother's recollections in the *Armley Album*. 'It were very hard work because you had to watch the white all the time and it made your eyes bad. If they got a break in the stuff, you couldn't see it too well because you got a sort of glare.'

Menders were paid by the piece but if the job was taking longer than normal then the supervisor would verify the difficulty and the worker went onto a time wage. Arthur Harrison's ensured that its burlers and menders took it in turns to get good as well as bad pieces to work on.

Should a particularly bad piece be encountered the other menders would stop talking to allow the mender concerned to give it her full concentration. Some mistakes could be expected but if too many occurred the supervisor brought the weaver responsible into the burling and mending department to see the poor quality of the work they had produced and be given the warning, 'Watch your work.' Every department had its supervisor whose job it was to see that everyone was kept busy.

The grease on the woven cloth was then removed in the scouring department, where it passed through a scouring machine containing a solution of ammonia and salt. The steamy room stank and, for the most part, the men there wore clogs as they clomped across the soaking floor. In the early years of the twentieth century, scouring still relied to a great extent on stale urine. At the Antwerp Mill on Whingate the all-male staff in the department used a bucket in the corner for urinating in. When it was full the contents were added to the scouring vat. In 1916 conscription during the First World War removed many young men from the mills. Females were then drafted in to the scouring department to join the older males. This meant that the bucket could no longer be used and the quality of the cloth deteriorated. The Antwerp Mill also had a stone vat erected in the area by the New Inn and the Carlton Laundry off Tong Road. The inhabitants of the old stone cottages were paid to put their urine in it. They soon realised that if they added an odd bucket of water it would bring them quicker returns. The Antwerp management realised what was happening and so reduced the price!

After scouring the material was fulled or milled to felt and thicken it. The finishing process saw the last pieces of woollen debris removed from the cloth. The piece was then taken to the cuttling machine where it was folded. Some firms, like Yates's, had their own dyehouses but others would send their cloth out for dyeing to such local firms as the Newlay Dyeworks, or the Butterbowl Mill. Certain mills would send their worsteds to firms such as Perrott's, the cloth finishers, to process it into non-shrinkable material.

During the first half of the twentieth century thousands of Leeds men and women continued the tradition of their forebears, spending their whole life in the industry. However, after the end of the Second World War wool manufacturing in Leeds went into terminal decline. By the 1970s there were just thirteen mills left in the city. The industry died as a result of a failure by some firms to invest in new production techniques and so compete with cheaper imports. An industry that had given Leeds an international reputation was gone, though many who had endured its hardships and yet enjoyed its camaraderie, still talk of it with affection and pride.

4

THE BIG CHILL: THE WINTER OF 1947

'The first fall of snow is not only an event, it is a magical event. You go to bed in one kind of world and wake up in another quite different.' When J. B. Priestley wrote that, he captured the idyllic, romantic image of wintry landscapes featured so frequently on Christmas cards and in the novels of Charles Dickens. The winter of 1947 did indeed produce a quite different world but it was a world that was neither idyllic nor romantic. It brought a winter of intense cold, treacherously deep snowdrifts, devastating fuel shortages, power cuts that brought the nation to its knees and chaos across the transport network as rail, road and water traffic ground to a halt. Of all the bad winters the people of Leeds have had to endure, 1947 was probably the worst.

It also came at a time when the country was slowly beginning to recover from a destructive war that had seen 25,000 of its factories damaged in air raids, making it impossible to replace worn-out equipment in mines, docks, power stations and on the railways. It was a period characterised by austerity: goods generally were in short supply, rationing limited what people could buy and queuing had become a regular part of everyday life. The last thing the country needed at that time was a seemingly endless winter of snow and ice.

Of course the town had experienced severe winters in the past. The great Leeds historian, Ralph Thoresby, recorded how, in 1684, the river Aire froze. Thoresby himself walked on the river from the parish church as far as the great mill at Swinegate as ox-roasting and sports were held on the iced-up waters. One hundred and thirty years later blizzards swept across Britain, leaving behind chaos. From 14 January 1814, Leeds found itself cut off. Only one coach, the *Telegraph*, bound for Newcastle, attempted to leave the beleaguered town but was soon forced to turn back. The winter of 1820 was no better. Snowdrifts once again held up coaches and the only mail to arrive was delivered on horseback. With the weather causing hundreds to be unemployed, a soup kitchen was opened with tickets issued to the poorest families and benefactors at the White Swan Inn gave loaves to the poor.

Almost a century later, in April 1908, unseasonable blizzards swept across Europe. For twelve successive days driving north-westerly and north-easterly winds battered Leeds. Part thaws in daytime and hard frosts at night produced the most treacherous streets in living memory for both pedestrians and horse traffic. Cabmen found that their horses could not move for fear of slipping on the icy cobbled setts. The postal authorities had a specific problem; how to transport the incoming mails from both Leeds railway stations over the frozen roads to the General Post Office in City Square. Eventually, sacks were laid down on the ice so that the horses could gain a sure footing. But there were those who found some humour in the snowfalls of that Easter week; at Meanwood, youths were reported going around singing Christmas carols.

There was little humour in 1940, however, when the winter was particularly severe. At the beginning of January temperatures plunged and there were extremely heavy snowfalls. The press called it the great 'freeze-up' but made no mention of it until the very last week of the month. Only then did the *Evening News* state that Yorkshire had had its fair share of freak temperatures. The reason for this reticence was censorship. In 1940 Britain was locked in war with Germany and no information was published that might help Luftwaffe bombing raids. Despite photographs in the press of wintry Leeds – and people skating on the lake in Roundhay Park – the *News* dutifully refused to use the word 'snow' in any of its reports.

Not that its readers in Leeds needed to be reminded of what had happened. Over a thousand burst pipes were reported on the

Sandford and Gipton estates. Several gas mains were fractured and twenty-one people were rushed to Leeds General Infirmary suffering from the effects of gas poisoning. Firemen, fighting a factory fire in Hunslet, saw their tunics freeze and then found that the nine miles of hose they had used was frozen solid and could not be rolled up. Bus services were seriously affected; one correspondent, calling himself 'Christopher', wrote to the *Yorkshire Evening News*, commenting on the 'indifference of the Transport Department'. It was a grim time, made even grimmer for one Leeds resident who attempted to clear the path outside his house by scattering salt on it. It was only when the snow failed to melt did he realise that he had used up the family's entire sugar ration for a week!

Then came 1947. The year began mild if a little unsettled but, on 23 January, light falls of snow covered Leeds and the *Yorkshire Evening Post* reported that the cold spell was the result of icy winds sweeping across the North Sea from Russia. Three days later, as arctic weather gripped the nation, blizzards swept across the county and Leeds was badly affected. But this was just the first of many Siberian-like snowstorms that would return week after week to besiege the city and drag on through February and into March. Some would last for twelve hours at a time and leave behind drifts between four and six feet deep at Adel, Shadwell, Halton and Middleton. It was a problem encountered by a *Yorkshire Post* photographer as he struggled to reach Eccup. His only means of finding the way was by following the telephone wires. When he arrived, he discovered what looked like a 'dead village'. In fact, the first human being he met was a German prisoner of war.

And it was bitterly cold. On the night of 28 January at Roundhay and Lawnswood the thermometer plunged to 21° Fahrenheit. It was not until early March that the first frost-free night of the winter was recorded in the town. Not surprisingly colds and flu struck in homes, schools, offices, factories and mills. Leeds Infirmary and Burtons tailoring factory on Hudson Road reported substantial absences. Leeds City transport department recorded that large numbers of its employees were off sick. At the

Norwich Union offices in the Standard Life building in City Square the management decided that the coal fires used to heat the building were inadequate for younger members of staff and issued them with mugs of cocoa.

By the end of the first week of February, it was estimated that two feet six inches of snow had fallen on Leeds in the previous seven days. The *Yorkshire Post* noted that by the middle of the month the town had experienced snowfalls on thirteen out of eighteen days. And the blizzards were still not over when February turned into March. Two days before the clocks were put forward to herald summer time, blizzards swept across the city from Cookridge to Middleton leaving behind huge drifts. For thirty-nine of the first seventy-five days of 1947 Leeds had suffered snowfalls. Drifts five feet deep were not uncommon. Some estimates of how much snow had fallen on the town put the figure as high as 2.75 million tons. The corporation claimed to have spent £250,000 in dealing with it.

To the country as a whole the cost was almost inestimable. Coal stocks were seriously affected and top priority was given to the Central Electricity Board (CEB). Distribution of coal ground to a halt as railways and road transport were unable to function. Pits were frozen, deep snow covered the coal yards and numerous railway lines were blocked. With the Leeds and Liverpool Canal frozen at Skipton, vital coal supplies for the West Riding mills came to a halt. By March coal production had plummeted. In desperation, some people in Leeds began to burn railings, old doors, oddments of wood and even shoes to keep warm. Few people had central heating and most families in the city spent the evening clustered round their fireplaces trying to keep warm. Hot-water bottles, heated oven-plates or hot glazed bricks wrapped in cloths were used to heat beds in bitterly cold bedrooms.

The police took the names of forty people desperate enough to raid coal stocks. At Morley, 14-year-old John Rimmington, along with his friend Derek Oliver, went to a local pit heap to scratch around in the mountain of slack for pieces of coal. The heap collapsed smothering John until only his feet were uncovered. His friend raised the alarm and the unconscious youth was finally rescued, badly bruised and shaken.

Before this bitter onslaught began, in December 1946, the CEB had issued warnings of the possibility of future power cuts. The government had begun to address the serious housing shortage by building more homes but that, in turn, meant that the number of people using electricity greatly increased. The *Yorkshire Evening Post* gloomily prophesied that, with a further 300,000 homes to be built, things would not improve until the supply of electricity was significantly increased.

When the cuts began they did so with a vengeance. On 24 January 1947, Roundhay, Oakwood and Gipton Wood had a 5 per cent cut at breakfast time. Soon, for a period of two hours, 25 per cent cuts blacked out Gelderd Road, Elland Road, Hunslet, Cross Gates, Halton, Whitkirk, Seacroft, Meanwood Road, North Street, the Quarry Hill Flats district, Camp Road and York Road. By February, domestic cuts from 8.30 a.m. until 11.30 a.m., and 1.30 p.m. to 3.00 p.m., were city wide. People became angry and frustrated. One correspondent to the *Evening Post* complained that the only way she could cook the weekend joint was by using her neighbour's gas oven. She signed it, 'All Electric and Fed Up'.

But gas supplies were also affected as the weather resulted in a huge increase in the use of gas fires. This caused pressure to be reduced, causing problems for cooks; Leeds housewives complained it sometimes took two hours to prepare a joint that normally took only an hour. 'Cynic' of Leeds lived up to his name. Writing to the *Yorkshire Post* he noted that John Strachey, the Labour politician, was in the USA arranging for a shipment of turkeys to be sent to Britain. 'Make sure they are cooked before despatch' was his advice!

The press remarked that reductions in street lighting saw Leeds's dimly lit streets brought back to 'almost wartime standards of gloom'. When the power cuts plunged the city centre into semi-darkness Lewis's, Woolworth's and Schofield's turned to old-fashioned hurricane lamps for lighting. The Grand Theatre and the Theatre Royal staggered their performances while city-centre cinemas delayed the start of their programmes. Leeds City Police headquarters was occasionally plunged into darkness but the inexpensive and popular British Restaurant, sited in the crypt of the town hall, was unaffected. By contrast, the restaurant of the Queen's Hotel suffered: the head chef, M. Eugene Brot, was forced to draft his menu by candlelight. And for hairdressers, laundries and factories across the city the cuts proved devastating. By the end of January the *Yorkshire Post* demanded that a rota system be introduced to give employers some opportunity to organise their workforces. The CEB agreed.

The clothing and woollen trades were badly hit. Dixon's work-force at Kirkstall was idle; Price's Tailors sent home 5,000 employees. Brown's at Bramley, the wholesale clothiers, saw 110 unable to work. Potterdale Mills and Service Tailors on Dewsbury Road were brought to a standstill and even John Barran's, the ready-made clothing company, was forced to adopt a three-day week despite having its own generator. Many others did the same. Probably the ultimate frustration was expressed by a manager at Grangefield Mills at Bramley: 'Yesterday and the day before we were idle for the want of coal and now we have an electricity cut!'

Every industry was affected. Hudson's jam-making factory announced that it faced closure if coal supplies did not arrive. Smiths and Booths of Rodley, the internationally renowned crane manufacturers, saw their vital export work held up. At least three hundred workers at the Silver Cross baby-carriage works in Guiseley were sent home. Kirkstall and Melbourne breweries suspended operations and, by the last week of January, Hammonds had only one week's supply of coal left, though Tetley's managed to continue production. The city's laundries, too, were seriously affected. Bennett Road, Headingley, Imperial and Grosvenor were but four that complained about the crisis; for this was a period when few people owned washing machines and laundrettes had yet to make an appearance in England. Some twenty thousand local people depended upon the laundries every week. In addition, restaurants and theatres, as well as three RAF units and other organisations, all needed that vital service. The Leeds employment exchange announced increases of between three and four hundred in the jobless figures.

However, there were those who, for a time, enjoyed the break from routine. Leeds schools closed in January due to a lack of fuel and children were free to roam the streets and build not only snowmen but also igloos. For some, sledging down Scott Hall Road or in Roundhay Park, snowballing whatever trams managed to come up Tong Road or trying to dislodge snow from roofs were considered great fun. The more enterprising pupils went snow shifting; clearing the pavement in front of someone's house to earn a penny or two. It was not to last. By the end of the month George Guest, the director of education, declared that all schools were finally to open, and in truth many children were happy to resume their studies, tired of their winter sports.

Sport was seriously affected. Rugby league matches for Leeds, Hunslet and Bramley were postponed. Elland Road was covered in snow, providing a cheerless prospect for Leeds United supporters with their team bottom of the First Division. The Football Association took a decision to extend the season to June if necessary. The only good news for Leeds sports' enthusiasts was that local man Len Hutton had scored a century for England against Australia in faraway Sydney, and even that was tempered by the fact that England lost the test. Nevertheless, by mid-March, 26,000 spectators braved the elements and turned up to the rugby league cup-tie at Headingley to watch Leeds beat Barrow 6–0.

But braving the elements was, at times, almost impossible. By the end of January the arctic weather had disrupted all traffic. Wolds villages were isolated and in Leeds hundreds were forced to walk to work. It was a mammoth operation trying to keep the roads open. Ploughs, mechanical shovels and manual labour were used, often for twenty-four hours at a time. Some 2,500 men from the cleansing department – aided by the Army, Polish volunteers and German prisoners of war – were deployed to clear the highways. An estimated 200 vehicles were involved, including bulldozers, to open up York Road. It was a heartbreaking task; just as progress was being made fresh blizzards swept across the country, bringing the 700 miles of roads in Leeds to a standstill once again.

Not everyone was satisfied with the efforts Leeds City Council had made. 'Suburban Ratepayer' in a letter to the *Yorkshire Post* protested that he had more trouble in negotiating one mile in Leeds than he did in driving thirty miles in the West Riding. He roundly condemned the chairman of the Leeds Cleansing Committee, a councillor Webster, for claiming that Leeds had 700 miles of roads. That figure included every back street in the city, he argued.

By the end of February only two roads out of Yorkshire were open. When trains could get through to Leeds those from the North were often over an hour late, those from the South up to two hours. Consequently, postal deliveries were often delayed. The RAC in Leeds warned that all Yorkshire roads were covered with hard-packed ice and recommended chains for use on journeys outside the city. Compounding the situation were seventy-seven trams in need of repair and the fact that even when roads were opened their surfaces could be treacherous. A bus bound for Headingley skidded at the junction of Park Lane and Burley Road and crashed into the window of a barber's shop; May Jewel of Newton Street was killed and three others were injured in the incident.

Impassable roads and interrupted transport affected not just commuters. Refuse collections were suspended for a time and supplies to the city came under intense strain. Reduction in the milk supply caused the gravest concern. By the beginning of February dairies were unable to bring in supplies from the Dales and Westmorland and this forced them to consider supplying priority permit-holders only. By 8 March, Craven Dairies was complaining that its supplies from Nidderdale and Settle were 'gravely interfered with'. The Leeds Industrial Co-operative Society Dairy had only enough to serve its priority holders but Provincial Dairies was more fortunate because it had managed to get a special tanker holding 1,000 gallons through. Supplies of food were affected. Fish deliveries from the East Coast were limited and further depleted as fishing boats from Whitby were hampered by gales and ice. Its effect on the fish fryers of Leeds was compounded by the need to reduce portions of chips by 20 per cent as a serious shortage of potatoes had developed. In Leeds Market, fruit and vegetables were in short supply: apples were available but oranges were scarce as were savoys and cauliflowers, with sprouts the worst hit of all. Pigeons, however, were still to be had in game row.

Even that availability was interrupted for a time when the glass roof of the market crashed down under the weight of snow and, for a while, brought trade to a standstill in several butchers', green-grocers' and florists' shops. A similar accident occurred at the Avro factory at Yeadon. Here six feet of snow piled up on the roof proved too much for the structure. These were not the only examples of dangerous roof falls. Seventy-year-old Mrs Ackroyd of Victoria Mount was completely buried when snow plunged off her roof. Neighbours summoned an ambulance and for fifteen minutes frantically tried to dig her free. The snow-blocked streets prevented the ambulance from getting within fifty yards of the accident and the unfortunate woman had to be carried by stretcher to the waiting vehicle. On reaching hospital she was found to have a fractured spine and a broken ankle. Six others were similarly treated at the dispensary, injured by snowfalls from roofs.

There were other accidents: Minnie Connor of Harehills lost her footing and fell through a shop window; Herbert Ward was thrown onto the pavement when his ladder slipped while he was painting Meanwood Baths. On a single day, fifty such accidents were dealt with at Leeds Infirmary; and by the end of the month 167 had been recorded.

People were forced to improvise. When Ernest Pullan died at Horsforth his coffin had to be dragged on a sledge across the icy fields as far as the hearse waiting on Scotland Lane. At Adel it was a happier occasion that necessitated unusual transport. Bride

Kathleen Bretherick had to be carried to church because the blocked roads stopped any vehicle from getting through. Others took on unusual tasks; May England of Lawnswood delivered coal for her father.

But then, during six years of war, women had grown used to taking on men's traditional roles. Readers of the *Yorkshire Post* in March 1947 may well have detected an indication of women's changing role in society. They, no doubt, formed their own views on the report in the paper that Mary Skasko, a New York secretary, insisted on being addressed as 'Ms'.

Life in Leeds went on despite the privations. Cinema newsreels, particularly the News Theatre in City Square, reported the world outside of frozen Britain. In the local press, people read about plans to establish a new university at York and to bring the Tudor room from Bretton Hall to Temple Newsam. In West Leeds, onlookers gazed silently at the simple notice fixed to the door of Armley jail, which announced the execution of Albert Sabin, a young soldier, for the murder of Horsforth psychiatrist Dr Neal McLeod.

There were those who laid the blame for the fuel crisis on the Labour government's policies and, in particular, on the nationalization of the coal industry. Mr Atlee, the prime minister, addressed the nation on the nine o'clock news at the beginning of February, appealing for a united effort to deal with the crisis. The *Leeds Journal*, the mouthpiece of the Leeds Chamber of Commerce, was adamant it was a crisis that was a direct result of 'bad housekeeping' and argued that 'drastic steps' to offset it should have been take as early as the previous October.

On the night of 4 March, for the first time for weeks, no frost was recorded in Leeds. But for some there was no rejoicing, for then came the great thaw and with it the fear of flooding. In Selby, 500 people had to be evacuated from a cinema in Millgate as the Ouse burst its banks. Nothing as serious as this occurred in Leeds, however. The Aire overflowed at Kirkstall, the East Leeds district suffered some damage and Rothwell Beck flooded. Nevertheless, the city, by and large, escaped any major damage, thanks in large part to the efforts made by the council to clear the 1,400 miles of gullies in the town of snow and slush and allow the surplus water to drain away.

It seemed that the *Yorkshire Post*'s plea to the 'gods of the weather' to recant had worked. 'If ever a people deserved a gentle ... thaw, we do' it wrote. For the people of Leeds had endured with fortitude almost three months of the worst weather the town had ever experienced. It was, indeed, a different world they had lived in and one that brought out the best in its citizens.

5

NEW YEAR HORROR

'Harrowing Scenes at Bazaar; Children in Flames'. This was the sensational front-page headline of the *Leeds Evening Express* on 2 January 1891. The rest of the Leeds papers also put the story on their front pages, and covered it in great detail. It was no wonder; the fire eventually claimed eleven lives, an event made more tragic by the fact that those who died were all young girls whose ages ranged from nine to fourteen. It was a tragedy set not in a dangerous industrial environment, nor against the background of a great natural disaster. It happened in the mundane surroundings of the school room of an English parish church in the suburbs of a provincial northern town at Christmas. The church still stands but the school room, where the tragedy occurred, is no more.

December 1890 saw the country gripped by bitter winter weather with snow covering Leeds. However it did not deter the residents of Wortley, in the west of the town, from going to church. Religion was important and places of worship were packed: by Methodists in the chapels at Branch Road, Silver Royd, the Bull Ring and Mount Pisgah; Catholics at Holy Family Church; Anglicans at St John the Baptist in Spence Lane and St Mary of Bethany on Tong Road. However, one of the biggest congregations was at St John the Evangelist, the parish church, and it was here that the tragic events unfolded.

St John's catered for an expanding community. Already to the north of the parish a mission school had been established at Silver Royd and the church offered a mother's union, men's Bible classes, cottage meetings, an adult temperance society and a Band of Hope.

Its combined Sunday schools boasted 700 pupils and an impressive library of 360 volumes. Both the Band of Hope and the hundred or so infants in the Sunday school were supervised by a 26-year-old clothing-company clerk, Eli Auty, who lived at 12 Oldfield Street. He had been associated with St John's since childhood, and would play an important part in the drama to come.

The new vicar, William Arthur Brameld, had taken up his position in August 1890. In November a new curate, Revd Ernest Freer Buckton, joined him. Christmas was approaching and plans had to be drawn up for the festive season. Among them was the suggestion for a bazaar to raise money for the new curate's stipend. Bazaars were a common way of raising money and almost all the local churches held them.

On 17 November the vicar chaired a meeting of the ladies' working party held in the schoolroom. It was agreed that Revd Brameld, Revd Buckton and Mr John Russell Willans, one of the sidesmen, should form a committee to organise the annual sale-of-work. They held no formal meetings but fixed the event for the last two days of December 1890 and New Year's Day 1891. The programme would include the Wortley Orchestral Band under Mr Robinson, a 'Fine Art Gallery' and Willans offered to direct what the *Armley and Wortley News* described as 'the notable play', *The Lodging House*. It was also felt that a children's concert should be included. Eli Auty, Charles Clegg, an active church member, and a 17-year-old servant girl, Eleanor Coleman, were given responsibility for organising the performance. The details of the programme were left to them.

Once the committee's wishes were known, Eleanor Coleman asked the Band of Hope children if they would participate but the response was poor. Auty went to her house and said he would arrange to get volunteers but it was Miss Coleman who came up with the proposal that the children should perform as Snowflakes. Later the vicar and other members of his committee would claim not to be aware of what this entailed. What was known was that the children at Mount Pisgah chapel had taken part in similar performances in recent times and Eleanor had witnessed a performance of Snowflakes at Lower Wortley only six months before.

She informed Clegg and Auty of the requirements for the presentation, explaining that the children needed lighted candles in paper Chinese lanterns and cotton-wool jackets and hats. Auty later claimed that he objected to the whole idea. In his words, 'It was a load of rubbish.' However, Eleanor Coleman later testified to the coroner's jury that, 'Mr Auty said he would very much like to have Snowflakes.' For his part, Clegg would tell the jury that he had initially said he wanted no part in the performance. Eleanor denied he had ever taken such a stance or that she had repeatedly gone to Clegg's house to persuade him to go along with the Snowflakes idea. Whatever had transpired, both Clegg and Auty eventually agreed to get involved in the production. The details of the performance were eventually drawn up but only just in time for the vicar to include them in the printed programme.

Clegg, Auty and Coleman made no mention of either the cotton-wool costumes or the lighted lanterns to Revd Brameld. Had they done so the tragic events that followed might have been avoided. Later, Mrs Brameld would remark on how two years before – when decorating their Christmas tree at the missionary college – she had used cotton wool to simulate snow. It had proved to be highly inflammable, caught fire and her husband had burned his hands putting out the blaze.

The programme proposed that the children would march around the very small platform carrying lighted lanterns and singing carols. In addition Ethel Fieldhouse, one of the older girls and a recent Sunday school prizewinner, would recite 'A Day in the Snow' and Caroline Steel – she was always known as Carrie – would give a rendition of Tennyson's 'Call Me Early Mother Dear':

> If you're waking call me early, call me early, mother dear;
> For I would see the sun rise upon the glad New Year.
> It is the last New Year that I shall ever see,
> Then you may lay me low i' the mould and think no more of me.

They were words that would take on a poignant meaning in the light of subsequent events.

Preparations for the performance moved on. Auty, with Clegg assisting, rehearsed the children on the Saturday and they met parents and asked them to provide the costumes. The coats were to be made of calico covered with cotton wool and had to reach the children's feet, while only a small cotton-wool hat was required. Neither parents nor organisers made any reference to the potential danger of cotton wool or lighted candles in paper lanterns. Auty offered to supervise the making of the lanterns and Eleanor Coleman advised him to fix a wire arm at the top to keep the lantern free. Once made, they were taken to Clegg's house where both men tried them out. Auty was not satisfied as to their safety and decided to cut a wider aperture for the candles.

Coleman also insisted that she had warned the children to carry the sticks with the lanterns upright at all times. Clegg later denied ever having heard her say this. Certainly, at rehearsals, Auty made it clear to the performers that should their paper lantern catch fire it should immediately be thrown away.

The schoolroom had to be prepared for the event. It was an L-shaped building with an exit next to a gate onto Lower Wortley Road and stood some distance from the church itself. The largest room was scheduled to hold the sale-of-work. Then at right angles to this, and parallel to the road, ran the rest of the building, divided into two smaller rooms. The first of these butted onto the sale-of-work room. It was here the performance would take place, as this room contained a very small stage. The stage had been temporarily extended but the extension had been erected in front of the door that led into the third room. It was this room that was to be used as the dressing room. The only exit from the dressing room was by climbing over the stage.

The stage was somewhat congested with a piano, a table, two chairs and a pair of steps. To reach the stage from the dressing room people had to climb on a wooden chair which had been placed there as a step. It was later generally agreed that the chair was too high for small children to climb on easily.

The dressing-room itself was crowded with benches, chairs and other pieces of furniture. A potential danger was the fire that burned in the grate of the fireplace on the end wall. A single gas-lamp with six mantles hung from the ceiling. A major factor in the tragedy was that the door from the entertainment room opened *into* the dressing room. It was not locked as local folk-legend has it. Confusion over this may have arisen because, in the December edition of the parish magazine, the vicar had warned that Sunday school classes were being so disrupted by latecomers that the doors would be locked once lessons started. The real danger, however, was that the performers tended to congregate in front of the closed door as they waited to go on stage and it would therefore be difficult to open in an emergency.

William Brameld prepared his January edition of the magazine for the printers during December and, addressing his parishioners, wrote, 'I begin the New Year with real hopefulness, and great thankfulness to ALMIGHTY GOD.' They were words that would have a hollow ring about them by the time they arrived in parishioners' homes. The magazine also contained an inserted section available to all parishes, *Home Words for Heart and Hearth*. Its January contents included – as well as its usual moralising serial, religious poems and thoughts for Lent – an article on the London Fire Brigade. In it the author pointed out that December was the most common month for fires and added a warning: 'Many may be traced to carelessness, especially the use of paraffin lamps, which should never be carried about lighted.'

At three o'clock on Tuesday, 30 December Mr T. Greenwood, one of the church's patrons, opened the sale and by the time it closed that day £74 3s. 10d. had been collected. On Wednesday the Hon Mrs Talbot performed the ceremony and £37 5s. 7d. was raised. The sale was heading towards being the most successful the church had ever held. Good-humoured crowds on both days virtually bought up everything on offer. The 'Theatricals', as Brameld referred to them, were a great success. That Wednesday, New Year's Eve, was the night of the first performance of the

Snowflakes. It was so successful that it was decided they should perform again on Thursday, the evening of New Year's Day.

Brameld had not seen the children's first performance. At the rehearsals he noticed the lanterns had not been lit. Had he known the performers were to carry lighted paper lanterns he later insisted, 'I should have prohibited it, for I should certainly have considered it too dangerous.'

For the second performance, Mrs Dixon of Amberley Road had gone once more to help to dress the children as her daughter was one of the Snowflakes. She left the room when the dressing was almost complete. Charles Clegg had also moved out of the room onto the stage to ensure that everything was ready there. Eleanor Coleman had made her way from the dressing room to the sale-of-work room. Fanny Craven, the 14-year-old pianist for the Snowflakes, and her sister Phoebe – who was to play a duet with her at some time in the programme – went into the dressing room. Auty asked them to stay but they failed to hear him above the excited hubbub and they left. The sexton testified later that the girls 'were laughing amongst themselves and knocking about'. But the adults' departures meant that Eli Auty was now left alone with fourteen young girls in the congested room.

At about 7.15 p.m. a bell rang in the sale-of-work room and it was announced, 'this way for the Snow Girls'. About a hundred people had gathered for the performance.

As Mrs Dixon left the dressing room, Auty began lighting the girls' lamps. Emily Tyrah, aged nine, was standing at the farthest corner from the door. Auty had taken Florrie Dixon's candle to light Emily's and then turned away. Florrie accidentally dropped her lantern on Emily's jacket and the cotton wool immediately took hold. Auty realised what had happened and swept Emily into his arms to extinguish the flames. Only then did he notice that the fire had somehow spread almost immediately to the other girls who were crowded by the exit ready to go on stage.

In a panic they struggled to open the door. When they succeeded, they scrambled up on the chair to reach the platform, their cotton wool dresses now ablaze. Charles Clegg, who was on the stage, leapt to do what he could. Another who reacted quickly was George Brookes, an Oldfield Lane butcher and part-time sexton and caretaker at the school. He whipped off his jacket to smother the flames and others in the room grabbed coats that were hanging up and tried to wrap them round the fleeing girls. The room quickly filled with smoke and Osborne Taylor, a local forgeman, pushed his arm through a window to let some air in as he looked for his daughter, Alice. She cried out, 'Oh father, come to me!' and he pulled off what burning wool he could from her clothes and then turned to help others.

Byron Cowling, taking admission fees at the front door, was alerted to the disaster when the curate, Revd Buxton, yelled 'fire!' Cowling looked up to see two girls, their dresses in flames, scramble across the stage and race through the entertainment room. He and Buxton threw coats and rugs over them. Three more panic-stricken children came fleeing after their friends with their clothes also engulfed in flames. Buxton and Cowling smothered the blazing dresses as best they could.

Fanny and Phoebe, the two pianists, were on the platform when the first burning girl appeared. Horrified, they fled, frightened that they too might be set on fire. Their friend, Ethel Fieldhouse, ran after them, her clothes still alight. Carrie Steel's younger brother dashed home to their shoemaker father. 'For God's sake come to school, sister's burning to death', he was reported as yelling. Mr Steel dashed to the school but by then his daughter had raced half a mile to her grandmother's house, her costume still burning.

From the time Auty noticed Emily's dress on fire to every flame being extinguished the time that elapsed, according to Revd Brameld, was scarcely more than five minutes. Word was quickly sent to two local doctors. Dr Henry Waite was halfway through presenting a New Year lantern slide show at Greenside Wesleyan chapel when he was told of the disaster. Within ten minutes he arrived at the schoolroom. There he found a scene of absolute chaos. The room was full of smoke. 'Demented people', as he described them, were rushing about getting in each others way. He declared he 'never saw anything like it.' Dr Scott was summoned to treat Florrie Brookes, the sexton's sister, at her home. He claimed that she was so badly burnt 'her features were scarcely recognisable'. He thought for a moment that she had stripped her clothes off and then realised they had been burnt off.

Someone had sped up the road to Wortley police station and from there the Leeds Police Fire-Brigade was telegraphed. By half-past seven the first engines were on their way. Some of the children were taken immediately to the General Infirmary on the top of the fire tenders, two were transported in cabs while horse ambulances, making two journeys, carried the rest.

But the burns were so severe there was little the infirmary staff could do. Emily Lister (13), the first to die, succumbed early on the Friday morning. She was followed at a quarter to seven when Carrie Steel (9) perished and a few moments later by Clarissa Roberts (11). Ethel Fieldhouse (14) died at eight o'clock. Maggie Kitchen (10) expired at a quarter to two in the afternoon and at ten minutes past six Ada Whitterton (11) passed away. In the days that followed the death toll continued to rise. Harriet Riley (12), Elizabeth Tingle (12), Emily Tyrah (9), Florrie Brookes (9) and Julie Anderson (9) all perished within a matter of days.

Alice Taylor (14) survived a few years. Sarah Kitchen (14), Maggie's sister, lived to be sixty-five and Miriam Stokes (10) survived to reach sixty but both were badly scarred and suffered their whole lives from the trauma. Charles Clegg, Eli Auty, Annie Tyrah, Osborne Taylor and Charles Clayton, a local warehouse-man, all needed treatment for burns as a result of their efforts to save the unfortunate children.

The following day – Friday, 2 January – a thick fog enveloped Wortley and the press saw it as symbolising the silent misery of the township. The Victorian fascination with death came to the fore. A knot of young sightseers gathered outside the schoolroom and the *Leeds Evening Express* reflected that the children 'stood marvelling with child-like wonder at the fate of lost playmates'.

It was a national disaster and like any national disaster attracted widespread attention. The London press carried reports and the *Daily Graphic* sent its artist to record the scene. Among his illustrations was one showing the dressing room in a state of chaos and another showing the doorway with the stage beyond and the chair that played such a crucial part in the escape route. Both the local *Evening Express* and *Evening Post* reproduced the pictures, as interest in Leeds was high. A special edition of the *Evening Express* published that Friday morning was eagerly snapped up.

Later that day at Leeds town hall, Mr J. C. Marshall opened the inquest but Buckton was too ill to attend and Eli Auty's hands were so badly burned that his doctors would not allow him to leave the infirmary. After taking some evidence the coroner adjourned the hearing until the following Wednesday.

Whilst Auty lay in the infirmary he protested that he would rather have sacrificed himself if he could have saved even one of the children. Some accepted his grief as genuine. Others, bitter and bloody-minded, began sending damning letters to his sick bed. Brameld condemned them. He also condemned those in the parish whom he considered had committed 'little short of downright blasphemy' by taking the view that the disaster was divine retribution. This was God's punishment, they argued, for allowing wicked 'theatricals' to be part of the entertainment.

The funerals began on the Sunday and thousands gathered to pay their final respects. That day, Carrie Steel and Maggie Kitchen were buried in the churchyard; Ethel Fieldhouse and Emily Lister at Oldfield Lane cemetery. The deeply emotional interments went on throughout the week. On Monday thousands gathered despite a blinding snowstorm to witness the burial of Clarissa Roberts. The *Armley and Wortley News*'s reports on the funerals resorted to cliché: 'Women and children sobbed and strong men were moved to tears' it declared. But irrespective of Victorian sentimentality, local feelings were genuinely sincere.

At least they were for most. William Robinson Lucas had travelled from Huddersfield on the Sunday to exploit the opportunity that the funerals offered. At Oldfield Lane cemetery he watched the mass of mourners occupied with the proceedings. He singled out a young woman absorbed in the service and picked her pocket. Fortunately for Minnie Thorpe she sensed the movement and Lucas was apprehended. The purse he took contained just two shillings and seven pence.

But Lucas was not alone in exploiting the melancholy affair. Unscrupulous printers began to produce mourning cards which they offloaded onto young boys, who in turn hawked them round the streets. Two confidence tricksters began circulating in the area collecting for the memorial appeal and authenticating their activity by showing a petition signed by Mr Brameld. The vicar had never seen the petition and in all probability the culprits were not from Wortley; for their most insensitive act was to call at the homes of one of the deceased girls and ask the parents for a contribution.

But the general response from the public was both sympathetic and generous. A relief fund to pay the funeral expenses was set up with the vicar as chairman and representatives of the community involved. Any surplus was to be given to the survivors, though squabbling meant that payment was delayed for some considerable time. A church memorial committee was also established and the Sunday school teachers and children offered to provide a new lectern as their lasting tribute.

Letters of sympathy poured into the vicarage from as far afield as London, Nottingham and Sunderland. Queen Victoria herself instructed the home secretary to convey her 'deepest sympathy' and enquire after the injured still in hospital. Donations large and small were forthcoming from all sections of the community. Records show that the Yorkshire Rugby Union contributed £50, the Wortley Conservative Association £1 1s.1d., children from Newham-on-Sea 11s. 0d. and, as the magazine described her, 'A Poor Woman 3d'.

But no matter how generous the response, the question had to be asked: who was responsible for the disaster? The reconvened coroner's jury listened carefully to the evidence. Buxton had to be assisted into court, obviously ill and very weak. Auty, his hands swathed in bandages, his neck showing traces of burns, gave every appearance of a man who had suffered grievously.

The jury was sympathetic to the suffering the men had experienced but its findings made grim reading. The crowded state of the room, the unguarded fire in the grate, the dangerous clothing and the lighted lamps were condemned out of hand. It remarked on children 'of tender age having no conception of the danger they were incurring'. Brameld, Buxton and Willans were criticised for not having 'exercised such forethought, care and supervision, as such duty imposed upon them'. Clegg and Auty were accused of 'great negligence' and the jury expressed doubts as to the truthfulness of some of Clegg's statements. However, it did express its admiration for the way Brameld and others had performed in the rescue operation and paid particular tribute to Eli Auty. It made one positive recommendation; that, in future, schoolrooms should be licensed just as other places of entertainment were.

In his February magazine Brameld responded. He accepted the principle of licensing. However, he defended the entertainment committee, objected to the slur against Clegg's honesty but acknowledged that as vicar he was solely responsible. He also bitterly condemned the London press.

But it was not just the London press that poured its opprobrium on the Wortley vicar and his helpers. The *Yorkshire Post* spoke of the 'fearful risk that these children . . . were permitted to run'; the *Armley and Wortley News* of a 'lamentable lack of caution'; the *Leeds Evening Express* that 'only the reckless and stupid' would have embarked on such a scheme; the *Yorkshire Evening Post* of the 'palpable lack of forethought and caution which led to the sad affair'; the *Leeds Daily News* reminded its readers that though Auty was guilty of negligence 'there must have been contributory negligence elsewhere'.

The national press was vitriolic. The *Standard* observed that the 'carelessness and foolhardiness . . . almost passed belief.' The *London Daily News* considered that what happened was 'criminally negligent'; *The Times* described the committee's actions as 'culpable folly'; the *Daily Telegraph* spoke of 'gross carelessness'; the *Newcastle Chronicle* lamented the lack of 'reasonable prudence'; the *Birmingham Post* claimed that a better situation 'could scarcely have been devised' to bring about such a catastrophe. Only the *Liverpool Courier*, arguing that 'good may come of its fatal consequences', and the *Daily Graphic*, that a valuable lesson had been learned, were more positive.

That was of little consolation to the relatives of the deceased. The horror of that New Year's Day passed into the folklore of Wortley and for years people there spoke of it in hushed and reverent tones. But in 2005 few people either in Leeds, or even in Wortley, are aware that such a disaster ever happened. A memorial was erected in the churchyard and is still there today – a testament to how the actions of sincere and good-hearted people, through ignorance and lack of thought, can be as devastating as those of the most evil of fiends.

6

LITERARY LOINERS

Why a person from Leeds is known as a *Loiner* has never been adequately explained. *Leodiensian* or *Leodensian* are more correct terms and yet *Loiner* is far more commonly used and widely known. It has been suggested that 'loin' is derived from 'lane' and certainly three of the principal thoroughfares of the city are lanes: Vicar Lane, Park Lane and Boar Lane, but the link seems somewhat tenuous. Others have suggested it comes from the fact that Leeds was originally called Loidis. Whatever the collective name for them, it is the efforts of those so-called loiners over the centuries that have shaped the destiny of the city.

Leeds has had its fair share of famous, even illustrious, figures. John Smeaton, the renowned eighteenth-century engineer whose works included the Eddystone lighthouse, was born and spent his life at Austhorpe near Leeds. Matthew Murray produced the world's first commercially viable steam locomotive in 1812 at his Round Foundry in Holbeck. In the world of photography, Frenchman Louis le Prince moved to Leeds and created a successful photographic business in Woodhouse Lane. More importantly, however, in 1888 he took motion pictures of Leeds bridge that were among the first anywhere in the world.

In art, Phil May, the great *Punch* cartoonist, was born in Wallace Street, off Wellington Road, the same street, incidentally, which some years previously had been the home of John Atkinson Grimshaw, the artist whose paintings brought to life the misty evenings and rain-soaked, glistening, gas-lit pavements of Victorian Leeds. Castleford-born Henry Moore began his studies at Leeds

College of Art in 1919. By the time of his death in 1986, he had lived to see his work recognised as a major breakthrough in sculpture using semi-abstract forms. His works now grace some of the world's greatest galleries, such as the Tate in London and the Museum of Modern Art in New York. In Leeds the Henry Moore Institute at the City Art Gallery was opened by the Queen in 1982.

No history of Britain is complete without reference to Richard Oastler, the factory king, who was born in St Peter's Square, Leeds in 1789. It was Oastler who led the campaign against the employment of children in factories, a crusade that eventually produced a more humane society. Joseph Priestley was born at Birstall near Leeds, became the minister at Mill Hill chapel in 1767 and the first secretary of the Leeds Library. It was while he was at Mill Hill that Priestley took up chemistry. He eventually became a pioneer in the study of gases and one of the discoverers of oxygen. And one Leeds man's invention can be seen in every city in the world: Joseph Aspdin, a bricklayer, was born in Leeds in 1779. With the building industry so dependent upon increasingly scarce and expensive timber, he sought a way of producing artificial cement. In 1824 he patented his new material made by burning and grinding clay and limestone. When set, it resembled Portland stone and so he named it Portland cement.

In commerce Joshua Tetley, an Armley maltster, took over Sykes's brewery off Hunslet Lane in October 1822 and created a brewery of national repute. In 1884 Michael Marks, a Polish Jew, opened his famous Penny Bazaar in Leeds Market and founded Marks and Spencer. Montague Burton, a Jewish immigrant from Lithuania, opened his bespoke tailoring business in Leeds in 1909 and by 1926 it was the largest clothing company in Europe.

In the field of acting Peter O'Toole became one of Britain's most accomplished performers. Born in Connemara in 1932, his family moved to Leeds where he studied at St Anne's Roman Catholic School. He made his amateur debut on the stage of the Civic Theatre in Cookridge Street, won a scholarship to RADA and began a career that has been divided between film, television and stage. In

1962, at only thirty years of age, he achieved international stardom when David Lean cast him as T. E. Lawrence in the epic film, *Lawrence of Arabia*.

Women have not featured prominently among the famous personalities of Leeds, though their role in the city's development should never be underestimated. Only two women, for example, have schools named after them: Lady Elizabeth Hastings and Agnes Stewart. Lady Elizabeth inherited the Ledston estate near Leeds in 1708, used her wealth to support educational charities, helped the young John Wesley and established an intellectual and religious retreat for women. Agnes Stewart, another religious bene-factor, was born in London but moved to Leeds in 1871. As a nun in the Church of England Community she created an orphanage in St Saviour's parish and then a girls' school, an infants' school and in 1880 St Hilda's School for boys. Agnes Stewart died in 1886.

But at least two Leeds women have achieved international recognition. The first was Sue Ryder, born in Leeds in 1923 to a wealthy family and determined from an early age to help people who were suffering. She married Leonard Cheshire, who had already set up homes for the disabled, but in 1953 she set out to develop a hospice movement herself. She was created Baroness Ryder of Warsaw in 1978 and, when she died in November 2000, had lived to see eighty homes opened worldwide. They were funded, in part, from the 580 Sue Ryder charity shops.

The second woman who helped to place Leeds firmly on the cultural map of the world was Fanny Waterman. She was educated at Allerton High School in the city, then at Leeds University and finally at the Royal College of Music. Although she became a concert pianist, her true vocation lay in teaching. Her reputation grew until, by 1969, *The Times* referred to her as the 'now legendary Fanny Waterman'. It was she, supported by Mrs Jeremy Thorpe and under the patronage of the Duchess of Kent, who was instrum-ental in inaugurating the Leeds international pianoforte competition in 1963. Through the medium of television, this triennial event has brought music to an international audience of millions.

Percy Alfred Scholes also helped to popularise classical music. He was born in Leeds in 1877 and, by the time he died in 1958, was recognised as a leading music critic, encyclopaedist and educator. Through his writings in the *Radio Times* and the *Observer* he did much to foster appreciation of the subject. He is best known for his *Oxford Companion to Music*, which ran into several editions.

He was but one of the writers associated with the town who have made a major contribution to literature. Some were born in the city, others have studied here or used it in their work. William Congreve, the Restoration dramatist, was born at Bardsey near Leeds and shaped his satirical portraits of fashionable society with such witty epigrams as: 'Heav'n has no rage like love to hatred turn'd, nor Hell a fury like a woman scorn'd'; and 'Music has charms to sooth a savage breast.'

Arthur Ransome, author of the *Swallows and Amazons* series, was born at 6 Ash Grove, Headingley in 1884. While he and his wife were visiting his mother in Leeds during 1929, he sat down one Monday in March and began to write *Swallows and Amazons*. Ransome little realised that he had embarked on a project that would make his name known throughout the English-speaking world.

J. R. Tolkien's link with the city is more tenuous. He was born in South Africa and appointed a lecturer at Leeds University in 1920 where he invented his Elvish language. But it was as a student at Oxford that he began work on his classic work, and in 1937 published *The Hobbit*. In 1954 and 1955 the *Lord of the Rings* trilogy appeared. Within a decade it was internationally celebrated, and has recently been made into a series of blockbuster films by Hollywood.

Though several Leeds writers have enjoyed international acclaim, only one has been made Poet Laureate, and even that was a questionable appointment. Alfred Austin, born in Leeds in 1835, became Poet Laureate in 1896. His appointment on the death of Tennyson was attributed more to his flattery of the prime minister, Lord Salisbury, than to his innate ability as a poet. Though his work often reflected popular feeling his official efforts left much to be desired. When the Prince of Wales fell ill, Austin penned the following doggerel:

Across the wires the electric message came
'He is no better, he is much the same.'

These less than inspiring lines led the *Daily Telegraph* to comment: 'Mr Alfred Austin has a clearly-defined talent, the limits of which are by this time generally recognised.' The Prince of Wales described his work much more succinctly; he called it 'trash'.

This description could hardly be applied to Charlotte Brontë. She was also well acquainted with Leeds. It was from Leeds that her father, Patrick Brontë, brought back a box of toy soldiers to Haworth for her brother Branwell and indirectly the soldiers started the sisters off on their writing careers. While researching *Shirley,* her novel about the Luddites, she sent to Leeds for the *Leeds Mercury's* report on the attack on Rawfolds Mill and in *Jane Eyre* Leeds appears as 'Millcote'. She sums it up as, 'a large manufacturing town on the banks of the A—; a busy place enough. . . . Not that my fancy was much captivated by long chimnies (*sic*) and clouds of smoke.'

Margaret Storm Jameson was another highly regarded Yorkshire author. She studied at the university in Leeds before embarking upon a literary career. From 1927 to 1968 her thirty books demonstrated wonderful storytelling ability. But it was in more recent times that a female writer born and bred in Leeds became one of the most successful novelists Britain has produced: her name is Barbara Taylor Bradford. By 2005, she had written nineteen bestsellers. The total sales of her books now exceed seventy million copies, and they have been sold in more than ninety countries and translated into over forty languages. Her most popular book, *A Woman of Substance,* is ranked among the ten best-selling novels of all time with twenty million copies sold. In 2003 the *Sunday Times* Rich List put her fortune at £90 million.

She was born Barbara Taylor at Upper Armley in West Leeds, a working-class area. Her father, Winston, worked for the local meter company and sixty years later was still remembered in the area as a smart-looking man. Her mother, Freda, was a cleaner and later caretaker at Northcote private school off Armley Town Street.

Barbara Taylor's beginnings were humble and typical of many in the area. She attended Christ Church Primary School, played out in the streets, visited the Pictodrome – the local cinema on Wortley Road – and scoured the steps for her mother. But if anything singled her out from the crowd it was her voracious appetite for reading. She had read all the works of Dickens by the time she was twelve but admits, 'Some of it was beyond me at that age, to be truthful.' She left school at fifteen, began work as a typist at the *Yorkshire Evening Post* but within six months was appointed a cub reporter.

She was an ambitious young woman. At eighteen, she was promoted to editor of the woman's page. At twenty she moved to London and become fashion editor of the weekly magazine *Woman's Own*. She married Bob Bradford in 1963, moved to the USA and has lived there ever since. It was he who would later turn several of her novels into television mini-series. But at first she continued with journalism, writing a syndicated column that appeared in 183 newspapers three times a week. Although she published children's books and eight books on decorating, she always had a strong desire to write adult fiction.

At first her efforts came to nothing but, in 1976, she submitted a ten-page synopsis and almost two hundred pages of a proposed novel, much of it based in Leeds and drawing upon her background in Armley. The book was, of course, *A Woman of Substance*, which now occupies a significant place in the pantheon of popular publishing.

It is the story of Emma Harte, a self-reliant young woman who becomes one of the richest women in the world through the business she establishes in Armley. It is a tale of ambition and adversity and Emma pithily sums up the main themes of the book as she reflects of Leeds: 'This city can either conquer you, or you can conquer it.' Simplicity is the key and Emma bases her strategy on two great Leeds businessmen: Herman Friend and Michael Marks. Friends's simple concept was the effective sub-division of his workforce, which enabled him to supply John Barran's famous ready-made clothing factory. The other influence, Michael Marks, was a Jewish immigrant from Poland. He had opened his Penny

Bazaar in Leeds Market in 1884 with the slogan, 'Don't ask the price, it's a penny'. His partnership with Tom Spencer established Marks and Spencer and, like Emma Harte's own business in the novel, it became a resounding success.

But *A Woman of Substance* is also a piece of social history, and Barbara Taylor Bradford brings the city of the early years of the twentieth century vividly to life. She describes how Emma wanders through the busy shopping centre gazing at the various stores, making mental notes for 'She could not wait until she owned her own shop.' Of course, the Leeds of 1910 had become a shopping centre of note: it had been transformed with its numerous arcades and the great stores lining Albion Street, Boar Lane and Briggate. It was a city where enterprise flourished; a city in which an enterprising woman like Emma Harte could prosper.

When Emma arrives in Leeds, one character, Blackie O'Neill, speaks of the city with its 'new manufactories going up and the mills and the foundries, as well as the handsome carriages and the elegant houses of the gentry'. But if Leeds is a thriving place, Emma also sees its worst aspects. She sees The Bank: 'this dreadful area of Leeds, off York Road, was bordered on all sides by tough neighbourhoods where grown men were not safe'. And the streets that stretch away from these slums are, 'narrow and ugly, with dark, mean-looking back-to-back houses pressing against each other, wretched dwellings for the working classes'.

Emma is befriended by a Jew, Abraham Kallinski, who tells her of the anti-Semitism rife in the city. 'Leeds is not such a law-abiding city in this day and age. We fend for ourselves as best we can. . . . We are despised by most,' he explains. By 1917 that bigotry manifested itself when anti-Jewish riots broke out in the Leylands district of the town where most Jews lived.

But it is in West Leeds, at Armley, that Emma makes her first foray into business by renting a property on Town Street, the main shopping centre of the district. There she opens a shop selling haberdashery and foodstuffs. In reality, Armley was not without its haberdashers and drapers at that time: in 1901 there was a large drapers, milliners and outfitters in Town Street trading under the name of E. Barnsbee and Co. It had opened in smaller premises off Theaker Lane but later moved to Town Street into an opulent building that boasted six bay windows. The building still stood at the beginning of the twenty-first century, with Anyan's, a local drapers, trading there. In 1901 a second draper, B. Smith & Son, also traded higher up Town Street but at the junction with Wortley Road.

Like Emma, Barbara Taylor would have walked countless times up the steep hill that led over Hill Top, for this had long been a popular Sunday afternoon stroll for locals. And, like Emma, she would have regularly passed the busy White Horse pub halfway up Town Street; it faced onto Armley Moor, the old tenter ground. Here Armley Feast, the local fair, was held annually on the first Saturday in September and has continued into the twenty-first century. Similarly, when in *A Woman of Substance* David Kallinski walks along Stanningley Road to the entrance to Armley Park and strolls up to the magnificent memorial-fountain built to celebrate Queen Victoria's diamond jubilee, he is simply retracing the steps of many other west Leeds folk.

It is on a bitterly cold Sunday in January 1906 that Emma catches a tram up Tong Road to Whingate Junction in Armley, the township where she is trying to make her fortune. Emma's journey is fictional but, on 3 September 1939, Tong Road registered in the memory of another Leeds writer, considered by the *Times Literary Supplement* as 'probably our greatest living dramatist': Alan Bennett. Bennett recalled how that fateful Sunday morning, 'found us on a tram going down Tong Road on a visit to Leeds'. Though Armley, Wortley and other ancient townships were absorbed into Leeds more than a century ago, the expression 'going to Leeds' is still used by locals. And Alan Bennett was very much a local person.

Bennett was born in Leeds in 1934 and for the early part of his life, like Barbara Taylor Bradford, lived in Upper Armley. His father was a butcher who worked at the local Co-op on Armley Lodge

Road. At the end of the war the family moved to Far Headingley where his father opened his own shop. In 1946 Bennett won a scholarship to Leeds Modern School, a grammar in the north of the city. His greatest claim to fame at that time was that he delivered meat to T. S. Eliot's future mother-in-law!

At Exeter College, Oxford, he got a first and for a time taught medieval history at Magdalen College. In the summer of 1959, the Oxford Theatre Group decided to put on a revue at the Edinburgh Festival Fringe. It was such a success that the Festival director invited Bennett, along with Peter Cook, Dudley Moore and Jonathan Miller, to put on their revue, *Beyond the Fringe*. Its subsequent success in London and New York played a major part in the satirical revolution that erupted during the 1960s. Bennett's career went from strength to strength, encompassing radio, television, the theatre and movies. Many of his works are set against a mundane lower-middle-class background and concentrate on such banal themes as holidays, hygiene, social proprietary and sexual repression.

In 1962 his first stage play, *The Blood of the Banbergs*, was produced. In 1965, his first television special – *My Father Knew Lloyd George* – was broadcast and in 1980 both his first radio play, *The Great Jowett* was broadcast and his first film, *Long Shot*, released. His successful films include the BAFTA-winning *Private Function* in 1984 and the screenplay for his classic play, *The Madness of George III*, which was first presented on stage in 1991. The producers, however, decided that the movie would have to be renamed *The Madness of King George* when it was released in 1995 as it was feared American audiences might wonder what had happened to *King George* parts I and II!

In 1982 he broke new ground on television with *Objects of Affection*, a collection of short stories. One story, *A Woman of No Importance*, featured a sole actress, Patricia Routledge, for whom it had been specially written. In the piece she speaks directly to camera and it laid the foundation for his acclaimed *Talking Heads* series. Though Bennett uses Leeds street names in the series, he insists that the locations are figments of his imagination.

In *A Woman of No Importance*, Patricia Routledge, playing Peggy, remarks on a 'blondified piece from the cosmetics counter of Timothy White's and Taylors' and Freeman, Hardy and Willis, the shoe shop, both very much part of the Leeds shopping scene. *Bed Among the Lentils* features Susan, an alcoholic vicar's wife, played by Maggie Smith, who has a relationship with an Asian shopkeeper. For this piece, Bennett created the character of Mr Ramesh, who owns a store sited behind Leeds General Infirmary, plays hockey for Horsforth and is a member of the Leeds Federation of Trade.

Thora Hird, as Doris in *A Cream Cracker Under the Settee*, finds herself on the floor of her home unable to move. As she lies there she reflects upon the frock she is wearing: 'A lame woman ran it up for me that lived down Tong Road,' she muses. David Haigh as Wilfred in *Playing Sandwiches*, ruminates on a Mr Kumar who 'got some decent digs in the Brudenells'. In *Waiting for the Telegram* Armley and Tong Road appear again. But these are not true Leeds locations. Bennett is emphatic, 'I hope no-one ever tries to construct an exact topography of these . . . because I use street names at random, generally picking out the names I remember from my childhood in Leeds.'

However, in his introduction to *The Complete Talking Heads* and his autobiography, *Writing Home*, he vividly brings to life the Leeds he knew. He remarks on 'the posh suburbs . . . Lawnswood and Alwoodley', on Mansfield's shoe shop on Commercial Street and on Marshall and Snelgrove's which stood on Bond Street and was 'a smarter store than Matthias Robinson's but both had the same hushed carpeted elegance, soft lighting and snooty assistants'. He recalls Mr Keen, the local dairyman in Armley with his horse and cart, ladling out the milk from his oval pail in gill measures; Slees the antique dealers on Boar Lane; the Number 16 tram running up Tong Road and 'the unchanging black silhouette of St Bartholomew's, and a few streets over, Armley Gaol.'

Bennett came from a working-class area of Leeds and attended a local grammar school. So too did Willis Hall. He was born in 1929, in a terraced house off Dewsbury Road and he went to

Cockburn High School. At fourteen he began his working life, first as an apprentice deck-hand, then with the *Yorkshire Evening News*. He finally ended up in the Army. While stationed in Malaya he began writing radio scripts. Back home his play, *The Long, the Short and the Tall*, opened at the Royal Court in 1958 with Peter O'Toole in the cast. Some of his most famous work, however, was in collaboration with another lad from South Leeds, Keith Waterhouse.

Their stage plays such as *England our England* and *All Things Bright and Beautiful* were successes and together they scripted two major British films, *Whistle Down the Wind* and *A Kind of Loving*. In Hollywood, they worked uncredited on Alfred Hitchcock's rather disappointing *Torn Curtain*. But their collaboration to adapt Waterhouse's novel *Billy Liar* for the big screen resulted in one of the most memorable movies of the 1960s. Much of it was shot in Leeds. One memorable scene features the town hall. From its steps Tom Courtenay – playing Billy Fisher, an undertaker's clerk with a Walter Mitty-like imagination – takes the salute as a fantasy army marches by. Even the half-demolished back-to-backs on Wellington Road were used in some scenes.

It was not the only time Leeds locations were used in a Waterhouse film. When his novel *There is a Happy Land* – set on a Leeds council estate – was filmed the schools on the Middleton estate that Waterhouse had attended were used as the backdrop. However, he was not born on a corporation estate, but in Low Road, Hunslet in 1929. His father was a heavy drinker who died when Waterhouse was three; his legacy was a brown suit and a ha'penny. It was then that the family moved to the council estate at Middleton before settling in the one at Osmondthorpe. From there he won a scholarship to the College of Commerce on Woodhouse Lane.

His first job was with an undertaker, a job that would one day provide the background for *Billy Liar*. Eventually he became a journalist on the *Yorkshire Evening Post*. His first report was simple enough: 'At 8*d*. to 10*d*. a lb, strawberries are cheaper and more plentiful at Leeds Market than they have been all season.' It was during his time with the *Post* that he got his first scoop when he revealed the corporation's plans to scrap the tramway system of Leeds and switch to buses. Eventually he moved to London where he became an established columnist, first with the *Daily Mirror* and then with the *Daily Mail*. But he continued writing books and now has fourteen novels and several works of non-fiction to his credit.

His most important work for the local historian is the autobiographical *City Lights; a Street Life* published in 1994. Gerald Kaufman, reviewing it for the *Guardian*, wrote that it 'stands out above everything else Waterhouse has created, earning my gratitude for giving back to me the Leeds that I loved, the Leeds that time and change has taken away.' Waterhouse captures a city now gone:

> Low Road, now largely urban desert, was one of the tram-rattling arteries running from the city centre, all of them lively thoroughfares lined with ironmongers' shops, newsagents and tobacconists, small grocers, family butchers, fish and chip shops, pawnshops, public houses without number, breweries, foundries, obscure little factories and workshops, and countless sooty red-brick terraces which stemmed off the main road on either side like herring bones.

He vividly recalls Hunslet Moor 'an acre of flattened cinders . . . where a great fair – Hunslet Feast – was held every August Bank Holiday'. He reflects on catching the No. 12 tram to Leeds and then Sammy Ledgard's bus to Horsforth to visit an aunt; and brings back to life City Square with its news scanner on the Majestic cinema, and the Silver Line taxis 'gliding in and out of the station' over the rubberised briquette roadway laid down so that the noise did not disturb the guests at the newly opened Queen's Hotel. But in Hunslet or Holbeck, he points out, 'when somebody was lying ill, the cobbles were still spread with straw to deaden the rumble of cart wheels.'

Richard Hoggart also drew on his experiences of Hunslet in his work. He was born in Chapeltown, in 1918, but following the death of his parents he went to live with his grandmother in Hunslet. From Jack Lane School he won a scholarship to Cockburn High School and then a senior city scholarship that gave him the opportunity to become a student at Leeds University.

No student of the social history of Leeds can ignore Hoggart's graphic descriptions and astute analysis of working-class life. His classic *The Uses of Literacy* (1957) analyses North of England culture in a completely new way. In the book he draws heavily on his experience of life in the back-to-backs. He examines working-class culture over the previous thirty to forty years and looks in particular at the way popular publications of the day affected the changes in that culture. His autobiography, *A Local Habitation* (1988), recounts in graphic detail life in the pre-war working-class areas of the city.

He describes the rhubarb fields of Leeds with rhubarb 'thick as a labourer's forearm'. He writes of clothing cheques where people are given a cheque to spend on clothes immediately and then pay off the debt weekly; of other club payments collected weekly to help pay for toys and hampers and Christmas decorations. He tells of the coal fire, 'a pivot of working-class life'; and the resentment some local folk held against the Jews of Leeds for their apparent prosperity but who forgot the 'poor Jews who worked very hard for low wages and never got out of Sheepscar'. He writes of the annual local feasts: 'the big stuff was in the middle; then sheltering under the rim of the big stuff, smaller stalls – hoop-la, rifle booths, dart-throwing stalls and the like.' And he explains what often proved a mystery to outsiders: how people in Holbeck or Hunslet could tell their area from others. 'How were the boundaries decided? By types of people and street furniture . . . or the division came at a main road or on each side of a medium-sized road . . . or the walls of a small factory marked the boundaries.'

Hoggart became assistant director-general of UNESCO and warden of Goldsmith's College at the University of London. He saw his *Uses of Literacy* translated into many languages and the concluding remarks of his preface are as relevant today as they were when they were written a half a century ago: 'One of the most striking and ominous features of our present cultural situation is the division between the technical languages of the experts and the extraordinary low level of the organs of mass communication.'

If Richard Hoggart, Alan Bennett and Willis Hall were products of local grammar-schools, Kay Mellor was most definitely not. She was born in Leeds in 1950, attended West Park Secondary Modern School but left at fifteen with no qualifications. At sixteen she was studying typing at Park Lane College but became pregnant and married Anthony Mellor in 1967. They are still married.

Her wish was to attend drama school and, after her second child was born, she returned to Park Lane where her tutor encouraged her to follow her ambition. Refusing to leave her family to study in London she applied to nearby Bretton Hall College and it was there that her literary talents began to emerge. Her play *Paul* was submitted to the National Student Drama Festival and although not a winner the feedback she got encouraged her to pursue the dream of becoming a dramatist. She formed the Yorkshire Theatre Company, contributed scripts for television soaps like *Albion Market* and *Children's Ward* and storylines for *Coronation Street*.

However, it was when she moved to a bigger house in West Park that she had the idea of writing a play about an older woman and it premiered at the West Yorkshire Playhouse as *Passionate Woman* in 1994. The theme of women's role in society attracted her and, in 1995, she tackled one of the most controversial social issues in the television series *Band of Gold*. Set against the grim backdrop of industrial Bradford, *Band of Gold* tells the story of a group of prostitutes each trying to forge their own destinies. It was an enormous ratings success and had an impact equivalent to a 1960s classic in the same mould, *Cathy Come Home*.

Two years later Sally Head, the executive director of *Band of Gold*, asked her to return to the theme of a woman striving to fulfil her destiny by adapting *Jane Eyre* for television. It was a dream come true for Mellor; *Jane Eyre* was her favourite novel. Since then more television plays and films have followed and, in 2003, the year that her play *Gifted* was produced, she received an honorary doctorate from Hallam University, a great achievement for a girl who left school without a qualification to her name.

Leeds can be rightly proud of its authors. Though they come from different backgrounds, their work forms a rich tapestry of human experience and reveals the passions, hopes and fears that make up life. In that they reflect the rich and diverse city from which they came.

7

BADGE OF COURAGE

On 5 December 1915 the night shift at Barnbow munitions factory in East Leeds had just begun work. Throughout the First World War the plant would produce some 500,000 tons of ammunition, making a vital contribution to the war effort. But producing bullets and bombs is a dangerous business. On that fatal Sunday evening, a disastrous explosion ripped through the building and thirty-five female workers perished. Those workers were fully aware of the dangers their work entailed yet they had committed themselves wholeheartedly to the task in hand.

Their names, the bravery they showed and the suffering they endured are known to few people today. Yet many Leeds women, sometimes at great personal sacrifice, have courageously served their country and many Leeds men have bravely taken part in some of the great battles in British history. James Barrass was a native of Holbeck and one of the six hundred cavalrymen who took part in the Charge of the Light Brigade during the Battle of Balaclava in 1854. He survived and died in Hunslet twenty-seven years later. Giles Salter of Leeds served as a Royal Marine during the same conflict and helped to put down a mutiny that broke out on-board ship.

John Greenhalgh, a Leeds coal miner, fought with Redvers Buller's column, which suffered serious defeats at the battles of Colenso and Spion Kop before relieving the besieged town of Ladysmith during the Boer War. Herbert Myers had his eye shot out in 1916 during the holocaust known as the Battle of the Somme. He was but one of the 400,000 British casualties from that engagement. He ended his days quietly, running a sweet and tobacconist's shop on Tong Road. In 1915 private Levi found himself cut off from his force and had to lie face down as shells exploded and Maxim fire rattled around him: 'It was horrible lying there hearing the wounded groaning and crying for water' he wrote home to Leeds shortly afterwards.

Ernest Boocock, a GPO engineer at the Armley telephone exchange, fought behind the Japanese lines in Burma during the Second World War. He too recalled how he and his colleagues lay in the jungle listening to the cries of wounded British soldiers knowing that the Japanese had left them there in the hope that rescue parties would be sent out and make easy targets for their snipers. And sixty years later he still recalled with some bitterness that, when supplies were dropped by the Allies, they had to pay for their cigarettes when they returned to base. Tom Page – who spent most of his life as a postman in Holbeck – was evacuated from Dunkirk in 1940 but on D-Day, 6 June 1944, he was back in France. By 6.30 a.m. he had established a forward observation post for the Royal Artillery.

There is nothing exceptional in their stories. Their deeds would be replicated time and time again by other Leeds men who performed similar acts of courage. Some, like major John Geoffrey Appleyard from Bramley, had their achievements recognised. He received the Distinguished Service Order, Military Cross and Bar for his outstanding work in the cross-Channel raiding group the SSRF, the Small-Scale Raiding Force, and the SAS, the Special Air Service. He died on active service in Sicily in 1943.

However, only a few men have been singled out for exceptional bravery in the face of insurmountable odds. For that they were honoured with the highest recognition for gallantry this country can bestow on any person; the Victoria Cross or VC. Between 1856 and 2003, 1,354 Victoria Crosses were awarded, eighteen to men either born in Leeds or closely associated with the town. The names of the Leeds recipients can be seen on a plaque near the Cenotaph by the Art Gallery on the Headrow.

The award was established during the Crimean War in 1856 by Queen Victoria and her consort, Prince Albert. It was presented to soldiers and sailors who had shown exceptional courage in the face of the enemy. The small bronze crosses, thirty-eight millimetres across, bear the simple words, 'For Valour'. They have always been, and still are, made by Hancocks of Burlington Arcade, from the bronze of two captured Russian cannons. Victoria and Albert's idea was to honour bravery irrespective of rank. One so honoured was John Pearson, a private, who was born at Seacroft, and became a member of the 8th King's Royal Irish Hussars.

Pearson fought in the Crimea at Alma, Balaclava and Sebastopol but in 1857 the Indian Mutiny broke out and he and his regiment sailed on the SS *Great Britain* for the subcontinent. Bitter at various reforms that were being introduced, at attempts to impose Christianity on them and the suggestion that new cartridges had been greased with cow and pig fat which was repugnant to Hindus and Muslims respectively, Indian troops mutinied and violence erupted.

At Gwalior in central India on 17 June 1858, Pearson's squadron encountered a rebel force. He was part of the charge and in the ensuing struggle suffered a severe sword cut to his right shoulder. The enemy regrouped and advanced under covering fire from both the town and the fort perched on a hill above it. Despite his wounds and constant attack from the Indian artillery, John Pearson led a charge against two enemy batteries. His comrades agreed that he, above all others, deserved to be recognised for his valour and accordingly he was awarded the VC, the first Leeds man to receive it.

Five years later on 7 September 1863, colour sergeant Edward McKenna of the 1st battalion 65th Regiment (later the Yorks. and Lancs. Regiment) enlisted in the town when he was seventeen and became the second Leeds man to be so honoured. He was serving near Cameron Town in New Zealand. In 1860 war broke out between the Maori inhabitants of New Zealand and the English settlers as the newcomers began to encroach onto Maori land. 'Let the mad drunkards get off to Europe' one Maori song defiantly proclaimed. Any help available to the beleaguered Europeans depended on what the British government could spare from its commitments elsewhere. Edward McKenna, along with his colleagues, was soon facing the crisis this policy produced. Heavily outnumbered, he saw both his officers shot and then took command. He led his small force in a charge through the enemy lines to safety, with only one of his comrades killed and one missing. He stayed in New Zealand and was buried in the cemetery at Palmerston North, on North Island, in 1908.

Troops maintaining the British Empire always faced the possibility of nationalist rebellions. The subcontinent of India was a volatile area. Captain Richard Kirby Ridgeway was an Irishman who, in 1879, was serving with the 8th Gurkha Rifles on the eastern frontier when he won his VC. On 22 November, during an assault on Konoma, his troops came under heavy rebel fire from behind a barricade. He raced forward to the fortification and began to rip the palisade-planking down in order to effect a breach and so enabled the British force to subdue the enemy. In so doing he was severely wounded in the right shoulder. He survived, eventually moved to Leeds and was cremated at Lawnswood crematorium in 1924, over forty years later.

The next major conflict in which Leeds men's bravery was so recognised occurred in South Africa during the Boer War. Sergeant Alfred Atkinson of Wortley and private Charles Ward of Hunslet distinguished themselves with their courage in the face of insuperable odds. Atkinson was born in Armley to a military family. His father, James Atkinson, was a farrier-major and legend has it that he was in the party that captured the cannons from which the original VCs were cast. Alfred Atkinson also joined the army, served his time and became part of the Reserve. However, with the outbreak of the Second Boer War he rejoined the colours, becoming a member of the 1st battalion of the West Yorkshire Regiment, the Prince of Wales's Own.

On 18 February 1900, the British Army intercepted general Cronje and his Boer army on the banks of the Modder River near

Paardeberg Hill. The Boers entrenched themselves in the dried-up river bed and a bloody exchange ensued. The incessant Boer fire raked the British lines, inflicting serious casualties. As the wounded lay helpless under the blistering sun, sergeant Atkinson took it upon himself to bring some relief to his injured comrades. Six times he ran the gauntlet of fire to carry water to the suffering men. On the seventh he was shot in the head and died three days later.

Charles Ward of the King's Own Yorkshire Light Infantry joined the 1st battalion of the regiment in 1897. Two years later, when the Second Boer War broke out, Ward became one of the thousands of British troops who were shipped out to South Africa. On 20 June 1900 he was part of a small British force with responsibility for defending the town of Lindley. Suddenly a Boer attack was launched. It became obvious that the vastly superior numbers of the enemy would soon overwhelm the defenders. Ward then volunteered to act as messenger and ran to the nearest signal station where an urgent request for reinforcements was sent. He then tried to rejoin his company, but Boer bullets cut him down and he was seriously injured. Fortunately he recovered and his bravery was recognised by the award of the VC. 'But for this gallant action the post would certainly have been lost,' the citation recorded. He was buried in Hunslet cemetery.

Ward had the distinction of being one of the last, if not the last, recipient of the medal from Queen Victoria herself. Alfred Atkinson received no such medal. Although the bravery of those who died in an act of courage was acknowledged in the official *Gazette*, the Victoria Cross could only be won by men who had survived their ordeal. In 1902, however, the new king, Edward VII, ordered that those who had died should have the award presented to their relatives. Thus Alfred Atkinson's relatives received his medal and it now lies in the Green Howard's Museum at Richmond.

The year 1914 heralded the outbreak of the First World War; the bloodiest conflict mankind has ever experienced. The people of Leeds bore a heavy burden; some 9,640 young men from the city perished.

The year 1915 saw two men who had spent much of their lives

in the town, though they were not born there, given a VC. Company sergeant major Harry Daniels of the Rifle Brigade distinguished himself in France when British forces launched a massive attack against the German lines at Neuve Chapelle on 10 March. Militarily it was a disaster. As Liddell Hart, the historian remarked, 'It was an isolated attempt with inadequate resources.' But that should never detract from the courage shown by the men involved. After a pounding from 400 guns and howitzers, the German lines were attacked by a combined force of British and Indian infantry. By 12 March, the British advance in the sector where Harry Daniels was stationed was being impeded by barbed wire. Daniels and his comrade, Cecil Noble, volunteered to go forward. Despite machine-gun fire sweeping the ground, they succeeded in cutting the wire and making an advance possible. It was not without personal sacrifice; both men were wounded and Cecil Noble later died of his wounds. Both received the Victoria Cross.

Private Charles Hull of the 21st Lancers was another such hero; though not born in Leeds he had close connections with it and was buried in Woodhouse cemetery in 1953. He won his VC in India on 5 September 1915. He was serving on the North-West Frontier, an unstable region where there was an ever-present threat to British forces from local tribes. On that fateful Sunday, a small British force suddenly came under fire from hostile tribesmen at Hafiz Kor. The officer in charge had his horse shot from under him and as the hail of bullets continued strafing the British force, Charles Hull rushed forward. He pulled the subaltern up onto his horse behind him and then, still under heavy fire, galloped to safety.

A month later, a Leeds police constable, now acting-sergeant John Raynes of the Royal Field Artillery was in action at Fosse 7 de Béthune in France on 11 October. His battery came under German shell fire. British casualties were high and, during the bombardment, a sergeant Ayres was hit. Raynes spotted his wounded comrade. Then, despite the constant barrage, he negotiated the forty yards that separated him from the injured man and set about dealing with his wounds. He returned to his own gun position but the shelling was so intense that he and two gunners were forced to stop firing and carry Ayres to a dugout. The two gunners were killed and then the Germans launched a gas attack. Raynes put his gas helmet onto the injured man. The next day he was caught in a second bombardment. The building he was in was struck and he was buried in the rubble. He was dug free and had his wounds dressed, but insisted on returning to fight with his battery. Still suffering from his wounds he returned home and served with Leeds City Police until ill health forced his retirement in 1924. When John Raynes was buried in Harehills cemetery in 1929 he was honoured with a civic funeral, one of the largest ever seen in the city.

The following year, 1916, saw the single most devastating day in the history of the British Army and the city of Leeds. During the course of a single day, 1 July, the British Army suffered 57,000 casualties. In the first attack of the Battle of the Somme some 900 men of the West Yorkshire Regiment, known as the Leeds Pals, were part of the assault and charged across no man's land. Seventeen returned. It was said that every street in Leeds had lost at least one man. The battle raged from July to November and, during that time, fifty-one men were granted the VC; two from Leeds.

Corporal George Sanders of the 1/7th, the merged battalions of the West Yorkshire Regiment, was born in Leeds in 1894 and was one of those involved on that first day on the Somme. He was advancing with thirty men across the battlefield at Thiepval, a small village on the Ancre River where some of the bloodiest fighting in the sector took place. It was there that he and his men became isolated from the main body of British troops. He insisted that they hold their position at all costs and set about organising defences. The next morning, despite a fierce German attack, they held their position and succeeded in freeing several British prisoners. Sanders survived and lived until 1950 when he was cremated at Cottingley crematorium.

The fighting at the Somme dragged on. During this protracted engagement, at Ginchy, a small hamlet north of the river Somme near the town of Combles, some of the worst casualties of the battle occurred. It was here that lance-sergeant Fred McNess of Bramley won his award. On 15 September McNess, of the 1st battalion Scots Guards, and his men were under heavy fire. Nevertheless, ignoring the bursting shells and rattling machine guns, Fred McNess led his men forward to the enemy trench. On reaching it he found his left flank exposed but still organised a counter attack. Despite being severely injured in the neck and jaw he ran the gauntlet of heavy fire to acquire further supplies of ammunition for his own men. Next he established a block to prevent the enemy from making further inroads into the British force. He went on encouraging his men until he was exhausted through loss of blood. In a romantic twist, he fell in love and finally married the nurse who cared for him during his convalescence. He spent his life working for the Leeds City engineers department and retired to Bournemouth. Tragically, he committed suicide in 1956.

The Western Front and its appalling casualties tended to dominate the headlines in Britain but, in the Middle East, a desert war was raging. Jack White, or Weiss, was born to a Jewish family in Leeds in December 1896. In 1917 he was serving as a signaller with the King's Own Royal Lancaster Regiment in Mesopotamia. On 7–8 March the force he was with was crossing the Djalah river on pontoons. Two came under heavy Turkish fire. By the time his own pontoon had reached midstream every man on board had been either killed or wounded. Twenty-year-old Jack White was the sole exception. Realising he was unable to navigate the craft, he tied a length of telephone wire round his waist, lowered himself into the muddy waters and hauled the pontoon slowly to the shore. In doing so he saved not only the men on board but also their arms and equipment. He died in Manchester in 1949 and was buried in the Jewish cemetery there.

Activity on the Western Front was increased when, on 23 April 1917, Sir Douglas Haig began his second thrust from Arras. Strong German resistance at Heniel and Wancourt held up his forces. Arras was to be one of the great battles of the war and was fought in almost winter weather. One Leeds man who took part was

David Philip Hirsch. He was born in Leeds and joined Leeds University officer training corps. Then, as a second lieutenant, he saw action with the Yorkshire Regiment, the Green Howards, at the Somme. On that April day at Arras he was acting captain of Y company on the right of the British line. He led his men in an attack on Wancourt, but in so doing was twice wounded. Despite the constant German fire he saw to it that a secure defensive flank was established. The position his men was in was exposed to extreme enemy fire but Hirsch moved along the line, encouraging his company to hold its ground. Despite heavy machine-gun fire and a German counter attack he kept up this devotion to duty until he was finally cut down. His name is recorded on the memorial to the missing at Arras.

Private William Boynton Butler was Leeds born, attending Upper Wortley Council School as a boy. He was a small man, so small that he was able to enlist in the 17th battalion of the West Yorkshire Regiment, specially created to cater for men of short stature and known affectionately as the Leeds Bantams. However, what he lacked in size he made up for in courage. On 6 August 1917 he was serving at Lempire on the Western Front. He was in charge of a Stokes gun when his trench came under heavy German fire. His gun malfunctioned. One of the fly-levers flew off leaving the unexploded shell in the emplacement. He picked up the live shell and carried it to the entrance only to find a party of infantry passing at that moment. He yelled at them to make haste as the shell was about to explode but turned so that if the worst happened his body would take the brunt of the impact and shield the passing troops. He then managed to hoist the shell over the parados (the mound at the back of the trench). Almost immediately it exploded. The trench suffered considerable damage but Butler was fortunate. The blast did not injure him, but left him in a confused state as to what had exactly happened. He received his VC and the people of Wortley also wanted to acknowledge their hero. On their behalf it was arranged for the vicar to present him with a silver tea-service at his old school. But his mother had to collect it for him – he was already back at the front. If he missed that ceremony he did at least live to attend another. In July 1962 he was invited to Buckingham palace with other VC recipients to meet the Queen. He was buried in Hunslet cemetery in 1972.

Ten days later, on Thursday, 16 August 1917, another Leeds man showed exemplary courage in the face of the enemy and was awarded a VC. Private Wilfred Edwards came to Leeds as a child. As a member of the 7th battalion of the King's Own Yorkshire Light Infantry he was serving at Langemarck in the Ypres salient in Belgium. This, the third Battle of Ypres, and often referred to as the Battle of Passchendaele, was an attempt to liberate Belgium. On that day Wilfred Edwards was in charge of a body of men. All their officers had been killed and heavy machine gun and rifle fire from a concrete fort held them in check. Edwards knew that the only way they could survive was for the fort to be silenced and its murderous fusillade brought to an end. Alone, he advanced on the fortified German position and proceeded to lob hand grenades through the loopholes. When his task was completed, he waved the company forward. The German occupants were now easily overcome; three officers and thirty other ranks surrendered. He then proceeded to guide the battalion through difficult terrain to safety. He was buried in Wortley cemetery in 1972.

During 1918 three more Leeds men achieved the distinction of being awarded Britain's highest award for bravery; Albert Mountain and Laurence Calvert were born in the city and Arthur Poulter came there as a young man of nineteen and made it his home for the rest of his life. His eight other brothers were also involved in the forces during that war.

Sergeant Albert Mountain of the 15/17th West Yorkshire Regiment was born in Leeds in 1895. On 26 March 1918 the combined battalions of the Leeds Pals, the 15th battalion and the Leeds Bantams, the 17th battalion, were at Harmelincourt in France. There he and his ten men faced a critical situation. A German patrol of 200 men was advancing towards them. Without hesitation he took a Lewis gun and sprayed the advancing enemy with deadly fire as they advanced. Having killed half of the attackers he then set about organising covering fire for his company to withdraw. While the main body fell back, Mountain and four men held back a further 600 Germans for half an hour. He then took command of a flank position which he held for twenty-seven hours before being surrounded. Not only was he awarded the VC, but was also the recipient of the French Croix de Guerre and Médaille Militaire. He was cremated at Lawnswood crematorium in 1967.

Private Arthur Poulter served with the merged 1/4th Duke of Wellington's Regiment in France and on 10 April 1918 he was acting as a stretcher bearer at Erquinhem à Leys. General Ludendorf had launched the last major offensive against the Allies and one that almost won the war for Germany. During the campaign of the Lys the British force was subjected to an intense artillery bombardment while small arms caused havoc. In spite of the barrage Poulter faced the lethal onslaught on ten occasions to carry wounded men to safety. Two of them were hit even as he bore them. So intense was the fire that the order was eventually given to vacate that side of the river Lys and withdraw to the opposite bank. Regardless of the danger Arthur Poulter crossed the river again to bring back yet another wounded man. In all, he bandaged forty wounded soldiers while exposed to enemy fire. It was an act of courage that earned him the VC. He was buried in New Wortley cemetery in 1956 and his medal now resides in the Duke of Wellington's regimental museum in Halifax.

Sergeant Laurence Calvert was born in Leeds on 16 February 1892 and attended Cockburn High School. He became a Territorial. By 1918 he was serving as a non-commissioned officer in the 5th battalion King's Own Yorkshire Light Infantry stationed in France. The month of September saw the Allies preparing to launch an all-out attack to break through the Hindenburg Line, which was known to the Germans as the Siegfried Line. This was a series of trenches strengthened by concrete bunkers and gun emplacements that ran roughly from Arras to Laon. The line itself snaked through the village of Havrincourt and it was here that Calvert's battalion was ordered to attack. At 5.25 a.m. on the morning of 12 September 1918 the assault began. Sergeant Calvert's C company, along with B company, were in the front line and ordered to take the south-west corner of the village. Heavy fire from Bogart's Hole pinned down the British force. Calvert realised that he had to act if the situation was not to deteriorate. He moved forward against the two machine-gun nests. Once there he bayoneted three German soldiers and shot four more, capturing the two machine guns in the process. Thanks to his action the British objective was attained without great loss of life and for his conspicuous act of bravery he was awarded the Victoria Cross. He died at Dagenham in Essex in 1964.

The Second World War saw just one VC awarded to a Leeds man for, as the official citation said, 'An example of devotion to duty which has been seldom equalled, never surpassed.' Arthur Louis Aaron was born in Leeds in 1922 and attended Roundhay School. In 1939 he began studying architecture at the Leeds College of Art and joined the air squadron at Leeds University. Two years later he had become a member of the volunteer reserve of the Royal Air Force and under its auspices was sent to Texas to learn how to fly. By 1942 Aaron was flying operational sorties and was awarded the Distinguished Flying Cross. On one occasion a fire broke out to the rear of the bomb door. Undeterred, he left two members of the crew to deal with it as he pressed on and completed the attack on the target.

Thursday 12 August 1943 was a busy day for the Allied air forces in Europe. American B-17s – led by the Hollywood star, captain Clark Gable – bombed the Ruhr and Bonn. In Italy more than six hundred RAF night bombers launched an attack on Milan and Turin. One of those bombers was a four-engine Stirling piloted by flight-sergeant Arthur Aaron. As it droned in over Turin an enemy fighter swooped and fired a devastating burst. Three engines were hit, the front and rear gun turrets were put out of action, the elevator control was damaged rendering the stability of the plane uncertain and the windscreen was shattered. Several crew members were hit and the navigator was killed.

Arthur Aaron was also hit. A bullet had crashed into his jaw and shattered his face. Another penetrated his lung, a third his right arm. He fell forward over the controls and the plane plunged several thousand feet. At 3,000 feet the flight engineer managed to halt the fall and levelled out. Aaron, unable to speak, indicated for the bomb aimer to take over the controls and a course was set for Allied-held Sicily or North Africa. The crippled bomber, with one engine completely out of action slowly made its way south while Arthur Aaron was taken to the rear and treated with morphine. After resting, he insisted on returning to the cockpit where he was lifted into his seat and his feet placed on the rudder bar. Twice he tried desperately to keep the course steady but the effort was too much. His crew finally persuaded him to relinquish the controls but, though racked with pain, he courageously issued instructions by writing with his left hand.

After flying for five hours Bône airfield in Algeria was sighted. Knowing that the undercarriage was retracted, Aaron tried to help his bomb aimer make the difficult landing. It took five attempts before the plane touched down safely. Nine hours later, flight sergeant Aaron died. His citation summed up his performance perfectly: 'In appalling conditions he showed the greatest qualities of courage, determination and leadership.' His VC is displayed in the Civic Hall in Leeds and his statue now stands at Eastgate roundabout, a fitting tribute to a brave Leeds man. He was just twenty-one.

Perhaps the courage and determination showed by these men and those other unsung Leeds heroes who fought for their country in the hope of providing a better world was best summed up by a young lance corporal, Andy Dodds of C company of the 7th battalion West Yorkshire Regiment. Writing home from the front in May 1915 he said, 'We shall win, maybe not in a month, or a year, but win we shall and the world will be sweeter.' He never posted his letter. His colleagues found it in his pocket after he had been cut down by a German sniper just seventy-five yards from the enemy line.

8

CRIME AND THE CITY

The time was 2.30 a.m. on 9 December. It was cold and misty when suddenly the silence was shattered by the rat-tat-tat of gunfire. Two rival gangs had opened fire on each other. Then one group took flight and drove off at high speed through the foggy streets. The other sped after them. The pursuing car eventually caught its quarry, or so the driver thought. The gunman inside blasted the vehicle it had been chasing with a shotgun. In the swirling fog, he hit the wrong car . . .

If this had been the Chicago of 1929 it would not have raised an eyebrow. In fact, it was Leeds in 2001 and just one more example of gun crime on the city's streets. The *Yorkshire Evening Post* put the story of the shooting – which took place outside the Casa Loco club on Templar Lane – on its front page when the case came to court. However, its editorial also highlighted another major problem the city faced. In just eight months 23,000 discarded syringes had been cleared from the city's pavements, footpaths and parks. Today guns and drugs, along with international terrorism, are the biggest challenges for the forces of law and order. But up to the 1960s neither the use of firearms, nor narcotics, were common in Leeds.

In the past, of course, the city had problems with crime. Thefts and burglaries were common. Cloth was frequently stolen from the tenter frames; two culprits, Green and Thackrah, were transported from the town for seven years for that crime in October 1800. Burglary then was a capital offence. Thomas Stearman and John Lucas of Leeds were convicted for burglary in Leeds and executed in

York in April 1792. Vandalism, too, was a problem: streets lamps were smashed in the town in 1800. And there were other anti-social activities that were common: women were attacked in South Parade in 1803; children were encouraged by adults to pilfer warehouses in 1811; prostitution was rife on the town's streets in 1813 and by 1859 Leeds had 120 'houses of ill-fame' as the chief constable's report described them.

Robbery was commonplace. The post-boy at Middleton was robbed in January 1797. Forgery at the time was a capital offence and Joseph Blackburn, a Leeds attorney, paid the ultimate price at York in March 1815 for forging a £2 stamp. Bodysnatching during the 1820s was regularly reported in the columns of the *Leeds Mercury* and the *Leeds Patriot*. The churchyards of St John's in Briggate and at Armley were both targeted whilst the parishioners of Wortley were so concerned that they built a small hut in the cemetery to guard newly buried corpses.

Inevitably there were less serious crimes. Two cabmen at a funeral at Beckett Street cemetery in November 1879 decided to break the monotony of the solemn occasion with a bout of fisticuffs, while William Fry got fourteen days on Christmas Eve 1908 for chalking on the pavement. The *Leeds Intelligencer* and the *Leeds Mercury* carried reports of such crimes but paid particular attention to murder and rape. Both editors protested that they were performing a civic duty by placing this information in the public domain, but they also recognised the commercial potential.

Mary Bateman, the poisoner, was without doubt the most notorious of these Leeds killers. Within a week of her trial in 1809, Edward Baines, the editor of the *Mercury* had published a pamphlet on the case. In four days, 1,000 copies had been sold and, in a matter of months, 10,000. The rape case of the decade also saw Baines quickly off the mark: even as the trial finished in August 1811 he announced that his one-shilling pamphlet would be available within a week and would include 'a GENUINE LETTER from WILLIAM HODGSON to his MOTHER after conviction.' There was outrage at the verdict, not least because Harriet

Halliday, the girl involved, had visited him in gaol. An appeal was made to the Prince Regent and Hodgson was eventually reprieved.

Crimes involving guns were few and far between. The most infamous of the gunman associated with Leeds was Charles Peace. Originally a petty thief, Peace gravitated to housebreaking and robbery. He shot a man in Sheffield over a squabble about the victim's wife and, in a separate incident, gunned down a police officer in Manchester. He was eventually arrested, made a vain attempt to escape from a moving train but was caught and hanged at Armley Jail in February 1879. His exploits continue to capture the public imagination: two films have been made of his life, books are still published about him, Madame Tussaud's gave him a place in the chamber of horrors and today the Internet tells of his misdeeds to a worldwide audience.

However, most Leeds murders did not involve firearms. The majority were domestic in origin and involved wives or girlfriends and were often motivated by jealousy. Of the men executed at Armley for murders committed in Leeds, four cut their victims' throats and five beat their partners to death. Only one involved strangulation, but it was the most talked-about crime during the inter-war years. Emily Yeomans was a waitress at Lyons café in County Arcade. Her body was found in Middleton Woods in October 1934. She had been strangled with her own stocking. David Blake of Beeston was eventually charged with the crime and executed at Armley on the day before his thirtieth birthday.

Theft accounted for two stabbings in Leeds that resulted in Armley executions. In July 1904, Edmund Hall – a labourer who worked at Greenwood and Batley's in Armley – stabbed his father-in-law to death in York during an argument and stole his watch and chain. And the last man executed at Armley Jail was also a petty thief. Zsiga Pantakai went to the home of Eli Myers, a market trader, in Chelwood Avenue, Roundhay one February evening in 1961. His object was to steal a vanload of clothes. Pantakai stabbed Myers to death and went to the gallows in Leeds Prison on 29 June that year.

The end of the Second World War was a watershed for crime

throughout the United Kingdom. Leeds did no more than follow the national pattern. Indictable offences recorded in the city during 1944 were 5,626. In 1946 they had soared to 6,072. The Leeds City Police response came in 1947 when a vice squad and an operations room were established. Some 1,891 emergency calls were received during that year; two years later the number had reached 10,629. Crime was on the march.

Gun crime became more of a feature. Albert Sabin, a guard from the prisoner-of-war camp at Tingley, was one of the first in Leeds to be part of this new culture. The soldier boasted, 'I always carry a gun about with me loaded.' On the afternoon of 21 September 1946 he was seen driving off with psychiatrist Dr Neil McLeod from his Park Square consulting-room. Sabin later testified: 'I made up my mind to have some money off him.' A struggle followed. The revolver went off and Dr McLeod fell dead. The doctor's body was later found in a ditch near the camp.

Guns were again involved in November 1949, when Walter Sharpe, a surgical boot-maker from Seacroft and Gordon Lannen, a 17-year-old from Middleton, broke into Linley's, a gun shop in Albion Street and stole four revolvers and some ammunition. A few days later they returned to Albion Street and entered Levines' jewellery shop, intent on armed robbery. In the bloody mêlée that ensued, Abraham Levine was shot in the head as he struggled with them in the street. Sharpe then fired above a horrified crowd of shoppers to frighten them off and the robbers ran up Woodhouse Lane pursued by members of the public. Armed police were quickly on the scene and the area, including the Gaumont cinema in Cookridge Street, was searched. Two days later the killers were caught in Southport. At their trial in Leeds town hall the judge commended those members of the public who had given chase, summing up his comments with the words, 'These men were brave and unarmed citizens. Leeds was not deficient in brave and gallant men that day.' The jury returned a verdict of guilty. Lannen, because of his age, was sentenced to be detained at his majesty's pleasure; Sharpe was hanged at Armley in March 1950.

If the Levine murder was clear cut, the shooting of Edward Watson, a car dealer from Ringwood Crescent, Leeds, was not. In May 1953, Watson met with Robert Moore, another dealer. They were to go and view a car in Harrogate. The full details of what went on between them are unknown, but what is known is that Moore shot Watson five times at point-blank range and buried the body near Swinsty reservoir. Moore was executed in January 1954. But murder was by now alarmingly common in the city, as was the use of guns.

Armed robberies escalated nationally during the 1960s and 1970s. At that time many workers preferred being paid weekly in cash and so payroll vans were easy targets. In addition, robberies of banks and post offices had become commonplace. There was a good example of the trend on 9 June 1966, when a gunman entered the Bridge End post office at the bottom of Briggate. He opened fire. The postmaster was wounded; the assistant killed. The raider escaped with £92 in notes. The police faced criticism for not catching the killer but their job was becoming more difficult with every year that passed.

As the century progressed acquiring guns became much easier. In pubs like the infamous Madhouse – more correctly the Market Tavern – at the junction of Harewood Street and George Street, or the Hayfield Hotel on Chapeltown Road, firearms were readily available, as indeed they were in many other establishments with dubious reputations. A criminal could either buy or hire one. Bullets were, however, expensive: by charging a high price for ammunition the owner hoped that the weapon would not be fired and used only to intimidate people. A used gun often had to be discarded.

Many young men in Leeds regarded guns as a status symbol, almost as a fashion accessory. The main source of weapons was the old Eastern bloc and, by the 1990s, the Balkans. Complicating the issue was the use of replica weapons, some of which could be easily converted to fire live rounds. By the 1980s the use of guns had become commonplace in Leeds, and two incidents involving firearms and police officers shocked the city. In October 1984 sergeant John Speed was shot dead while investigating two men acting suspiciously outside Leeds Parish Church and, on the afternoon of Boxing Day 2003, constable Ian Broadhurst was gunned down in the Oakwood area as he made enquiries about a stolen BMW car.

Conventional armed robberies on banks, building societies and security vans, in which firearms were used, were still relatively rare. Most robberies involving guns were directed at corner shops, and were carried out by young drug addicts wielding a real, or an imitation, firearm. Alternatively guns were used for settling differences between rival gangs or between drug dealers. To combat the growth of drug-related crime, a specialist squad was formed in Leeds as early as May 1967.

In 1985 the *Yorkshire Evening Post* reported that, 'The Hayfield Public House in Chapeltown, Leeds resembles a street bazaar as young blacks compete openly to sell a wide range of cannabis products. Harder drugs are said to be available by special arrangement.' At the time heroin could be bought there for £10 a wrap. The Hayfield was regularly cited as a source of drugs. Customers were reported driving up to its well-lit car park in an assortment of expensive cars. The police were criticised for not closing the place down but they argued that it was a focal point for drug dealing and, by keeping it open, they could keep an eye on what went on. One WPC, however, added her view in May 1985 that 'if we arrest too many we are going to cause a riot.' The *Evening Post* quoted the landlord-tenant, George Binger, who said he was not aware of any drug-dealing being carried on there at all.

The Hayfield was not the only place in Leeds where drugs were available. The Gaiety on Roundhay Road and the Silver Tree club were other well known sources. Cliffs' blues club in Markham Avenue offered sensimilia or bush (cannabis) but denied handling heroin. Two doors away was the 99 club in Spencer Mount. A *Yorkshire Post* reporter went there in May 1985 as part of the paper's investigation into drugs in the city and graphically reported the scene: 'Deafeningly loud reggae music made concentration difficult. The air was thick with the pungent aroma of cannabis cigarettes.' Again it was claimed no heroin was sold but a white youth in the Strega nightclub told the journalist that smack (heroin) and speed (amphetamines) were readily available if you asked 'in 99'.

The authorities faced a constant battle to contain the problem and in 1991 the British Transport Police in Leeds recovered twelve kilograms of heroin from Pakistan. The drugs were found in a locker in Leeds City station and had an estimated worth of £1.5 million. In 2002, the West Yorkshire force launched a major operation against the Yardies (Jamaican drug dealers) and claimed 200 arrests, more than 100 deportations and the seizure of drugs worth more than £1 million.

To help addicts an addiction unit was opened in Clarendon Road in 1982. Solvent abuse had also grown alarmingly in schools during the late 1970s and by 1985 a third of children surveyed in seventy-five city schools claimed to have tried it. By then the council had also identified 600 heroin users in Leeds. Apart from the physical damage from the drugs, violence was an integral part of the scene. In November 1998 Colin Joyce, a heroin addict from Middleton, was battered to death with a baseball bat in broad daylight.

Weapons became essential to drug syndicates in the city as trafficking, particularly in crack cocaine, increased and gangs needed to arm themselves to defend their territory against interlopers. In Leeds the police had to deal with an increasing number of what they termed 'black-on-black killings' as Yardie gangs fought turf wars. One such drug-related incident happened in Leeds in November 1998 when Orville McIntosh was shot dead outside a 'blues' illegal drinking club in Cowper Street. Detective superintendent Brian Steele had no doubt: 'This is nothing less than a cold blooded execution.'

By the end of the twentieth century shooting incidents in Leeds were commonplace and often only came to police notice when hospitals reported treating patients with gunshot wounds. They were almost all drug-related. Originally drug dealing was predominantly carried out by West Indians in the Chapeltown area. But as the market expanded – particularly in inner-city areas such as Burley and Hyde Park and on council estates generally – dealing by whites became more common. Asians too became involved and conflicts between rival gangs escalated.

A dramatic example occurred in December 1993. Clifton Bryan and Robert Samuels were hit by bullets outside the Continental off-licence on Hamilton Place. The would-be assassins were said to be three armed men belonging to a gang from the Halton Moor area. The injured men sped to St James's Hospital with the would-be assassins in pursuit. At the hospital more shots were fired and the police were summoned and forced to mount an armed guard to protect the two wounded men.

Running parallel to drug-related violence was a general increase in crimes of violence: domestic assault, muggings, the wounding of total strangers and murder. In 1950, 99 such crimes were reported but by 1961 the number had risen to 212. In 1973 one staff nurse at Leeds General Infirmary commented that Friday nights were 'teeming with assault cases'. The trend led detective chief superintendent Denis Hoban to remark that the city faced an 'unprecedented spate of murders and attacks' adding 'youngsters today see violence all around them'. Pamela Babington, a 14-year-old, even complained in the *Evening Post* that her youth club meetings 'usually end up with a fight on the street'.

By the mid 1970s, the Merrion Centre, Kirkgate, the Corn Exchange and the junction of the Headrow and Vicar Lane were considered dangerous places to be late at night. Knifings and beatings with baseball bats and chains were reported. In October 1973 Newton Samuel ended up with forty-two stitches in his face after a fracas at the Cabana club on Roundhay Road. At the same time a gang of ten Hell's Angels armed with knives and chains attacked a young couple in York Road.

The Hell's Angels rode powerful motorbikes and tended to defy the law, often indulging in violence. They originated in the United States during the 1940s but spread to various countries and formed a chapter in Leeds. However, in the 1970s the City of Leeds Chapter of Hells Angels was replaced by a rival organisation, the Blue Angels. They established links with Blue Angel chapters in Glasgow and Belgium which supported each other. When a Blue Angel shooting took place in Holbeck, the Belgium chapter took the wanted man in. But a bitter rivalry developed between the Blue Angels and the Hell's Angels.

Some Leeds Blue Angels were law-abiding but others were heavily into violence. One novice member (known as a prospect), who came from the Seacroft area, had to prove his worth to become a full member. To this end he was taken to the Jockey pub in Wakefield. A total stranger standing at the bar was selected and the prospect was ordered to attack him with a hammer. He did so, fracturing the man's skull. The accused was acquitted. All the witnesses at the trial suffered from selective amnesia!

Intimidation of witnesses was by now a serious problem in poorer areas such as Halton Moor, Seacroft and Harehills. Following a serious disturbance in North Yorkshire involving the Leeds Blue Angels, one witness refused to attend court. He had been threatened and was concerned for the safety of his family. As a result Darren Sheldrake was so terrified that he went on the run for twelve months. When he did return to Leeds he was attacked in his home by a gang using baseball bats and knives. Even so he did not report the matter to the police. It was only when further threats were made to him, and he feared for his life, that he took action. The police arrested the culprits at gunpoint. During the trial in 1996 the judge was so concerned about the possibility of violence that he ordered armed police to be placed on guard outside the Crown Court in Leeds. Attempts were made to threaten Sheldrake if he testified and, when the case was over and the miscreants convicted, the police had to rehouse him in another part of the country.

The battle against crime has seen the establishment of neighbourhood-watch schemes across the city. Similarly the police, Leeds City Council and community groups have co-operated to make Leeds safer. Each year scores of innocent people are victims of lawlessness. Much of the crime in the city is related to ignorance and poverty; much to the greed and selfishness generated by a materialistic society. It has long been recognised that many Leeds villains came from families with criminal backgrounds that went back generations. But how to break that cycle of criminality is still an open question.

9

CHAPELTOWN BURNING

Just after dawn had broken on Monday, 13 July 1981 a car made its way cautiously up Roundhay Road from Leeds city centre and then drew to a halt. Its four bewildered black occupants slowly climbed out and raised their hands in the air. Before them stood a complete riot squad of police. The men realised there was no escape and reluctantly admitted that they had just burgled a jeweller's in the Huddersfield area. They surrendered their loot but were mystified as to how the West Yorkshire force had responded so quickly and in such numbers. With a smile on his face, an officer explained, 'You were just unlucky.' The burglars had no idea Chapeltown had erupted that night and caused some of the worst civil disorder ever seen on the city's streets and that a massive police operation had been mounted to maintain order.

The spring and summer of 1981 saw racial discontent manifest itself in outbreaks of violence across the country. It had started in Brixton in April and by July fighting between white and Asian youths had broken out in Southall. It was followed by an explosion of street violence in the Toxteth area of Liverpool, Manchester's Moss Side, Leicester, Bristol and Halifax. Multi-ethnic Chapeltown in Leeds was no exception.

Street violence was not new in Leeds. Troops had fired on a mob in Briggate in 1753 protesting over turnpike charges; in the nineteenth century Luddites and Chartists clashed with the authorities and in the twentieth century several strikes led to violence. The 1960s was a watershed as left and right-wing activists took to the streets for a variety of reasons. This tendency became more pronounced in 1968 when Enoch Powell denounced mass immigration from the West Indies, India and Pakistan in his famous 'rivers of blood' speech. While some were appalled by his views others welcomed the comments; dockers held demonstrations in support of Powell and described him as 'good old Enoch'.

In November 1968, Patrick Wall, an authority on law and order and immigration, and the Tory MP for Beverley and Haltemprice, was invited to Leeds University to speak to the Conservative Association. The University Union's *Left Wing* bulletin was disgusted at the prospect and thundered: 'Students must therefore organise in the university to smash racism whenever it raises its head . . . We therefore urge all students to attend the "meeting" on Friday to oppose this Tory "gentleman".' They did. Seven hundred packed the hall, hundreds more were gathered outside. Nazi salutes were given as the MP arrived and cries of 'Enoch! Enoch' rang out.

Despite the constant heckling, Wall spoke for twenty minutes and on leaving the hall violence broke out. The national press highlighted the story and claimed that he had been spat at and his wife had been tripped and kicked. The behaviour of the students outraged considerable numbers of Leeds people across the political spectrum and was bitterly condemned by many for preventing freedom of speech. Others, however, felt that a public denunciation was essential in the fight against racism.

In less than a year, on 26 July 1969, racial discord had surfaced in the city. It began as result of a Saturday night squabble in Woodsley Road, Burley, when Bhupinder Singh pulled a flick-knife on Kenneth Horsfall and stabbed him to death. Singh and two associates were arrested and clashes broke out between white and ethnic minority youths in Burley Lodge Road and Burley Lodge Place. Stones and bottles were thrown at homes owned by immigrant families, forcing some to flee to relatives in Bradford. The streets were littered with bricks, windows were smashed and a car was burnt out. There was more trouble on the night of Monday, 28 July. People from ethnic minorities were warned to stay indoors and licensed premises in the area were closed.

Barrington Black, the defence solicitor, declared, 'There is a simmering volcano of racial disharmony on the verge of erupting in this area.' Community leaders were appalled at the remark with the Revd Furness, of the Leeds Council of Community Relations, stressing that these were 'beer riots' not 'race riots'. A local priest, Father Cairns, pointed out that the area had a relatively small immigrant population and that the different ethnic groups in Burley usually enjoyed an excellent relationship. The lord mayor, alderman Bretherick, emphasised that, 'There is no racial problem in Leeds.' But the left-wing *Leeds Weekly Citizen* warned that 'the community leaders must shake off their complacency' and an editorial in the *Yorkshire Evening Post* made a clear point: 'The editor's postbag confirms there is a strong anti-coloured feeling among some people.'

The city council and various community groups worked hard to defuse the situation, though the Oluwale incident in 1971 did little to ease the tension. When a Nigerian vagrant, David Oluwale, was discovered dead in the river Aire, two policemen were found guilty of assaulting him. There were many supporters of the police who pointed out that Oluwale had been a public nuisance for some time. But there were others who disagreed and believed that certain Leeds officers showed what later became described as 'institutional racism'. The home secretary, Reginald Maudling, ordered a special inspection of the Leeds Police force.

One event that regularly occupied the local police at this time, and was peculiar to Leeds and certain surrounding districts, was Mischief Night. Traditionally 4 November had seen children and teenage pranksters roam the streets playing tricks on people. Knocking on doors and running away were accepted as harmless capers but through the years the pranks degenerated into vandalism. Fireworks were put through people's letterboxes, garden gates were stolen and car tyres were slashed. Matters came to a head in 1974 when a gang of youths set upon police officers and firemen in Moortown, injuring six of them as they answered a 999 call.

Throughout the 1970s an underlying trend of violence marred society generally. Football hooliganism raised its head while violent industrial disputes and political demonstrations all too often ended in clashes between protesters and police. Relations between the forces of law and order and ethnic minority communities became extremely strained at times. Fascist agitators contributed to the tension as claims were made that in Compton Road library, for example, books dealing with political issues were defaced with National Front stickers. Complaints were raised by some that books bought by local libraries in the Urdu and Punjabi languages were a waste of public money. At the same time Peter Lazenby of the *Yorkshire Evening Post* pointed out the underlying reasons for the dissatisfaction found in immigrant areas. He graphically commented on the 'appalling squalor for black and white families alike and massive unemployment.'

Another factor exacerbated the situation. Rastafarianism, a Caribbean religious cult, emerged in many West Indian communities in Britain during the 1970s. Many young Afro-Caribbeans in Leeds identified closely with it, listening enthusiastically to Bob Marley's songs. *Catch a Fire* came out in 1973; *Burnin' and Lootin'* in 1974. In 1975 those lyrics were to become a reality on the streets of Leeds.

On Mischief Night 1975, gangs of youths roamed through the Chapeltown area. Bricks were hurled through windows, a new car on a garage forecourt was overturned and a parked van was pushed down a hill into a lamp-post. The following evening, on Bonfire Night, missiles were thrown through a car windscreen on Spencer Place. Police cars were attacked as a large mob of mostly black youths raced through the streets of the district indiscriminately throwing missiles and fireworks. Reports estimated the numbers at between 150 and 300. The main trouble spots were Spencer Place, notorious as a red light thoroughfare, and Grange Avenue. At 9.35 p.m. an abandoned CID car was overturned and in the ensuing chaos another police car crashed into a tree and seriously injured two officers. It appeared that the newly formed West Yorkshire Police force was unprepared for such an emergency and the vast majority of both black and white citizens of Leeds were shocked by the lawlessness.

The *Chapeltown News*, however, was scathing in its condemnation of the police who, it said, 'must take a large share of the blame for what happened.' It accused the force of violence, intimidation and both destroying and fabricating evidence. When an all-white jury acquitted twenty-one out of the twenty-five apprehended during the riots, the paper heralded the verdict as 'a great victory for the Black youth and indirectly a victory for all of us who are struggling for equality.' The left-wing *Leeds Other Paper* denied *Yorkshire Post* reports that the youths 'rampaged' through the streets and claimed that it was the police who chased the youths. It also introduced an economic dimension into its argument, pointing out that 25 per cent of Chapeltown's youths were unemployed. A small core of young black activists saw the whole incident as a legitimate political protest in a society where their views accounted for little. As one remarked, 'We want to be looked upon as human beings, we want them to leave us alone.'

Following the 1975 disturbances the city council, religious bodies, multi-cultural organisations and the police made strenuous efforts to create harmony and were relatively successful. However, in 1981, national events overtook them and Leeds once again was faced with mayhem.

It started with an April race riot in Brixton. By July similar outbreaks across the country shocked the nation. *The Times* reported violent outbursts in Blackburn, Blackpool, Bradford, Cirencester, Crewe, Derby, Gloucester, Halifax, Hull and Leeds. On Saturday 11 July the *Yorkshire Post* headline succinctly summed up the situation: 'Street Warfare Sweeps Britain' and went on to identify London, Liverpool, Preston, Ellesmere Port and Hull as places devastated by such actions. In Leeds a Jewish baker's shop and an Asian post office had their windows smashed that Friday night but nothing more serious occurred.

However, people in the community had known for some weeks that trouble was brewing in Chapeltown. John Gill of the Gilclive Electrical shop was told that an outbreak was imminent. One West Indian made it clear: 'This had been coming for a long time. The tension has been building up and it was bound to erupt sometime.' At about half past two in the early hours of Sunday 12 July his prediction came true when a gang of about 150 gathered outside the Gaiety pub on Roundhay Road.

Youths, some as young as twelve, poured onto the street. A car was torched and an attempt made to set fire to an Indian restaurant. Rival gangs fought pitched battles, particularly around Hamilton Avenue and Grange Avenue as white skinheads joined up with blacks. Property in Nassau Avenue, Mexborough Avenue and Cowper Street went up in flames. Windows of property on Roundhay Road were smashed. Ajmer Singh Sian, an electrical retailer, was threatened at knife point and hi-fi equipment worth £8,000 was stolen from him. The off-licence on Hamilton Avenue had its stock looted. They were just a couple of about two dozen shops whose stock was stripped bare. Police did their best with riot shields to control the mob but it took four and half hours to regain control.

On Sunday evening all was calm when the police paraded opposite Chapeltown police station. They were dressed in their normal uniforms but each man was also issued with a green helmet with a visor – similar to those used by the military in Northern Ireland – a four-foot-high polyfibre shield, hockey shinpads and a cricket box.

Just before midnight, news came in that rioting had started in Chapeltown near the Hayfield public house. About a hundred youths were gathered there stopping cars coming up Chapeltown Road. As the sixty riot-trained officers came into view the mob started yelling abuse. The force moved forward to disperse the crowd and the throng then scattered down the side streets near the old synagogue. The police were ordered to follow them. Too late, they realised they had been drawn into an ambush. Hundreds were lying in wait and slates, bricks and other missiles were hurled at the advancing officers.

Under a hail of fire the police were driven back up Chapeltown Road. Petrol bombs were thrown and it became obvious that further supplies of these Molotov cocktails were readily available. In the fighting several people were injured, some seriously, yet ambulances could not get through. The Standard Tyre and Exhaust Company was burnt out and some of the mob began looting. Shops such as Crocketts were ransacked. Those that had been boarded-up earlier in the day saw their protection ripped away as looters emptied their shelves. The Private Shop, a local sex shop, was a particular target.

Meanwhile some of the rioters who were not looting began wielding sledgehammers at police and throwing paint over their shields and visors, while petrol bombs burnt several officers. For some reason senior ranks failed to release the reserve riot squads and the ragged line of policemen was forced back up Chapeltown Road under a hail of missiles and Molotov cocktails. Reports emerged that the mob intended to attack Chapeltown police station in order to burn it down. At the old rugby league headquarters on Chapeltown Road the retreating force formed the final defensive line; it had to be held at all cost. 'It was like Rorke's Drift' mused one officer.

The mob then singled out senior officers for attack and badges of rank were torn off as a precaution. The hail of missiles continued. The besieged force was under orders not to retaliate but the men were relieved when finally two CID men arrived with CS gas launchers. Their elation was quickly dispelled, however, when it was realised that no gas canisters had been issued.

Then, at three in the morning, police reserves were released. A charge was ordered and the mob fell back in disarray and fled. A few more petrol bombs were hurled but, finally, control of the streets was reasserted by the forces of law and order. At the junction of Spencer Place and Roundhay Road a line was thrown across the road. And it was here some little time later that the four unfortunate burglars came to a standstill in their car. The riot was over. As one weary officer remarked, it had been 'a night of madness'.

The analysis then began. Councillor Cedric Clark pointed out that, 'Everyone in Chapeltown and Harehills knew a time-bomb was ticking.' The police tried to play down the political element. The *Guardian* quoted a West Yorkshire police spokesman as saying, 'As far as we are concerned this is just pure hooliganism.' Ronald Gregory, the chief constable, argued that the riots had been stage-managed, that extremists from outside had fomented trouble and that CB radios had been used to co-ordinate attacks. Errol James, a community leader, admitted that youths were seen in the area who were unknown to locals. Many feared that left-wing infiltrators had been at work. Mr Narayan, defending those arrested that night, agreed that the community feared that outsiders had exploited the situation but also stressed that police repression of black youths had played its part.

There was no doubt that community relations had been severely damaged. Complaints were raised about the lack of legal facilities made available to those later accused of rioting and violence and cries of 'lies' and 'disgusting' emanated from the public gallery of the court. Some innocent people contended that they had been persecuted unjustly. Mark Leopold was a case in point. He claimed he had been going to a party when he was pounced on by police and beaten with batons. The police had suffered immeasurably. Unquestionably, many officers conducted themselves with extreme bravery in the face of fearful provocation and several officers suffered serious injuries. Equally disturbing was the fact that police morale had plummeted as many of the rank and file felt that senior officers should have released the reserve force sooner and sanctioned the use of CS gas to give protection to the besieged force.

There seemed to be no doubt that in the wake of the street disturbances nationally, a copy-cat element had triggered off much of the violence in Chapeltown with some using it simply as an excuse for hooliganism. Nevertheless, there were other factors. Discrimination in jobs, police harassment, unemployment, poor housing, racial discord and the overall depredation of the Chapeltown area, had all played their part. The *Come-Unity News* for August was adamant that following 'harassment, abusive and racialist remarks . . . it had to happen.' The Revd Glendenning saw the reasons behind the events as economic and social rather than racial. 'The problem is not of black people but of urban decay,' he argued.

The council tried to be conciliatory and the Labour and Conservative parties agreed not to debate the issue. They felt to do so would 'do nothing to help the cause of race relations in the city'. The Liberals disagreed, but were outvoted. Estimates put the damage at around £2 million. An action desk to deal with the matter was set up and George Mudie, the Labour leader of the council, brought together community leaders to identify solutions. Major steps forward were taken, though even today much remains to be done.

The situation improved in the week after the riots as the city focused on Headingley, where England and Australia were due to meet in a test match. Then, a fortnight later, the nation came together to celebrate the wedding of Prince Charles and Lady Diana Spencer. Peace may ostensibly have been re-established in Leeds but many of the underlying causes of the riot still festered. If the authorities and community leaders thought the problem was almost solved, they were in for a sad awakening. Violence was to flare up yet again.

Chapeltown was again at the centre of lawlessness during the nights of 21 and 22 June 1987. The outbreak began when police were called to a domestic dispute in Grange Terrace at about half past three on the Sunday afternoon. It was triggered by rumours that two youths had been beaten up by police officers on the Friday evening and the simmering resentment towards the police once again exploded. Petrol bombs were thrown, arson committed, passing vehicles were stoned, a mini-supermarket looted and a sex shop extensively damaged. Fortunately, no serious injuries were reported and damage to property was limited. The following Monday evening the police withdrew from the area in order not to provoke further disturbances and left the restoration of peace to volunteers and youth workers from the Mandela Centre and the Palace youth project. Senior officers insisted that their intelligence indicated that the rioting had been planned for weeks and the discovery of a cache of petrol bombs and missiles showed that the outburst was not spontaneous.

March 1990 saw Leeds involved as one of a number of cities caught up in a series of national demonstrations held against the community charge (or poll tax, as most people called it) introduced by the Conservative government. Although many agreed with the principle of such a charge, a significant number expressed deep antagonism. When the Labour council in Leeds set a charge of £348 some three hundred protesters battled with police outside the Civic Hall and the building was daubed with slogans such as 'Break the poll tax, not the poor.' A torchlight procession of about two thousand marched through Leeds but it was believed that the protest had been engineered by two left-wing groups, Militant Tendency and the Socialist Workers' Party.

If the poll-tax protests unified sections of the community, the resentment of ethnic minorities in Leeds about discrimination resurfaced in 1994. Early on Saturday 15 October police went to Reginald Terrace in Chapeltown to investigate a suspicious BMW car. A mob suddenly gathered and surrounded the officers. Reinforcements were drafted in and for two hours a running battle was waged and police cars damaged. One officer, constable Martin Wharam, was saved by his belt buckle when an assailant tried to stab him. But the violence was not all one-sided. The police were accused of brutality and an allegation was made that a boy of thirteen was kicked in the face by three policemen.

The root of the problem lay in resentment, not only of the police but also of authority in general. Many in Chapeltown felt that society had failed them. Equally there were many who pointed out that people there had done little to support the police in their attempts to clamp down on prostitution, gun crime and the drug culture. In fairness, desperate efforts had been made by responsible men and women to help the district shed its seedy image. But it was an uphill battle, especially when the national press got involved. The visit of the Queen in March 1990 was intended as recognition of how the area had tried to improve. The local newspaper, the *Leopold Times*, bitterly pointed out that it hardly helped when Fleet Street concentrated more on vice in the area. Typical was *The Sun* headline: 'Tarts Take Day Off to See Queen'.

Drugs were at the root of the outburst in Leeds in July 1995 but it was the Hyde Park area, not Chapeltown, which saw two nights of mindless fury cause £500,000 worth of damage to property as 150 youths ran wild. Cars were burnt out, windows smashed, petrol bombs hurled arbitrarily and the Jolly Brewer, originally known as the Newlands public house, was gutted. Two years later violence again returned to Hyde Park when, on 16 May 1997, gangs involved in drug trafficking provoked the disorder. It was sparked off when police went to a local public house to investigate dealings in crack and heroin. About fifty youngsters, some as young as twelve, burnt out cars and ran amok. Fortunately no-one was seriously injured.

The summer of 2001 saw race riots break out again in Britain. The most serious occurred in Oldham where police and local councillors blamed National Front and British National Party activists for fomenting the trouble. The British National Party denied this and accused Asian racists of being the instigators. Other riots were reported in Burnley, Bradford and Leeds. It was estimated that about two hundred went on the rampage through the Harehills district on Tuesday 5 June and missiles were thrown at passing buses and cars. Some cars were burnt out and the police resorted to using CS gas. They were accused of heavy-handedness, but in turn, they claimed that much of the disorder was premeditated, with outsiders precipitating it. The actions were, in the police view, 'criminal activity, pure and simple' and the use of closed-circuit television for the first time enabled many culprits to be apprehended.

In the early years of the twenty-first century, tensions still lie beneath the surface. However, since that night of madness in 1981, and despite numerous setbacks, great efforts have been made through the years by the city council, voluntary organisations, ethnic groups, churches and the police to create a peaceful community. Following the riots of 2001, it was a voluntary worker, Razaq Raz, who offered hope for the future when he observed that, in Harehills, 'People from all races live there together very happily.' There are many who would claim that sentiment could be applied to Leeds as a whole.

10

THE HOOLIGANS OF ELLAND ROAD

At the start of the twenty-first century the people of Leeds had every reason to be pleased. Their city was vibrant with a flourishing economy and an environment that was being rapidly regenerated. But it was the performance of its football team, Leeds United – particularly in the European arena – that had brought the city international fame. However many regretted that the team, its supporters and the city in general had been tainted by a hooligan element associated with the club.

Leeds United had been formed in 1919 following the demise of Leeds City. However, it was not until Don Revie became the manager in 1961 that the club achieved any real success. Yet for all the triumphs, Leeds under Revie acquired an unsavoury reputation for being 'the hardest and most uncompromising team in the football league'. Later, Johnnie Giles, a key player, admitted they 'overstepped the mark a bit'. Revie's response was pithy: 'Don't worry about the press . . . what matters is that they are talking about you.' But it did matter, and the name 'dirty Leeds' stuck.

The team's image was not improved when, in December 2001, two Leeds players were in court charged with attacking an Asian student in City Square. Jonathan Woodgate was found guilty of affray. Lee Bowyer was cleared. The National Civil Rights Movement described the Bowyer verdict as 'perverse' and the *Daily Mirror* hailed him as a 'scumbag', urging him, into the bargain, to sue. Many of the fans were disgusted at the players' behaviour but many endorsed Bowyer's acquittal. A banner supporting the player was unfurled during the Everton match at Elland Road and a hooligan element in the crowd chanted loudly and in unison, 'You can stick the *Daily Mirror* up your a***.'

Hooliganism and football have long been bedfellows. It was even recognised as a violent game in medieval times. Despite playing the game himself – he certainly owned a pair of football boots – Henry VIII banned the game in 1548 because of the riots it caused. Anti-social behaviour at football matches was also common in the nineteenth century. In 1888 press reports of Preston North End's five nil win over Aston Villa described the crowd as 'howling roughs' who had pelted both teams with stones and then assaulted them.

In April 1906 Leeds experienced similar behaviour when some of the 10,000 crowd at Elland Road took exception to refereeing decisions during the Leeds City versus Manchester United match. When the final whistle blew, missiles were hurled at the unfortunate Mr Campbell. Although anti-social behaviour during the 1920s and 1930s did result in occasional outbursts such occurrences were uncommon. But the 1960s brought an eruption of violence among football followers that became known as the 'English disease'.

Despite this trend Leeds fans, at first, were placid. So much so that the *Yorkshire Evening Post* was able to state, in April 1967, that: 'The Elland Road crowds, large as they are, are far better behaved than most big city clubs although there have been signs, home and away, of a small but loud minority of hooligans among them. United have already taken steps with the police to control them.'

It was a premature observation. That small but loud minority soon came to the fore. In May a crowd of over 36,000 gathered for a home game with Liverpool. Violence erupted, the referee was attacked and the match was halted while the Leeds chairman, Harry Reynolds, addressed the crowd: 'If you want the ground closing, we don't' he warned. Phil Brown, the *Post*'s sports reporter, commented that, 'Elland Road has never seen worse conduct'.

In the 1967 FA Cup semi-final at Old Trafford, Everton fans

invaded the pitch and Leeds supporters retaliated by hurling pennies, toilet rolls and abuse at them. At Elland Road in January 1969 Leeds played Manchester United. The ground was filled to capacity with 48,000 inside and a further 2,000 locked out. The crowd spilled onto the pitch, fifty spectators were injured as bottles and coins were hurled indiscriminately and the St John Ambulance volunteers were in constant demand. Alderman Woodward, the chairman, insisted 'the majority of Saturday's crowd were well behaved'. It was true that the vast majority of supporters in Leeds, as elsewhere, were not only well behaved but also strongly disapproved of the hooligan element.

Like other clubs Leeds worked tirelessly to eradicate the problem. The next time Leeds and Manchester United met many youths wearing crash helmets and heavy boots, and sporting Manchester's red colours, were removed from the ground. Attempts were made to separate the supporters but fans disregarded the segregation. Fighting broke out and one senior officer reported that evictions from the ground were so fast 'we couldn't count them'. But the troubles were not confined to the stadium. Mr Redmond, the licensee of the New Peacock, reported that records had been stolen from the jukebox and chairs broken. People in the area were terrorised. Hooligans smashed windows and 200 marauders swept down Creskeld Street making their way to City Square, pursued by police. William Horsfield, landlord at the Imperial Hotel on Princes Street, reported that he had had £100-worth of windows smashed. It was nothing new. Residents claimed that it happened every time Leeds had a home game.

The club banned crash helmets, steel-capped boots and banners and the police were instructed to look out for those wearing 'aggressive clothing'. Court cases followed. Twenty-two-year-old Kenneth Nicholas Wilson, the so-called 'King of the Kop', was found guilty of assaulting two police officers in the north stand while PC Doherty explained that much of the violence at Leeds matches was directed at the police. Don Revie argued, 'Hooliganism at football matches has been getting out of hand.' The outspoken Judge

Pickles remarked that 'In many young men . . . violence is bubbling beneath the surface.' In September 1970 it again rose to the surface as fighting between Leeds and Chelsea fans continued before, during and after the game. In mid-October Manchester United were the visitors to Leeds and once more trouble broke out. But the Leeds board, working with the local police, were taking effective action. 'They deal with trouble properly at Leeds' was the comment of the Manchester United chairman.

Leeds supporters reserved their most vehement dislike for Manchester United. The more fanatical supporters of both clubs clashed throughout the final decades of the twentieth and on into the twenty-first century. The bitterness became extreme. One Leeds supporter would not even use a Vodafone mobile because the company sponsored Manchester United and the Lancashire team were generally referred to by Leeds supporters as the 'scum'.

Why this should be the case is not clear. Some accounts have it that, in the 1970s, Manchester United fans had claimed in the tabloid press to 'rule the roost' whenever they went to Elland Road and that this incensed Leeds fans. Certainly, by the 1990s – when the Reds were the most successful team in the Premiership – jealousy may have played a part. The bitterness between the two sets of hooligans is best demonstrated by two examples.

In February 1958 the plane carrying the Manchester United team home from a European cup tie crashed at Munich airport in the snow. Twenty-three people were killed. Matt Busby, the manager, survived but eight players – the 'Busby Babes' – perished. Over forty years later Leeds fans still taunted the Manchester contingent when they visited Elland Road by singing:

> Whose that dying on the runway?
> Whose that lying in the snow?
> It's Matt Busby and his boys,
> Making such a f****** noise
> 'Cos they can't get their aeroplane to go.

Manchester fans retaliated by unfurling a banner bearing the words 'Manchester United – Istanbul Branch'. It was a direct reference to two Leeds supporters who had been stabbed to death in Istanbul on the night before Leeds were due to play Galatasaray in the UEFA Cup semi-final in April 2000.

Some people wondered whether the Leeds hooligans simply reflected the uncompromising attitude shown by the team on the field. But Terry Brindle in the *Yorkshire Post* saw the national press view of the team's approach as part of the North–South divide. Leeds United, he pointed out 'still smart under a lingering reputation which denies their skill and emphasises their toughness south of The Wash'. But talk to ex-Leeds hooligans and you will hear them speak of the excitement of the moment. The buzz. The challenge to authority in the guise of the police. The ability to stand up to an enemy and fight for your team and your city. And it should be remembered that this was not just a Leeds problem but one endemic in football generally.

Certain teams' supporters were always singled out for particular attention. During the 1970s a bitter rivalry grew up between the fans of Leeds and Chelsea. Such conflicts did not always occur at the ground. In December 1975 Chelsea and Leeds fans met by chance at Birch services on the M62. The *Leeds Other Paper* carried an eyewitness report of what happened next: 'Once the Leeds lot took the concourse they just went mad . . . they were smashing the glass of the bridge [over the motorway] – booting, hitting, some just nutting panes. They were knocking down trees outside . . . ripping them out of the ground and whirling them around their heads.'

Though such outbursts could never be justified, there were factors that ignited violence. One was poor decisions made by referees. Over the years mistakes made by officials have repeatedly aroused reactions but these usually went no further than the crowd yelling abuse. However, in 1971, a decision by a referee precipitated a pitch invasion at Elland Road that brought serious consequences for the club. With only four matches left to play that season Leeds knew that if they won them all, they would be league champions. The first was at Elland Road against West Bromwich Albion. A crowd of almost 37,000 gathered on Saturday 17 April to cheer Leeds to victory. They were to be disappointed. Leeds played sluggishly and with twenty minutes to go West Brom scored one of the most controversial goals of the decade. Referee Ray Tinkler was adamant it was a goal and some thought he was right to award it. But the Leeds supporters in the ground, and millions watching later on *Match of the Day*, believed that Jeff Astle, the scorer, was clearly offside. Several incensed supporters ran on the pitch and harassed the referee and the linesman. Fighting broke out with the police, the game was held up for five minutes and twenty-seven people were arrested. Leeds eventually lost by two goals to one and a mob besieged the club's offices trying to get to the unfortunate Mr Tinkler.

Though Leeds won their remaining matches, that loss against West Brom meant that Arsenal became champions by one point. Don Revie even tried to justify the actions of the crowd. 'Can you blame them for what happened today?' he asked. Percy Woodward, the chairman was also furious. 'It is appalling that nine or ten months work by all of us . . . should be destroyed by one man. . . . I am not blaming the spectators. There was every justification for it. I am sorry it happened but there it is.' However, Leeds City councillor Bernard Atha argued that Woodward's comments were 'disgraceful' and the FA took a serious view of the whole matter. They decreed that the first four home matches of the following season would be played away from Elland Road.

In the next few years Leeds made serious efforts to change their image and gave some superb performances on the field; performances that got plaudits from football enthusiasts across the world. At the end of the 1974/75 season – now under the managerial eye of Jimmy Armfield – the club reached the final of the European Cup. Leeds would play Bayern Munich at the Parc de Princes in Paris for the most prestigious trophy in club football. A crowd of 48,374 gathered on the evening of 28 May 1975 in the French capital, while millions watched on television.

Leeds dominated their German opponents but when Peter Lorimer, the Scotland striker, scored in the sixty-seventh minute the referee disallowed the goal for offside. Neutrals were outraged. Later, accusations of bribery were made against the official. A section of the Leeds supporters reacted, frustrated in part by the team's performance and by a decision considered by many as one of the most unfair in any game. A full-scale riot ensued. Seats were ripped out and hurled across the stadium. The police waded in wielding batons in an attempt to restore order. Security men and police fought with the hooligans and millions of pounds worth of damage was done. The world watched as the carnage unfolded and the good citizens of Leeds could only wring their hands in despair.

The financial costs were enormous but relatively insignificant compared to the damage done to the reputation of Leeds United. It seemed that all the efforts to improve the club's image had been jettisoned in a few moments of madness. The body that controlled European football – UEFA – held Leeds to account. Jimmy Armfield, known as an honourable man, argued cogently on behalf of the club and, persuaded by his presentation, those who heard the case reduced their original ban on the club playing in European competitions from four years to two.

But that did not deter the hooligans. In 1978 mounted police had to gallop onto the pitch at Elland Road as the cup tie with Manchester City was held up for twenty minutes while thugs were arrested and missiles cleared from the pitch. The following September, in a league match against the same team, and again in January 1980 during the Nottingham Forest game, missiles were thrown. When Newcastle United visited in October 1982 ball bearings were hurled indiscriminately from the crowd and the players had to be taken off the pitch on safety grounds. Most of these troubles emanated from either the Kop or the south stand and, at times, both areas were closed.

By the early 1980s the policing of football matches had become more sophisticated with the advent in stadiums of technologies such as closed-circuit television. Grounds like Elland Road had fences erected to prevent crowd invasions and Leeds was the first club in the country to create a police compound where arrested thugs could be held. Although these measures were successful in damping down much of the trouble at grounds, disturbances increased in town centres and motorway service-stations. In order to reduce the chance of rival supporters clashing, special trains were laid on and away fans were escorted by the police from the station to the ground. When the match was over the away fans were detained for anything up to an hour – until the home contingent had dispersed – and were then escorted back to the station.

Alcohol, however, was not sold on these trains. Thus a small group of Leeds supporters who were not hooligans, but enjoyed a drink before a match and resented being herded like sheep, decided on a new strategy. They chose to catch the service train to away games and consequently became known as the Leeds Service Crew.

Although the train fare on the service train was higher than on the football specials the advantage of travelling without a police escort and the opportunity to buy drink was appealing. The Leeds group attracted more supporters, some of whom were violent, and so the Leeds Service Crew developed a reputation for hooligan behaviour. This was not an isolated phenomenon. Many teams developed similar groups of aggressive young supporters, known as 'firms': Aston Villa had its Steamers, Birmingham City its Zulu Warriors, Burnley its Suicide Squad, Chelsea its Headhunters, Manchester United its Inter-City Jibbers and Millwall its Bushwackers.

The Leeds Service Crew was a mix of working-class men and successful businessmen, most of them well able to afford trips around the country. The poorer members found the problem of raising their train fare eased when Persil washing powder put tokens on its packets, which could then be exchanged for cheap tickets. The company little realised that the Service Crew would make such good use of the promotion. Meanwhile the Crew's reputation through the years became one of the worst in the country, a situation that the press exploited. Some of the original members – who regularly met in the Black Lion in Bishopgate

Street before the match and did not resort to violence – were approached by reporters from the *News of the World*. The journalists, eager to learn about the supporters' exploits, were willing to pay for rounds of drinks if the fans would talk. 'We just made it all up,' one fan later said, 'as long as they were prepared to pay for the beer, we'd tell them anything they wanted to hear.'

Unfortunately, not all the Crew's behaviour could be described as fictitious and vicious attacks by the Leeds Service Crew were common. By this time Elland Road was considered to be the best-policed ground in the country but that did not stop Leeds fans from creating mayhem at away games. In fact Leeds, along with Chelsea had, by then, the worst record of any club in the Football League.

The end of the 1981/82 season saw thousands of Leeds supporters visit the Hawthorns – the home of West Bromwich Albion – for a relegation decider. As Leeds headed for defeat its fans began ripping down the fencing and mounted police were brought onto the pitch even while the game was in progress. Leeds lost; rioting followed. It did not end there. Travelling home to Leeds virtually every motorway service station on the M6 was vandalised.

In May 1985, Leeds, now in the Second Division, approached the last game of the season with an outside chance of promotion. The game was to be played at St Andrew's, home of Birmingham City. There, one of the worst riots in British football took place as rival supporters clashed. Tragically, 15-year-old Ian Hanbridge of Northampton – watching his first league match – was crushed to death. The incident, however, received much less coverage than normal. That day the nation was horrified when reports began to filter through that the main stand at Park Avenue, home of Bradford City, had caught fire; 56 people were burned to death and a further 200 injured. Attention was focused on the West Yorkshire tragedy and the reports of the Leeds and Birmingham riot was little mentioned.

The *Birmingham Evening Mail*, however, launched a bitter attack on the so-called supporters of both clubs. Leon Hickman of that paper wrote a passionate piece under the headline, 'The sad face of British soccer':

> Football became an obscenity on Saturday at St Andrews. An excuse for mob violence on a scale that sent shudders through the heart of our nation. . . . It was anti-police, anti-society, anti-civilisation. . . . Hundreds among the Leeds supporters came with pre-meditated ideas how they would make Birmingham City pay. . . . It was the final beanfeast of the season. A chance for the Leeds louts to show again the blooded flag of anarchy, just as they had three seasons before at West Brom where relegation was made certain. . . . In their darkened world of hatred, these youths could reason that frustration inflamed by drink led to these outrages, nothing of the sort could be claimed for the Blues rioters.

Trouble started when the home team scored and missiles were hurled at the Birmingham goal. From the Leeds fans in the Tilton Road End volleys of plastic seats, blocks of wood from a burnt-out catering hut, chunks of terracing and bottles rained down on their opponents. Eddie Gray, the Leeds manager, made a despairing appeal for reason but a hail of missiles was the response to his request. Only after a delay of thirty-two minutes was it possible for the game to restart.

When the final whistle blew a full-scale confrontation followed between the police and Birmingham City fans. Mounted police were driven back with many of the horses struck by missiles. Red flares were fired into the police lines and more seats ripped out and hurled in defiance. Some ninety-six police were injured as well as about fifty supporters. In the mayhem a twelve-foot-high wall collapsed under the pressure of the Leeds section of the crowd. Young Ian Hanbridge was trapped beneath. Bizarrely, both rioters and police stopped fighting to free the injured youth but he died later in the Midland Centre for Neurosurgery in Smethwick.

The scenes outside the ground were equally disturbing. Cars were wrecked, and two hundred Leeds fans attacked a coach carrying guests from an Indian wedding in Preston that just happened to be passing. Bricks were hurled at the vehicle, windows smashed and five people injured. The driver accelerated away from the trouble.

'I put my foot down. . . . They would have lynched all of us if I'd stopped,' he remarked. The racist aspect of the incident could not be overlooked; nor could the fact that some Leeds supporters were seen wearing swastika armbands and chanting 'Sieg Heil'.

In May 1990 the last match of the season again saw Leeds fans involved in violence. Leeds, away from home, needed to beat Bournemouth to win the old Second Division and guarantee promotion. Dorset police anticipated trouble and urged the Football League to reschedule the game. They refused. Thousands of genuine Leeds supporters as well as the hooligans wanted to be present for the historic occasion and invaded the resort. The problem was that Bournemouth's Dean Court stadium could only hold 10,000 spectators and this was compounded by the fact that high-quality forged tickets had been on sale in Leeds for days before the game. A further complication was that Saturday 5 May was on a bank holiday weekend and there was limited accommodation in the seaside resort.

Mark Jones, the *Bournemouth Evening Echo* reporter, had little doubt about where the blame lay: 'A hard core of Leeds followers were clearly geared up for a fight when they gathered outside . . . the Dean Court ground. There was hatred in their faces. Many were drunk.' For a couple of hours before the kick-off there were clashes between the police and Leeds fans. The police had the responsibility of stopping those without tickets invading the ground and were subjected to a hail of stones hurled from the car park. The police charged. Hooligans clambered over cars to escape and then retaliated with further missile attacks using bottles, cans and pieces of wood.

For the rest of that bank holiday weekend Bournemouth was subjected to violence. Holidaymakers were stoned, deck chairs and rubbish bins were set alight and at least one car was overturned. Many supporters camped on the beach and the clashes between police and fans continued into the night. The *Echo* claimed there was evidence that the worst violence was orchestrated by so-called 'generals'. By now a national football intelligence unit had been established and Dorset police hoped that by co-operating with the

West Yorkshire force the main culprits would be identified and later brought to justice. Councillor Les Carter, the lord mayor of Leeds, summed up the attitude both of the general public and decent Leeds supporters: 'Like the rest of the genuine Leeds fans, I am totally appalled. They are not fans, they are just thugs.'

But many believed they were political thugs, Fascists using football for their own ends. In 1988 the Leeds Trades Union Council and the Anti-Fascist Action group published their findings in *The National Front, Football Violence and Leeds United*. They launched a campaign, supported by local MPs, to condemn it. Leaflets were handed out at Elland Road denouncing 'the appalling racism that has plagued Leeds United in recent years' and discussions were held with the council and the club.

Racism was not new in football. In the 1960s Albert Johanneson, Leeds United's first black player, was often subjected to racist abuse from both opposition players and fans, with the Liverpool supporters on Anfield's Kop chanting 'Oh! Ooh! Coco Pops!' whenever he touched the ball. Other clubs were known to have Fascist sympathisers among fans and Elland Road had long been targeted by the National Front. During the 1970s copies of its newspaper, *Frontline*, had regularly been sold there and its leaflets freely distributed. The *Bulldog*, a Fascist youth paper, even ran a league identifying those clubs with the highest levels of racism. Leeds was never far from the top: in issue No. 40 Newcastle United took over the top position, Leeds was second, then came Chelsea and West Ham. Perhaps the editors had taken heed of a letter they received from 'Dave, Leeds United Service Crew'. He wrote to the paper expressing dissatisfaction about how the tables were compiled: 'Isn't it about time that those who organise the Racist League should play the White man? I am talking about putting the true Whites of Leeds United's Service Crew on top where they rightfully belong. Why is it that West Ham and Chelsea are always joint first and Leeds following up just behind?'

At Elland Road racist chanting, Nazi-style salutes and repeated abuse of black players were regular occurrences. The national press repeatedly carried reports condemning the antics of that Leeds minority. One black player – Luther Blisset, of Watford and England – commented to the *Daily Mirror* in April 1987: 'Normally the abuse comes from the terraces, but during one Leeds game whole groups in the stand were doing Nazi salutes and shouting "Sieg Heil".' *The Sun* quoted Andy Gray of Crystal Palace: 'They are thugs and their racist abuse is aimed at coloured guys like me . . . Elland Road is the worst ground of the lot.' The *Guardian*, in January 1988, reported Aston Villa's game there but began its piece by describing how, when the players ran on to the field, 'the usual boos and offensive chants greeted them . . . their black players received bananas.' The *Independent* in March that same year reported how Leeds was 'praised in NF publications for the "patriotic whiteness" of the team.' And it was not just Fascist insignia that were on display: at the playoff at the end of the 1986/87 season against Charlton Athletic at Birmingham, the Red Hand of Ulster flags of the paramilitary Ulster Defence Association were flown by some Leeds fans.

Only days before that incident, while returning from a match at Oldham, a mob of about twenty Leeds supporters – ironically from York – raced through a Trans-Pennine train pursuing a group of black youths. Armed with fire extinguishers, sticks and metal rods they moved along the corridor chanting, 'Let's throw the black bastards on the track.' Fortunately the guard, Clifford Jamieson, had the presence of mind to lock the black youths in the guard's van but, in the ensuing struggle, an off-duty guard, Ronald Norman, who had gone to help, was kicked and punched.

In 1986 two *Yorkshire Post* undercover reporters, Tony Watson and Richard Donkin, penetrated the National Front. In February that year they revealed the unsavoury behaviour of many of its Leeds members. They argued, 'While it is difficult to establish whether the NF and other interest groups have orchestrated the violence on the terraces, there is little doubt the party has actively encouraged it.' One supporter, claiming to be a lapsed member, described the Service Crew as all 'NF supporters. We go to away matches and have battles with other fans. . . . We carry plastic

Stanley knives 'cos they are easy to hide. Sometimes at weekend we look for blacks and Pakis to do over.' And the Leeds hooligan presence was seen far from Elland Road. *Searchlight*, the left-wing magazine, reported in January 1988 how, during a Fascist march through Stockholm, several National Front skinheads were seen wearing Leeds United scarves.

In Leeds four city-centre pubs were the favourite meeting places for National Front members before a match: the Whip, the Viaduct, the Duncan and the Black Lion. It was in the Lion that the original Crew members had gathered and this could have led some to make a connection between the Crew and the Fascists. Many long-standing supporters admit that though racist comments were chanted and 'Sieg Heil' salutes were given, the majority who indulged did so simply for devilment.

'We throw bananas to wind up coloured players' one remarked. It was seen as no more offensive than the insults yelled at opposition players such as the chant composed for one player, whose wife had just had a baby: 'Hope your kid dies of cancer.' Chanting 'Sieg Heil' and giving the Nazi salute, it was claimed, was the best way to rile the police. The problem has not yet been eradicated: *Private Eye* made reference to it in December 2003 when it accused Leeds supporters of chorusing to Leicester City supporters, 'You all live in a town of Pakis.'

The experience of Leeds United over the years has simply reflected the national trend. The press have rightly focussed attention on it, though the emphasis on Leeds thugs has been exaggerated, for the hooligans at Elland Road are no better or worse than those of many other football clubs in the country. But what must never be forgotten is that the club has striven assiduously to eliminate the problem. Equally, the vast majority of Leeds supporters have always wholeheartedly condemned the conduct of that small, but vociferous, minority whose antics have soiled both the name of the club and the city.

11

THE HOME GUARD IN LEEDS

In June 1940 Britain stood alone. Europe had been overrun by the Germans and only good fortune and a brave rearguard action saved 330,000 Allied troops stranded on the beaches of Dunkirk. The situation was desperate. Invasion threatened. People had already seen the horrors of Nazi occupation as nation after nation succumbed to the armies of the Third Reich. In May, Reinhard Heydrich, Himmler's subordinate, had ordered the 'special search list, GB' to be drawn up. It contained the names of 2,300 prominent people in Britain who were to be arrested once the German occupation had taken place.

As might be expected Winston Churchill, the prime minister, and his deputy Clement Atlee were on it, but it also contained five Leeds citizens. Two were classed as immigrants: Theodor Plaut and Robert Bloch, both professors at the University. A third professor on the list was Selig Brodetsky, the celebrated mathematician and Zionist leader, of 3 Grosvenor Road, Headingley. All three men were wanted for matters relating to 'cultural spheres'. Another name on the list was that of a Leeds engineer, Herbert Purcel Astbury, who was sought for matters relating to defence and the armed services. The fifth was Karl Eschka, wanted for passport offences by the German police. It was even said that, had the invasion taken place, Quarry Hill Flats were designated for use as the local German headquarters. Meanwhile there were those who hoped for a miracle after reading an article in the *Leeds Weekly Citizen* that the paper republished from a secret German socialist magazine. It explained how Hitler might be overthrown.

But the reality was that a mighty military machine was poised to attack. The *Daily Express*, putting a brave face on it, claimed that the 'Army command is inclined to welcome an attempt by the enemy at invasion'. Churchill was more of a realist and, anticipating the imminent threat, he defiantly announced: 'We shall fight them on the beaches, we shall fight them on the landing grounds . . . we shall never surrender.' The problem was, with what would the British fight? The Army had lost a considerable number of trained men and most of its equipment at Dunkirk. In the event of an invasion, support would be needed from every quarter. In October 1939, when Churchill was still first lord of the admiralty, he had written to the home secretary to ask: 'Why do we not form a Home Guard of half a million men over forty?'

The idea was not new. In the early years of the nineteenth century Britain had faced a similar threat when Napoleon's 'Army of England' camped at Boulogne waiting for the order to invade. In July 1803, the government had been forced to introduce a Levy en Masse Act which empowered it to train every able-bodied man if sufficient volunteers were not forthcoming. Initially Leeds had shamed itself when only twenty men in the town offered their services, but a week later the *Leeds Mercury* was delighted to report that 'Leeds is herself again!' as a thousand of 'her chosen sons' came forward.

It was a different matter in 1940. This time there was no holding back. On Tuesday 14 May, Anthony Eden, the secretary of state for war, broadcast a personal appeal to the nation asking for men to join the Local Defence Volunteers (LDV). Almost before Eden had finished speaking those butchers and bakers, bank clerks and shop assistants and thousands of others not engaged in military service, but aged between seventeen and sixty-five, flocked to recruiting offices. They came from all walks of life: in Leeds, H. D. Bousfield was a partner in the solicitors Dibb and Lupton; Joseph Brodwell was a skilled leather-worker; Clarrie Thornton was a brickyard labourer. His namesake, Joe Thornton, was a socialist and a regular contributor to the *Leeds Weekly Citizen*, the local Labour newspaper. The paper itself had considered conscription 'unwelcome and most inopportune' in May 1939 but now it accepted the need. Joe Thornton recognised the impending danger. He was incensed when someone questioned his wisdom in volunteering for the Leeds LDV. Was he prepared to submit himself to military discipline and all without pay, his critic asked? Thornton was. He saw the new organisation in terms of a 'citizen army', and one he added 'that might play a big and perhaps decisive part in this titanic struggle'.

Cecil Aspinall of Easterly Crescent anticipated Eden's broadcast and arrived at the Leeds City Police offices to volunteer on the Monday morning, twenty-four hours too early. He was turned away. Within minutes of the broadcast finishing volunteers began to arrive at recruiting offices in the town. In the first hour Leeds registered eighty men; by nine the following morning 2,600 volunteers had registered.

Within four days of Eden's broadcast, a captain Ward called a meeting at Roundhay Mansion to discuss how Eccup reservoir could be guarded day and night. The water supplies to the city from Fewston, Lindley Wood and Swinsty reservoirs as well as from the river Ure had to pass through Eccup and sabotage there would have been disastrous to both the people of Leeds and the city's war effort.

Not everyone in Leeds agreed with this response to the war. Within days of Eden's appeal, one correspondent raised a point in the *Evening Post*: 'If volunteers are issued with rifles and uniforms, how would the enemy construe this? (Knowing them as we do.) Would private houses be considered as barracks by Hitler and consequently military objectives?' he wrote.

There were also those who held sincere beliefs about the evil of war and so a register of conscientious objectors was drawn up. The York Objection tribunal sat in Leeds to determine how genuine such cases were. In May 1940, John Herbert Parkes of Headingley opposed the war and his case was considered sincere as he was acting as an unpaid secretary to the Leeds branch of the Jewish Anti-Nazi League. His name was added to the register. Renton

Pullan's was not. He flatly told the tribunal he would not be in the least alarmed if Hitler ruled Britain, adding that he thought the system in the country was worse than in Nazi Germany. John Edward Parris, however, was included, and volunteered to train with a Quaker ambulance unit. He argued his conscience would not allow him to join the LDV for that would mean he would have to bear arms; he would not become a 'parashootist'.

'Parashooters' was a common nickname for the new force. In April that year German paratroops had been used for the first time in a major conflict when Denmark and Norway were overrun. This new form of warfare, like the threat of air raids, was uppermost in people's minds. Not surprisingly newspapers, like the *Sunday Dispatch*, featured articles on 'How to spot paratroops'.

If paratroops posed a real threat it was obvious that these would be the very troops LDV members would have to face and so in less than a week their nickname was quickly established: 'Parashooters'. It was kinder than some they were given – Last Desperate Venture, Long Dentured Veterans, or Look, Duck and Vanish. The government considered changing the name with Churchill pointing out that the word 'local . . . was uninspiring'. Herbert Morrison suggested 'Civic Guard' but Churchill preferred the title he had thought of in 1939 and in July its name was changed to the Home Guard.

The 9th battalion, raised by colonel H. D. Bousfield, was based north of the river Aire and was one of several set up in Leeds. Bousfield was an experienced soldier having commanded the 5th battalion West Yorkshire Regiment in 1917. His battalion was responsible for an area that stretched from the river Aire as far north as the boundary of the area covered by Otley's 30th battalion. These battalions were affiliated to the West Yorkshire Regiment and each battalion was divided into companies. C company, the largest in the 9th battalion, was set up after a mass meeting in Moortown.

The 7th battalion was organised in East Leeds incorporating Seacroft, Temple Newsam and Halton. Among its duties was the manning the anti-aircraft (AA) batteries at Cross Gates. The 8th battalion – which included at least two holders of the Victoria Cross in its ranks – reached from its most northerly point at Newlay to Middleton in the south, Stourton in the east and New Farnley in the west. It eventually rose to some five thousand men and was finally split into two, forming an additional battalion, the 18th, under lieutenant colonel C. W. Mustill and based at Bramley Barracks. The city centre itself was defended by the 16th battalion and a detachment of men from the Royal Army Pay Corps.

Each company had its own headquarters. The headquarters of Q company of the 8th battalion, for example, was based at Elland Road. Companies were further broken down into platoons who had their own small areas to defend. They also had their own local headquarters. The 8th battalion's F company number 4 platoon, responsible for guarding Silver Royd Mills and Tong Road, met at 2 Whingate Road, a large house opposite the Commercial Hotel – a fact not lost on some of its members!

Static units were also formed by local firms. The Blackburn Aircraft company on Roundhay Road, Montague Burton's, the ready-made clothing specialist, Greenwood and Batley's, the armaments manufacturer, Lewis's department store on the Headrow, the Leeds Industrial Co-operative dairy department, the Thrift stores and Kirkstall Forge were but a few of the firms in Leeds who raised their own units. Leeds Corporation was not to be outdone and the highways department also formed a static unit.

There was always a constant drain on Home Guard manpower. Anti-aircraft batteries were established at sites in Garforth, Yeadon, Post Hill at Farnley, Adel and Knostrop. Commanders of the 9th battalion complained bitterly that their men were regularly being directed to supplement the latter two sites and, to compound the problem, it was often expert Browning machine gunners they were losing. The *Evening Post* also reported that both the Air Raid Precautions (ARP) and special constables were drawing men from the Home Guard volunteers in Leeds.

Communication with new volunteers left much to be desired. The *Daily Telegraph* reported that many of those who had rushed to offer their services in May 1940 had still not heard anything from the authorities by mid-June. Others also felt ignored. Some offered their help through the press. 'Ex-Instructor KOYLI' wrote to the *Evening Post*, 'I would be quite willing to teach any young man how to use a rifle.' And there were those like an 'Ex-Regular NCO' from Leeds who was experienced in arms drill and felt that the new force was singularly lacking in this area. He wrote to the same paper in May 1940 complaining that men like him were not being used to train volunteers. He said he had witnessed how incompetently some LDV men were being trained and how dangerously they handled their rifles.

The shortage of equipment also handicapped training. In the first months of the new force's existence the city had just eighteen rifles per four hundred men. Appeals for private weapons were made and a steady stream of sporting rifles, shotguns and revolvers appeared at police headquarters for use by the LDV. Leeds Police initially opposed the use of revolvers but, facing the reality of a shortfall in weapons, they relented. It was, however, bitterly resented in Leeds that, when the war was finally over, the Home Office introduced legislation to prevent the police renewing firearms certificates for revolvers. It was a point strongly made by colonel Boyle.

Boyle was also critical of the War Office's provision of equipment, which was quite inadequate. In a letter to the Leeds press in June 1940 he made his point and stressed that as the new force was a voluntary one it had to provide much of its own resources. He appealed for help from the public. As funds began to run low the 9th battalion attempted to raise money by arranging functions. These included two concerts at the Grand Theatre in 1943 and 1944 and an exhibition of service pigeons at the Art Gallery, some from the royal lofts at Sandringham.

The War Office, however, did make some provision. The summer of 1940 saw the first supply of 300 rifles from the United States, which meant that some of the Home Guard's .303 rifles could be transferred to the regular Army. But even by March 1942 the 8th battalion's F4 platoon had just twenty-four rifles between forty-five men. In Leeds a few Tommy guns were available and these were eventually replaced with the more flexible Sten gun, a cheap, reliable and mass-produced sub-machine gun. However, by 1944 almost every man in the city was equipped with either a rifle or a Sten gun. Leeds also had two flamethrowers but as these proved to be as dangerous to the operator as to the enemy they were soon withdrawn. Browning machine guns, anti-tank Blacker bombards and Mills bombs were also eventually supplied and special stores were built in remote locations across the city to hold the equipment.

Dissatisfaction about government support was still being raised by Leeds company commanders who complained that even by 1941 there was a lack of greatcoats for their men. The local authority was also criticised for failing to issue free tram tokens to men going on duty. Eventually, however, every man in Leeds could boast that he had a greatcoat, battledress, gaiters, gas cape, steel helmet, forage cap and respirator.

Ammunition, particularly in the early months of 1940, was in desperately short supply. When the first American rifles arrived in Britain only fifty cartridges accompanied each one. The government, exercising extreme caution, released just ten rounds to each volunteer. To conserve ammunition an order was issued forbidding any Home Guard to shoot at enemy aircraft. The ultimate in military parsimony happened to the 9th battalion. Their entire Sunday was occupied with an exercise that saw them undertake a fifty-mile round-trip to the Strensall rifle range near York for target practice. Each man fired just one round! In 1940 Churchill even complained to one brigadier that a single practice round was too much!

Through the long, hot summer of 1940 Hitler's aim of launching Operation Sea Lion, the invasion of the United Kingdom, stuttered to a halt. He had always insisted that certain conditions had to be met before that invasion could take place. Control of the air was one and here the Luftwaffe failed to achieve superiority as RAF Hurricanes and Spitfires helped win the Battle of Britain. On 17 September the

German war diary announced: 'The enemy Air Force is still by no means defeated. . . . The Führer therefore decides to postpone "Sea Lion" indefinitely.'

But if the threat of invasion had receded, there was still a threat from saboteurs. To combat this, the Home Guard in the Leeds area trained assiduously. Some training was done by the 9th battalion at the University's playing fields and instruction was given in its lecture halls, though a rent had to be paid. Occasionally a cinema might be used for a mass meeting, as when the 8th battalion used the Lyric in Tong Road. Drill was regularly carried out and not always appreciated by the men. Company sergeant-major Fletcher's domineering attitude antagonised many of the 9th and in May 1943 he was finally replaced by two more popular men: company sergeant-major Donegan and staff sergeant-major Saxby.

It was not simply a question of knowing how to present arms or clean a rifle. Small-arms drill, bayonet practice, fieldcraft, camouflage, movement by night, map reading, message writing and operating under a gas attack were all skills that a Home Guard might need. Even crossing a river by means of boats constructed from four stretchers and a tarpaulin lashed round them was practised on the Aire at Kirkstall. Men learned how to make 'Molotov' cocktails – bottles filled with petrol and gas tar with fuses attached by means of adhesive tape. The Leeds battalions persevered in preparing their men for any eventuality, though it was agreed that gas training was never a popular exercise.

As ammunition became more readily available, target practice was held at a variety of ranges including Briggs quarry, Meanwood quarry, Ingham's Brickyard quarry in Wortley, Eccup embankment, Bramley, Clayton Wood and Stairfoot while live bombing was practised at Belle Isle. Anti-tank training with Blacker bombards was undertaken by more experienced men at Little Almscliffe though every man learnt to lob Mills bombs and hand grenades. At Golden Acre live ammunition was used as machine guns were fired over the troops and time bombs exploded to prepare trainees for battle. One Home Guard reflected on his Golden Acre experience: 'The regular soldiers – God bless them! – lobbed eight-inch cracker-jacks at you. They stung a bit.'

Exercises could be dangerous and on 17 January 1943 a fatality was recorded. The men concerned were practising with a Blacker bombard anti-tank weapon at Kirkstall Forge. Believing it to be unloaded they fired. They were mistaken. The live shell smashed through a garage wall, destroyed a director's car, injured private Claughton and, tragically, killed private McGowan.

Night training was also undertaken. An *Evening Post* reporter joined one platoon for an exercise on a local golf course. He describes 'crawling through grass, seeking cover behind bushes, taking shelter in sandy bunkers . . . (and) firing imaginary rounds at the enemy.' The night ended in bathos, however, when a suspicious-looking man was apprehended. He turned out not to be a dangerous German spy but someone simply looking for golf balls. But golf courses were no bad places for training exercises. Both the *Yorkshire Post* and the *Leeds Mercury* had suggested them as ideal bases for Home Guard units as they were obvious targets for an airborne assault by German paratroopers.

Exercises elsewhere were also arranged. Weekend camps were held at the Leeds waterworks site at Arthington whilst at Wigton Moor troops used 'home made smoke bombs' before the normal supply was received. Some large-scale operations in the city involved the local ARP, the National Fire Service, Leeds Police, the city engineer's department and the Women's Voluntary Service. The attempt to create a realistic scenario saw ambulances called in to remove the 'wounded'. It was after one such occasion that the 9th battalion discovered it had managed to acquire forty-eight blankets from one of the other support services!

Effective communications were essential. Pigeon fanciers in Leeds were enrolled as members so that their birds could be used. Carrier pigeons were a useful addition to any network should other systems fail or if radio transmissions were prone to interception by the enemy. Cadet cyclists were employed and later wireless operators were used. Signalling equipment using landlines was not always successful. Often when an exercise was scheduled linesmen in Leeds had to report for duty hours earlier than the rest of the men in order to replace missing stretches of wire. It was not secret agents or fifth columnists who were responsible for the missing cables but local gardeners who found the wire useful for repairing fences.

Training was carried on for all ranks. Leeds officers were sent to Osterley Park at Hounslow, the best known of the training centres. Here they were instructed by, among others, Spanish Civil War veteran, Tom Wintringham, on guerrilla tactics. Most of the Home Guard subaltern trainees realised the value of this new approach. But women in the force were a different matter and the War Office hardly helped matters by christening those females who came forward to help as 'Army followers'! Later their official designation became 'Nominated Women' and eventually 'Home Guard Auxiliaries'.

Their role included operating telephones, signalling equipment and dealing with intelligence. Colonel Boyle bitterly complained that in Leeds they were expected to accompany their menfolk but without helmet, respirator or greatcoat. Some were given rifle practice with .22s and several national shooting competitions for women volunteers were organised at the Swinegate tram depot where an excellent firing range had been created.

Kirkstall Forge Company, however, cocked a snook at officialdom. Initially formed as a static unit in 30 May 1940 it became a full Home Guard company in its own right and one that carried out its duties enthusiastically. Here thirty women volunteers enrolled for non-combatant duties. But the forge disregarded the order to restrict rifle practice to .22s. Under corporal Miss Hilda Hampshire, a tracer and technical illustrator in the drawing office, the girls trained with service rifles and Sten guns using the miniature firing range that had been created on the top floor at the forge and the range at Toads Hole Wood.

They joined the men in exercises at Golden Acre, were subjected to the same military discipline and marched on parades. Officially their only distinguishing mark was a small gold-coloured brooch made of bakelite with 'HG' inscribed on it and pinned to their civilian clothes. That was not good enough for the women at Kirkstall Forge. First they made up their own uniforms consisting of navy-blue slacks, white blouses and blue berets. Then by a variety of subterfuges they scrounged full khaki uniforms making it difficult to distinguish between male and female.

But the Home Guard should not be seen as an organisation characterised by endless fruitless exercises and amateurish incompetence, as exemplified by the popular television programme *Dad's Army*. Should the secret code word 'Bugbear' be issued, its duty was to respond as secret orders of 8 February 1941 laid down: 'to hamper and impede the enemy no matter in what direction his attack may come'. Strategies were developed in the event of an invasion, with Headingley tram depot and Kirkstall Brewery designated as possible headquarters. Duties included manning AA batteries, guarding roadblocks at places such as Otley Road, King Lane and Whitecote Hill and defending Viaduct Road where there were bridges over the river and the canal. But one of their most important functions was the guarding of Eccup reservoir and its outlet valve. From 1941, the registration and inspection of petrol pumps also became part of Home Guard responsibilities.

During air raids, Home Guard personnel were called upon to help deal with fires as incendiary bombs caused havoc. The worst raid on Leeds was the night of 14/15 March 1941. The infirmary, the town hall and City Museum in Park Row were all hit. Two other buildings struck by incendiary bombs were the market and City station. Fortunately, at Kirkgate Market, private John Hoddell of the Home Guard was on duty. He knew the building well and was to able minimise the damage. A similar situation occurred at City Station where Sergeant H. José climbed onto the roof of the building and took action. Both men were awarded medals for gallantry.

On Tuesday 6 June 1944, the *Yorkshire Evening Post* appeared with a headline proclaiming the news that the nation had waited four long years to hear: 'Invasion of Northern France goes according to plan.' First editions of the paper were sold out as people gleefully welcomed the news. Two French airmen at the YMCA threw their berets in the air. 'Vive la France!' cried one; 'I want a drink to celebrate!' cried the other. Unfortunately, he failed to appreciate Leeds licensing laws: D-Day or not, the city's publicans were not able to open their doors until 11.30 a.m.

However, if Leeds people and Allied servicemen felt euphoric about D-Day the results of the invasion placed a serious strain on the Home Guard in the city. From 1944 they were called upon to guard wounded enemy prisoners in the city's hospitals night after night. Armed with Sten guns, Home Guards reported for duty at the end of a day's work. Next day they were expected to return to work without any rest. The physical strain was considerable and those who were too tired to work next day lost a day's pay. Some men even left prisoners unattended so they could get back to work on time and not lose wages. Employers, who in the past had been supportive, became antagonistic and morale among the men sank.

By the end of 1944 the need for the Home Guard was over and on Sunday 3 December they were officially stood down. King George VI took the salute in Hyde Park and Leeds sent a handful of men from its Home Guard to represent the city. These included lance corporal Pickering who held the Military Medal and 70-year-old private Raby. As they marched through the streets of London, Cockneys shouted in appreciation, 'Good old Tykes!' The Leeds Home Guard women's auxiliaries did not take part and even the King failed to recognise their role in his broadcast that night when he said, 'Officers, non-commissioned officers and men, you have served your country with a steadfast devotion.' There was no reference to the women who had selflessly served their country.

That same Sunday, as heavy rain fell on Leeds, thousands lined the Headrow to pay tribute as the citizen army of the town held its final parade and marched into history. Some four thousand men representing the city's different battalions paraded through Victoria Square, where major-general Shears took the salute with home secretary Herbert Morrison and lord mayor Alderman C. V. Walker in attendance. Once again the Leeds women's auxiliaries did not share in the triumph. At least Arthur Merrill of the *Yorkshire Evening News* pointed out that they too had 'given enthusiasm and valuable support' in the struggle.

In the decades that followed, the Home Guard faded from the public consciousness. Eventually it became a vehicle for good-humoured fun as *Dad's Army* entertained the nation. But at a time when Britain faced one of the most desperate periods in its history those now-forgotten men and women of Leeds, as elsewhere, came forward to serve the nation and face whatever fate had in store.

12

THE CAPITAL OF FISH AND CHIPS

When Gerald Priestland, in his classic book *Frying Tonight*, declared that Leeds had 'a fair chance to claim to being the intellectual capital of fish and chips' his tongue may have been in his cheek but his remarks did contain an element of truth. For well over a hundred years fish and chips have played a significant part in the life of the town.

It is likely that the first enterprising individuals to start selling fish and chips together did so during the 1860s in Oldham and London, probably cooking in the set-pots usually used for heating water and washing clothes. In Leeds the honour goes to Edward Lewis, a London businessman who owned both shops and hotels. By 1881, he had opened a shop at 5 Marsh Lane where he was listed in White's *Directory* simply as a 'shopkeeper'. A year later his designation was changed to that of 'fishmonger'.

In 1886 he had installed Alfred Stone as his manager in Marsh Lane. Stone is described in Kelly's *Directory* for that year as a 'fried fish dealer' but what made the Marsh Lane shop different from other fried-fish shops was that it also offered chips. Lewis's advertisements for the time bear this out: 'Excellent suppers of fried fish and chipped potatoes (à la mode de Paris) cooked in the best dripping . . . may be had every evening from 6 p.m. to 11 p.m.' It is thought that Lewis opened a second shop in West Street and that same year Henry Hardisty at 69 West Street is described as running a fried-fish shop though whether he was acting on his own or as Lewis's manager is uncertain. Within a few years many other shops had opened across Leeds: Isaac Simpson on York Road, Lander Jowett at Whingate, James Annal on Kirkstall Road, Hannah Fox in Meadow Lane and James Wightman on Town Street at Beeston were but some of the local men and women who saw the opportunities offered by this new idea.

By 1909 the number of shops in Leeds had risen to around eight hundred, with Mr Potentier owning a chain. However, almost all of these outlets were concentrated in the out-townships, or on the periphery of the town, and there were none in the city centre. Part of the reason may well have been that the trade was considered by many to be offensive. The stench of the cooking – whether by cotton-seed oil or by beef dripping – was deemed unacceptable. Concern over its anti-social impact was such that the Town Council Act of 1925 effectively banned fish-and-chip shops in controlled developments but, by the end of the 1920s, Leeds City Council allowed limited provision in the new housing estates. Nevertheless, John Bryan was fined £5 for setting up a shop at Horsforth without official permission as late as 1931. It was not until October 1940 that fish frying ceased to be classed as 'an offensive trade'.

But despite the official view the trade was growing and eventually fish shops and fish restaurants opened in the city centre. Henry Youngman established his business in Hunslet in 1885 and then moved to the Headrow in 1914 where he opened a fish restaurant. He ultimately relocated to New Briggate in 1928.

But 1914 had a greater significance than the opening of a new fish restaurant in Leeds. The First World War actually saw the number of shops decline throughout Britain, and Leeds followed this trend as its outlets fell to about five hundred. Supplies of fish were severely restricted and price increases became inevitable. Haddock had always been the most popular fish sold in Leeds but shortages meant that ling, catfish (or Scotch hake as it was some-times called) and coal fish were used as substitutes but Youngman later admitted that if possible he avoided telling customers what they were eating.

In Leeds fish and chips were available every evening, except Sunday, from about 6.30 p.m. to 11.45 p.m. and on Fridays and Saturdays at lunch time, known locally as dinner time. One abortive attempt to open on Sunday by Bridge End Fisheries on Wellington Road in 1931 proved unsuccessful. As late as 1980 one Leeds fish fryer was prosecuted for selling fried fish on a Sunday yet ironically in Wetherby, Guiseley and Boston Spa no such restriction applied.

The early evening demand through the week was often for chips bought by factory hands on their way home from work. For some people there were times when chips was all the family could afford but when money was available fish and chips provided a tasty, inexpensive and convenient supper. It was common for some households to enjoy them three or four times a week. They were also popular in local factories for dinners. In 1931, Montague Burton's, the Leeds clothing company, installed its own fish-frying range so that it could produce up to two thousand fish-and-chip dinners for workers.

There were few back-to-back streets in Leeds that did not boast a fish shop in the immediate vicinity. At night, queues would regularly form at the more popular fryers. The fish on sale in Leeds, unlike in many towns, was skinned before frying but they were only half the size of those sold in fish shops at the end of the century. Another local variation was Leeds fish cakes. In most places these were a form of rissole; mashed potatoes mixed with minced fish and then fried. In Leeds, and some other West Riding towns, fish cakes were simply minced fish placed between two slices of potato and then battered. Cheaper offerings in Leeds shops were fish tails – smaller and cheaper than the normal fish – and scallops, a slice of potato dipped in batter and fried.

The Majestic and King Edward potatoes, which were generally used, needed considerable work after peeling in order to remove the many eyes and cracks that invariably defaced them. The problem has now all but disappeared thanks to improvements in potato growing. New potatoes, however, always presented difficulties. They cooked too quickly and were too small to make fish cakes. Leeds proprietors often displayed notices apologising for the fact they were being used and for the price increases they generated. However, when old potatoes once again became available the price dropped back.

Jewish fish-and-chip shops, which had developed in the North Street area of the town, offered an added, and sometimes free, attraction; a kind of pickled gherkin known as an 'ugegkie' ('uggerky') or a 'dill'. In Leeds mushy peas – which became very popular in later years – were not usually sold. To buy these, and the pork pies that normally went with them, people had to go to either their local pea-and-pie shop or to one of the many tripe shops.

Leeds fish shops were mainly family businesses with the husband usually frying and the wife serving. The Johnson family was the exception in that they owned six shops in the town by 1929. But large or small, Leeds traders felt that some form of association would be beneficial to their trade and, following the example set by Rochdale in 1904, tried to establish one. It was not a success. However, when the National Federation of Fish Fryers (NFFF) was formed in 1913, Leeds proprietors joined and by 1927 the federation moved its head office to Hunslet Hall Road. The following year, as if to demonstrate its commitment to the city, it entered a float in the annual Children's Day procession. By 1941 it had a prime site in Albion Street and then relocated to Dewsbury Road where it remained until its move to Meanwood in 1992.

During the 1920s Leeds was gaining a reputation as the centre of the trade. Shop owners generally bought high-quality fish and claimed to be 'proud and careful of their trade'. But Henry Youngman recognised the need for change and pointed out how dark and dismal some shops were. He advocated the introduction of tiled interiors with colourful pictures of animals, romantic sailing ships or swimming shoals of fish portrayed on the tiles. Hygiene regulations were not as strictly enforced as they are today. In some fish shops the pet cat could be found strolling through the fish-preparation room. Recognising the importance of the issue to the public, Kitson and Seniors of Holbeck emphasised that their new ice chests were 'hygienic'.

Attempts to combat poor nutrition were introduced by the Leeds education committee. It provided a mixture of cod liver oil and malt to needy pupils and from 1929 enabled children to buy a third of a pint of milk a day in school. But some medical officers of health argued that poor nutrition was a direct result of eating fish and chips and the using of tinned foods. These, they argued, were no more than conveniences latched onto by lazy mothers. Dr J. Johnston Jervis, the Leeds medical officer of health whose campaigning zeal led to life expectancy being markedly improved in the city, disagreed. He argued that fish and chips contained 'all the necessary vitamins to build the body tissue of the human body'.

Around the same time another Leeds physician, Dr Vining, speaking at a meeting of the Leeds Poor Children's Holiday Camp Association agreed with his colleague. He claimed that 'it would be beneficial for every child to be able to partake in a meal of fish and chips every day'. Not unnaturally the April edition of the *Fish Fryers Review* seized on his comments and gleefully reported them. Leeds traders saw their opportunity and soon posters proclaiming Dr Vining's message appeared on the streets. Vining was furious. His solicitors, Catlow and Wormald, took up his objections pointing out that it was unethical for doctors to advertise. The argument with the fish fryers rumbled on until the end of the year.

Apart from the nutritional dangers, fire was the most obvious hazard the trade faced. During 1935 alone twenty-five Leeds shops reported incidents as pans overheated and fire broke out. Experience in frying was essential as there were no thermostats on frying ranges in those days so the fryer had to determine the heat in the pan and this he controlled by topping up the fat in order to reduce the temperature. Ironically the most successful shops were more prone to have fires. Frying produced scraps of batter that were usually given away. But shops generated more scraps than could be given away and any surplus was thrown in a bin. In the less popular shops, the scraps had time to cool whereas the busier establishments produced scraps at such a rate that the cooling process was hindered. Internal combustion occurred and fire often broke out, usually several hours after the shop had closed. By the 1930s around six hundred shops were operating in Leeds, and fire was a constant hazard in all of them.

The demand from fish shops spawned several ancillary industries in the area. The Acme Engineering Company of Holbeck offered its Lancashire frying range from £47 10s. while Wm Brooks & Son Ltd of Copley Hill was advertising New Coke burning ranges. In 1928 the Leeds Association discussed the advantages of using gas as an alternative fuel and by 1940 the *Fish Fryers Review* claimed 212 fryers in the city had chosen this option. Coal was still popular in the 1930s; the firms providing it included Lodge's of Cross Flatts and McKay's based in the Corn Exchange, which specialised in supplying the frying industry. Potatoes were available from Dandy's of Horsforth and dripping from a variety of suppliers in the town including both Webster's and Norbury's on Skinner Lane, and Calvert's on Vulcan Street. Some fryers had already moved onto buying ready-made batter from firms such as Arnold Grimshaw Ltd of Hunslet Hall Road – which supplied the unoriginally named BATTA powder – but many still preferred to mix their own. Fryers jealously guarded their secret methods of mixing batter. Some simply used plain flour, baking powder and water; others added eggs or vinegar and some even a bottle of Guinness, to give it flavour!

Originality was not restricted to batter. Some fish fryers developed innovative ideas to increase sales. In 1922 W. H. Boomer of Leeds fitted out a one-ton Ford van to produce one of the first mobile fish-and-chip shops. With its white-topped roof, and bright red and gold sides, it proved a popular attraction in outlying villages. Others also worked hard to expand their businesses. One trader sold wet fish, which he hawked round the neighbourhood on a cart. Another fried fish in olive oil, which he then sold cold for workers to put in their sandwiches. But the most successful entrepreneur in the Leeds area was Harry Ramsden.

After several unsuccessful business ventures he bought a lock-up fish shop on Wibsey Lane, Bradford and then one on Manchester Road. But in 1928 he purchased a lock-up shop at Guiseley on the outskirts of Leeds. Three years later he opened his fish-and-chip restaurant there, and of course it became world famous. Wall-to-wall carpeting, glittering chandeliers and his entrepreneurial zeal gave the business a reputation that other restaurateurs could only envy. Brass-band concerts and clock golf were just two of the attractions he organised for customers.

In 1952, to celebrate twenty-five years at White Cross, he surpassed himself in showmanship when he decided to sell fish and chips on 7 July at the 1912 prices his father had charged: fish 1*d*. and chips ½*d*. Parties came from as far afield as Huddersfield and Halifax. Brass bands performed, a rhythm choir sang, a firework display illuminated the sky and it was estimated that eight thousand people took advantage of the offer. In 1954 Ramsden sold the business. The name was kept alive, however, and at the beginning of the twenty-first century it was internationally known as restaurants were opened in places as far flung as Blackpool, Glasgow, Florida and Saudi Arabia.

Not all fish fryers were so successful and, perhaps sensing the difficulties as the shadow of Nazism fell across Europe, Mr A. Schofield – who had been a fish fryer for many years – told a meeting of Leeds Fish Fryers Association in August 1939 that he would not advise young people to go into the trade. The declaration of war that year certainly did present difficulties for fish fryers in Leeds, as elsewhere.

Supplies of fish were immediately affected as the Admiralty commandeered a number of trawlers. Major Milner, MP for South-East Leeds, pointed out that some shops in the city were being driven out of business. Leeds fryers complained about the disruption to supplies and that dripping was harder to get. A further cause for concern was that one Leeds merchant held about a thousand tons of dripping in his store and local fryers feared that if his warehouse received a direct hit during an air raid the loss would have a catastrophic effect.

Wrapping paper was also in short supply. Newspapers and magazines were collected as salvage to be recycled. By collecting salvage, Middleton Council School raised £100 in just six months to support children in blitzed areas. With the shortage of paper, customers were asked to bring their own wrappings or a basin to put their fish and chips in. One enterprising Leeds firm advertised it had a consignment of wrapping paper available. Some gullible shop owners placed an order and paid for it, but when the delivery arrived found it consisted of old pamphlets and booklets which were of no use whatsoever.

More serious was the extensive operation of the black market. Though fish and chips were not rationed, retailers had a limit placed on their supply. By November 1941 some fryers were prepared to pay more than the government's maximum price to ensure a steady supply and keep their shops open. When stocks began to dry up they secretly bought additional supplies of dripping and fish; and when potato supplies began running low they short-circuited the system by buying directly – and illegally – from local farmers. Henry Youngman, president of the Fish Fryers' Federation in Leeds, demanded that a blacklist be drawn up of such people as they were jeopardising the industry. The same could be said of the fish cakes from one unscrupulous Leeds shop. C. H. Manley, the city analyst, at the request of the *Yorkshire Evening News*, investigated the content of its fish cakes: only 3 per cent was fish, 21 per cent was batter and 76 per cent was potato.

However, most Leeds fish fryers fulfilled their responsibilities to the war effort both legally and patriotically. The Leeds branch of the NFFF raised money for the Spitfire Fund by contributing £55 8s. 8d. Most accepted the restrictions stoically and often with a sense of humour. Perhaps it was best summed up in a notice displayed by Bertie Wilson on the wall of his Addingham Street fish shop in Armley: 'Owing to Hitler, your fish'll be littler.'

When the war ended society changed. Acme was still supplying its fish-frying ranges in 1965 as it had for almost the whole of the century but Brian Parker, president of the Leeds and District Fish

Fryers' Association recognised that innovation was essential if the trade was to survive. He urged members to diversify by installing microwaves at a cost of about £185 and, like him, to sell pies and pasties. Many fryers were reluctant to alter their traditional habits but realised there was a growing market for sausages, peas, beans, beef burgers, chicken and curry.

The alteration in licensing hours was another factor. The new legislation that allowed pubs to close at 11 p.m. meant that people no longer bothered calling for fish and chips after closing time as they had done when pubs shut at 10 p.m. Often cinema audiences – leaving after the first house at about 8.15 p.m. – would call at a fish shop but the decline of cinema-going during the 1960s and 1970s also contributed to a drop in demand. To combat this many shops opted to open at teatime instead and markedly reduced their evening openings.

A further threat came first from Chinese, then Indian take-aways and latterly from fast-food chains like McDonald's and Kentucky Fried Chicken. The growth was rapid and was considered such a threat by some Leeds councillors that, in 1991, they objected to the proposal to open a fifth takeaway on Whitehall Road, which already boasted two Chinese, an Indian and a pizzeria. Added to the threat of competition were increasing health fears over the use of fat and so many Leeds shops started to use vegetable oil for frying. In 2002, there were still some 120 fish-and-chip shops and fish restaurants in the Leeds area but the national trend in takeaways was changing. Sales of Chinese and Indian takeaways had declined by about 10 per cent, and one market research organisation claimed that fish-and-chip sales were down 11 per cent.

Despite this, fish shops in the city – though much changed in appearance and in the range of products available – were still extremely popular and retained considerable goodwill. Among the most popular over the years have been Dennis's, Youngman's and Bryans, which all built up strong followings; while Brett's, opposite Headingley, has long been a favourite with cricket journalists.

In 1972, the monthly magazine, *The Chipper*, claimed: 'In its 57 years of existence the Leeds association has enjoyed the highest reputation in the trade in the North of England.' No doubt some towns would disagree, as they would with Priestland's claim that Leeds is the 'nation's intellectual capital of fish and chips'. But in 2005 local fish shops have a place in the hearts of Leeds people as they have done since Edward Lewis established his shop in Marsh Lane in the Victorian heyday of the 1880s.

13

THE RIPPER YEARS

At about eleven at night on Friday 2 January 1981 the last act in Britain's biggest-ever murder hunt was played out. Sergeant Robert Ring and probationer constable Robert Hydes of the South Yorkshire Police had come across a suspiciously parked, brown Rover 3500 with its lights off in the isolated drive of the British Iron and Steel Producers' headquarters in Sheffield. When questioned, the female passenger claimed that she was the driver's girlfriend. However, when the driver was challenged he had to admit he did not even know her name. It was a charade that was bound to be exposed as the officers recognised Olivia Reivers as a prostitute. As Hydes questioned the couple, sergeant Ring contacted the police national computer at Hendon to check the number plates. It showed that FHY 400K belonged to a Skoda and not to a seven-year-old Rover. The plates were obviously stolen and the driver was arrested on suspicion of theft.

The crime having occurred at a scrapyard near Mirfield in West Yorkshire, the accused man was taken to a police station in Dewsbury. However, the name of anyone arrested with a prostitute had to be passed on to Millgarth police station in Leeds, the headquarters of the squad set up to apprehend the man known as the Yorkshire Ripper. The Ripper was a pathological killer who had sexually assaulted and brutally done to death thirteen women across the north of England and attempted to murder seven others. During an interview with detective inspector John Boyle of the Ripper task force, Peter Sutcliffe, the driver, was confronted with the fact that the police had retrieved a ball-peen hammer and screwdriver from the gateway in Sheffield where he had hidden them. At 2.40 p.m. on that Sunday he was asked, 'What about the Ripper?' It was only then that the 35-year-old quietly admitted, 'Well, it's me. I'm glad it's over.'

On 22 May 1981 an Old Bailey jury, by a verdict of ten to two, found Peter Sutcliffe guilty of murder. He showed no emotion at the verdict. The prosecution argued that he had carried out a crusade against prostitutes and women he considered to be promiscuous. His defence counsel said he believed that he was carrying out divine retribution. The truth was never established. What had become clear, however, was the effect his attacks had on the people of the north of England in general and of Leeds in particular. Mr Justice Boreham, sentencing him to life imprisonment, commented on those he had terrorised for six years: 'It is a population which to my knowledge does not lack fortitude. But I am left with no doubt that women from wide areas were in the deepest fear, and I have no doubt, too, that fear spilled over to their menfolk on their account.'

Fear had spread across the North during that harrowing period. In Leeds it was most acutely felt for it was here more than anywhere else that Sutcliffe carried out his vendetta. The press called it 'a reign of terror' and it had indeed tested the 'fortitude' that Mr Justice Boreham had praised. It generated an atmosphere of fear that people had never experienced before. It was a fear that for some, even with the passage of time, never went away. As one Leeds woman remarked, twenty years later: 'Since the Ripper, I have never felt safe to go out alone at night.' It also provoked bitter criticism of the shocking incompetence of the relatively newly formed West Yorkshire Police. None was more vociferous than the feminist lobby in Leeds.

The 1960s had seen a revolution in social attitudes in Britain and life in Leeds reflected the growing trend in licentiousness. Leeds had always had red light areas. In the early 1940s and early 1950s Bond Street in the city centre was notorious, as was the infamous Robin Hood pub on Vicar Lane. By the 1960s, prostitutes had moved to the Chapeltown area where Spencer Place and Grange

Avenue both developed reputations as centres of the trade and it was here that Sutcliffe would carry out his first attack. Violence towards women was becoming more of a problem. The Salvation Army converted its crumbling Mount Cross maternity home for unmarried mothers on Broad Lane at Bramley into flats for deprived woman and children. Volunteer groups established, at different times, two women's refuges in the Burley area despite Leeds City Council's refusal to apply for a government grant to help fund the projects.

It is against this background that the story of the Ripper must be seen; a story that started early on the morning of 30 October 1975. Alan Routledge, helped by his younger brother Paul, was out delivering milk in Chapeltown. On a sloping grass embankment some twenty-five yards from the caretaker's bungalow of the Prince Philip Centre on Scott Hall Avenue they found what at first sight appeared to be a children's discarded guy. It was in fact the body of a local prostitute, Wilma McCann. She had been struck on the head and stabbed. The *Yorkshire Evening Post*'s headline read 'Murder in Fog – Savage and Sadistic Attack in Leeds'. Detective chief superintendent Denis Hoban took charge of the case.

Twelve weeks later Emily Jackson, another prostitute, was battered to death and her body dragged to a derelict property in a cul-de-sac at Sheepscar. She had been stabbed fifty-one times. The *Evening Post* drew comparisons with the McCann murder. Posters were distributed across the city and loudspeaker announcements were made to the crowds at Headingley and Elland Road grounds appealing for help in catching the 'manic knifeman who has murdered two prostitutes'. Vans with six-feet-high placards toured the Roundhay, Harehills and Chapeltown areas. Police leave was cancelled, 150 detectives were drafted onto the case and Hoban remarked, 'He is the type who would kill again'. He did.

Two more Leeds prostitutes were attacked. After failing to kill Marcella Claxton in May 1976 at Soldier's Field, Roundhay, the killer struck again at the same place in February 1977 and stabbed Irene Richardson to death. Detective chief superintendent James Hobson, now in charge of the Leeds investigation, announced that 'no prostitute in Leeds is safe'. The reality was that no woman, prostitute or not, was safe. In June 1977, he attacked and murdered 16-year-old Jayne MacDonald, a respectable teenager, near the Chapeltown Community Centre.

Nor were his victims restricted to Leeds. Patricia (Tina) Atkinson in Bradford in April 1977 and Jean Jordan in Manchester the following October were both sadistically despatched. At Bradford, Yvonne Pearson in January 1978, and ten days later Helen Rytka in Huddersfield, became victims. That same year, on 16 May, Vera Millward from Manchester was brutally murdered. Twelve months later, Josephine Whitaker at Halifax in April, and in September Barbara Leach, a student at Bradford University, became victims. Another seven women managed to survive his savage attacks, though many of them were left mentally scarred.

By now the press and public were referring to the killer as the Yorkshire Ripper. In September 1979 the *Yorkshire Post* and *Evening Post* offered a reward of £5,000 (a considerable sum at the time) and within a few months West Yorkshire Police Authority was offering £25,000 for information leading to the man's arrest. Assistant chief constable George Oldfield was put in charge of the investigation.

One of the survivors, Marcella Claxton, gave the police a description of the man who had attacked her but the police argued that had she been a Ripper victim she would not have lived to tell the tale. Four of the other women survivors also gave descriptions but their evidence, too, was considered unreliable. The police had made a fundamental error of judgement.

Over a period of time three letters from the North-East, and claiming to be from the Ripper, arrived at police headquarters. Then, in June 1979, a cassette tape was received by Oldfield with a chilling, taunting message apparently from the killer. He was a man with a Sunderland accent: 'I'm Jack. I see you're still having no luck catching me . . . I reckon your boys are letting you down, George. They can't be much good.' Oldfield was convinced that both the tape and the letters were from the Ripper himself, saying that he was '99 per cent certain they were authentic'. He went on to announce, 'We are definitely looking for a man who originated in the North-East.' The police spent £1 million on publicity in their search for the elusive Geordie and a confidential memo was sent to other forces advising them to eliminate any man from their enquiries 'if his accent is dissimilar to a North-East (Geordie) accent'. The police had made another serious error.

They made yet another over the killing of Joan Harrison who was murdered in Preston in November 1975. The police assumed this was another Ripper killing and forensic evidence from the scene indicated that the killer's blood group was 'B' positive, the second rarest in the country. Thus after each murder, the Blood Transfusion Service at Seacroft was contacted. But Sutcliffe had not murdered the Preston woman; nor was he 'B' positive.

Leeds colleges were asked to examine the records of students from the North-East. A dedicated telephone line was available twenty-four hours a day for anyone wishing to hear the tape again. The press asked its readers: 'Do you know a father, brother, son, fiancé, boyfriend or neighbour with access to a car whose whereabouts on the murder nights are not known?' Officers visited local Leeds clubs and pubs playing the tape to customers. Publicity leaflets and posters were circulated round the city pleading, 'Help us to stop the Ripper from killing again.'

The public responded and thousands of letters and telephone calls were made to Ripper headquarters. Some estimates put the number of calls as high as 50,000, making them almost impossible to collate. Computers at the time were relatively unsophisticated: the police computer at Hendon simply recorded the registration number, owner and make of cars. For the rest, manual card indexes were used, making cross-referencing extremely difficult.

Suspicions now ran high in Leeds. People looked with misgivings on those with Geordie accents. Lifelong friends and neighbours looked for unusual traits in people they had known for years, Geordie accent or not. The moral dilemmas some individuals faced were enormous. One anonymous woman with a Scottish accent contacted the solicitor of Anthony Steel. He was being held, accused of another murder, of Carole Wilkinson, a bakery worker at Bradford. The caller claimed that her son had committed that crime but was afraid to come forward to clear Steel's name for fear of being accused of being the Ripper. (Steel was found guilty and imprisoned. He was pardoned in 2003.)

Elsie Henderson of New Wortley agonised for weeks over what she should do. Her ex-husband was from the North-East, had a Geordie accent, enjoyed the company of prostitutes and at times resorted to violence. After talking to her family she decided to go to the police. As she later said, 'I couldn't have lived with myself if I'd kept back information which led to another killing.' She plucked up courage to contact the task force, was thanked for her public spiritedness but was told that her husband had already been interviewed five times.

In August 1980, at Farsley on the outskirts of Leeds, the killer changed his modus operandi. After beating Marguerite Walls with a hammer he strangled the civil servant with a loop of hemp. Her body was hidden under a pile of leaves in what was known locally as 'the Secret Garden'. The police disregarded the Ripper connection. They argued that the use of strangulation ruled the serial killer out. It was another disastrous misjudgement. Their response was similar over the next attack.

Dr Upadhya Bandara had arrived in Leeds from Singapore on a World Health Organisation scholarship. On 24 September she was walking home through Chapel Lane at Headingley when she was seized and viciously assaulted. The would-be killer was disturbed and fled. The police, however, once again refused to accept she had been attacked by the Ripper despite her giving the same description of him that the other survivors had. At the beginning of November Theresa Sykes in Huddersfield was attacked and only saved when her boyfriend arrived on the scene. The police again disregarded the Ripper link.

Less than a fortnight later the Ripper struck for the last time. Jacqueline Hill was a student at the University of Leeds. On the night of 17 November 1980 she had attended a seminar in

Cookridge Street, then caught the Number 1 bus home to Headingley. Sutcliffe, sitting in the Kentucky Fried Chicken restaurant, watched her alight at 9.23 p.m. He followed her to Alma Road, a dimly lit street off the main thoroughfare, and attacked her. Dragging her to some spare land, he savagely stabbed her to death. Her bloodstained handbag and glasses had been left lying in Alma Road and were later found by some students who summoned the police. Spending just a few minutes, two officers carried out a cursory search. It was not until just after ten the next morning that the body was found. The *Yorkshire Post*'s headline, 'Police doubt Ripper link in student's murder' was soon disavowed. The Ripper had indeed struck again.

It was this murder that roused the public to anger and generated an atmosphere of fear and even panic. In Leeds women now tended to go out in the evening escorted by men. Colleges, clubs and pubs changed their routines. Students at Trinity and All Saints College at Horsforth organised lifts in private cars. Understandably, the impact at Leeds University was particularly felt. Since the murder of Bradford University student, Barbara Leach, Leeds University authorities had taken some protective measures such as laying on buses from discos and pubs. But for many that was not enough. One student claimed, 'I hate Leeds now. I'm scared and all my friends feel the same.'

In the Headingley area, frequented by students, Salvo's Italian restaurant reported a marked reduction in trade. Letters to the press suggested women wishing to go out should travel in groups. Many did. The managements at the Cottage Road cinema and the Original Oak pub commented that it was noticeable girls no longer arrived alone. Some schools closed early to let children get home in daylight and girls were advised not to leave the building alone; others cancelled their after-school activities. Hospitals took particular care after Leeds General Infirmary received a hoax letter saying one of its nurses would be the next victim. Some 91 per cent of Bramhope residents called for street lighting to be installed. Debenhams scrapped its plans to open late for Christmas shoppers.

Some Leeds prostitutes began moving out of the Chapeltown area. Others, despite the obvious danger, continued to solicit. As one prostitute philosophically admitted, 'You take a risk all the time.' Nevertheless, when Christine Brent was arrested, she was found to be carrying a knife for self defence. She was not alone. Many other women began carrying knives, sharpened steel combs, hatpins and alarms. Following Jacqueline Hill's murder, some three thousand mugger alarms were sold in Leeds stores in a matter of hours.

A clairvoyant, Nella Jones, who claimed to have seen the Ripper's face and had predicted he would strike on 17 November, came forward to offer help. The *Evening Post* suggested that doctors' files should be made available but only to police surgeons in order to maintain patient confidentiality; the British Medical Association insisted it would have no objection to the proposal. The Department of Health and Social Security trawled its records.

In Leeds questions were asked in workplaces and supermarkets, in pubs and bingo halls. Why had the police spent only two to three minutes searching near Jacqueline Hill's bloodstained handbag? Why was the murder squad not even told that the handbag had been discovered? Why were callers – who rang other city police stations when they could not get through to the Ripper headquarters or police area headquarters at Brotherton House – told brusquely just to keep trying? In response to this criticism ten new numbers were made available. The National Breakdown Recovery Club, in conjunction with Marcus Fox, MP for Shipley, appealed for £100,000, which would be offered as a reward. But the police seemed to be in a hopeless situation. It led one senior officer ruefully to quote G. K. Chesterton: 'Society is at the mercy of the murderer without a motive.'

That may well have been true but there were many in Leeds who believed that the city was also at the mercy of an incompetent police force that seemed incapable of apprehending the killer. The force also faced criticism for failing to catch a hooded rapist who had committed twelve rapes in the Bradford area around the same time.

The *Evening Post* admitted, 'People are beginning to say, "No wonder they can't catch him".' There were those police officers who felt the investigation was getting nowhere and went on to describe it as the 'Ripper Circus'. Even more critical were some members of the public who cynically claimed that there were probably certain officers happy for the case to continue in order to line their pockets with overtime. Five days after Jacqueline's death, the *Yorkshire Post* pithily summed up public feeling in the city: 'Current opinion in saloon bars is that, if they are going to get him, pretty soon would not be soon enough. . . . Five years is a long time; thirteen murders is thirteen too many.' Its sister paper the *Evening Post* was equally critical: 'Any force which has failed for five years to catch a madman who has killed thirteen times . . . must expect criticism.'

Along with the *Morley Advertiser*, the *Post* launched a poster campaign proclaiming: 'The Ripper is a Coward – Let's Catch Him'. Workers at the Burton group supported the strategy but the police did not. They considered that such an approach was inflammatory and likely to provoke more violence from the elusive killer. Other posters displayed by the police and at the university simply stated the obvious: 'Do not go out alone', and 'Stick to well lit streets'. And there were those, like one correspondent to the *Evening Post*, who bitterly observed that the police were powerless: 'too numerous do-gooders and successive feeble governments have seen to that', she wrote.

But something had to be done even though local politicians were divided over what that should be. The North-West constituency Labour Party called on the party and local Labour councillors to take all possible measures to ensure the safety of women. Stanley Cohen, MP for South-East Leeds, suggested that Scotland Yard be called in. Merlyn Rees, MP for South Leeds disagreed. He argued that as all police forces now had the resources for an investigation of this magnitude it was unnecessary. In fact two senior Scotland Yard officers had been called in to give advice for two weeks in November 1979. Their conclusion was that everything that could be done was being done.

Meanwhile Sir Donald Kaberry, the long-standing MP for Leeds North-West, voiced the views of many; 'If ever there was a case for capital punishment surely it applies to this man.' The *Leeds Other Paper* took issue with what it termed these 'Neanderthal MPs' and their call to bring back hanging. It also condemned the *Evening Post* for carrying a pin-up on its front page next to its headline on the Jacqueline Hill murder: 'Leeds Killing – it's the Ripper'. It deplored the way that the press generally referred to the women victims as 'respectable or not', and argued that police efforts had only accelerated when non-prostitutes were murdered. It demanded a curfew on men in the city and urged the police to publish all the information they had received from the Ripper. It alleged that of the 750 words in the letters only 170 had actually been made public.

Television too played its part. As early as July 1977, Yorkshire Television devoted a *Calendar Special* to the affair in which Marilyn Webb, the reporter, toured the Chapeltown area with George Oldfied interviewing residents and prostitutes. Following the Jacqueline Hill murder, BBC 2 allocated a seven-minute slot in its late-night programme, *Newsnight*. Thames Television went to Leeds University for a discussion programme on the case. Bob Southgate, the presenter, was heckled when he allocated only the last ten minutes to the 150 women who made up the invited audience.

George Oldfield, who had publicly stated that the issue was a now 'a personal matter between him and the killer', suffered two heart attacks and chief superintendent James Hobson was placed in charge of the case. He commented that they would not eliminate anyone simply because they did not have a Geordie accent and assured the public that the 'morale of the force is high'. He added that he felt that the police still had 'the public confidence'. The *Yorkshire Post* begged to differ and insisted that, 'It is clear something would have to be done to restore public confidence.'

Correspondence in the press revealed the extent of that loss of confidence. Dennis Edwards of Rothwell wrote of 'a force beginning to lack credibility'. From Huddersfield, A. Schofield wrote: 'the obvious bungling by the police . . . makes one wonder if he ever will be caught'. The police did have their supporters. One writer commented, 'it would be wrong to make scapegoats of the police' and spoke of 'the ability to be wise after the event'.

But many argued it was outside help, not wisdom, which was required despite chief constable Ronald Gregory's decision not to seek it. Politicians, press and public demanded a new approach, and a special Ripper squad was formed from the best-available officers. They included commander Robert Harvey, adviser to the chief inspector of constabulary and, on the recommendation of William Whitelaw, the home secretary, Stuart Kind, of the Home Office Research Establishment. They would work under Hobson though Oldfield was retained as titular head of the investigation.

Some members of the West Yorkshire Police committee, however, felt that they had been misled. They said that they had been told that the new 'super squad' would be involved directly in the investigations, now they discovered that the new officers were to act only in an advisory capacity. But the criticism of the committee was nothing compared to the condemnation of the authorities by women's groups.

At the time many were incensed about the treatment of two sisters in Bradford, Charlene and Annette Maur, who had just been jailed for the murder of their brutal father. It was seen by many as symptomatic of the attitude of the authorities towards women. Some decided that more positive action was required. The Women's Action Group at the university demanded better campus lighting, emergency phones, late-night transport and complained that, 'Women are virtually under curfew in West Yorkshire.' Other women insisted that some had been forced to give up their studies and jobs. Activists made it abundantly clear, 'We are directing our fear into anger and we are not going to be terrorised off the streets.'

For some Leeds women the issue became part of a wider political agenda. They condemned those whom they felt were exploiting the situation for commercial gain such as the manufacturers of alarms, though they said nothing about the number of women in the city who were eager to buy those alarms. They condemned taxi drivers for making excess profits as women switched from public transport. However, they failed to mention that many taxi drivers, after dropping off their fares, waited until they saw their passengers had gone inside their homes to safety.

Some criticism was harsh. It was argued by a few women that all men were simply waiting for an opportunity to attack, rape and murder any female. Audrey Marlow, in the *Leeds Other Paper* objected to this view: 'I can see no evidence that this is true of more than a socially sick minority,' she wrote. Nevertheless, some women took practical action to deal with the threat of attack. Self-defence classes were organised by the Women's Self-Defence Group. A national conference of Women Against Violence Against Women had already been convened at Royal Park Middle School, Leeds for the weekend of 22/23 November. Ironically it fell at the end of the week in which Jacqueline Hill had been murdered and the place chosen for the gathering was less then two miles from the scene of the crime. Initially the intention had been to discuss women's issues, examine graphic cases of rape and hold self-defence classes. Now – disgusted at the perceived injustice of the Maur trial and the lack of progress on the Ripper case – a protest march was organised.

Five hundred women gathered in City Square and marched up Briggate to the Odeon cinema, which was showing *Dressed to Kill*, a film that 'exploited' the sexual aspects of killing. They stormed the building, hurled red paint at the screen and then moved on to the Plaza cinema, famed for its soft-porn films. A cordon of police, however, stopped the assault and the group moved off, making their way up Merrion Street to Woodhouse Lane. Fights broke out as police prevented them from entering the BBC studios and the Fenton public house. En route cars had been damaged and some men were physically attacked, including reporters from both the *Yorkshire Post* and the *Morning Star*. The women, however, claimed that men had provoked them by shouting obscenities. Frustration had led to their anger and their spokeswoman claimed, 'We have made our point'. For the *Yorkshire Post* they had proved themselves 'at best second-rate men'.

Then, suddenly, it was all over. On the evening of Sunday 4 January 1981 the police called a press conference. Gleeful chief constable Gregory, flanked by Oldfield and Hobson, announced that a man had been arrested. 'He is being questioned in relation to the Yorkshire Ripper murders . . . I can tell you we are absolutely delighted with the developments at this stage. Absolutely delighted,' Gregory smiled. It was one more error of judgement. Members of Parliament condemned such comments as premature and Sir Michael Havers, the solicitor general, emphasised that there was an 'obligation to be discreet in what one says so as not to prejudice any prosecution'.

The media had a field day when the case came to court. The *Daily Mail* sent thirty-two reporters and cameramen to cover proceedings. When it resorted to cheque-book journalism even the Queen took the unusual step of publicly admitting she shared 'the distaste of all right-minded people'. Many in Leeds agreed. The city had undergone one of the most traumatic periods in its history and to see it exploited for commercial purposes was anathema to them.

During his trial Sutcliffe argued that 'they knew it was me for a long time'. But he had escaped because, 'It was in God's hands . . . God was controlling me.' The hoax letters and tape were 'an indirect line to God . . . so that I could be left to carry on'. While he was in Armley Jail awaiting trial he boasted he 'might do only ten years in a loony bin'. Mr Justice Boreham ruled he must serve a minimum of thirty years.

Some £4 million had been spent on the investigation: 250 detectives had been employed full time for three years and thousands more at different times; 21,000 interviews had been conducted; between 500 and 1,000 letters a day were sent to Ripper headquarters; and forty primary suspects were identified. Astonishingly, Sutcliffe was not included on the list, despite the fact that he was interviewed by police on several occasions and was repeatedly spotted in red light areas in his car.

So ended the biggest murder enquiry in the history of the British police. Recriminations followed at the end of the trial. Bob Taylor, who was involved in the investigation, and who later became a detective chief superintendent, acknowledged that the police had 'lost control of what it was doing'. The home secretary, William Whitelaw, set up an inquiry under Lawrence Byford, an inspector of constabulary. Five months later his damning 156-page report accused senior officers of lacking imagination and flexibility. But there were those who argued that, had the old Leeds City Police, a smaller force, been in charge, a more effective outcome would have been achieved in far less time, with much less tragic circumstances.

14

A YEAR OF PESTILENCE

On 27 December 1918 readers of the *Leeds Weekly Citizen* looked at its 'Review of the Year'. Understandably, the local paper reflected on the horrors of the bloody conflict that had ended only a month before. The First World War was over at last. But even as victory was being heralded, the worst cataclysm that mankind had ever experienced swept across the world and left between twenty and forty million dead. The *Citizen* noted that, 'Its effects touched every street and almost every home. It proved a sadly fatal epidemic.'

But it was more than an epidemic; it was a pandemic. The deadly virus struck from Australia and New Zealand to Canada and the United States; from Russia and Germany to Ethiopia and South Africa. Britain was no exception, and Leeds was but one of the cities that saw its population smitten and almost two thousand of its citizens die. The year 1918 was indeed, as the *Citizen* called it, 'a year of pestilence'. It was the year of the 'Spanish flu'.

Influenza was not a new disease. Some experts believe that flu can be traced back to the ancient world but it was not until 1743 that it acquired the name 'influenza'. Like other towns Leeds would not have been immune from that infection any more than it was from many other contagious diseases. In 1801 a fever raged with such ferocity through the poorer areas of Leeds that it was decided to open a house of recovery on Vicar Lane. For three months in the spring of 1809, a measles epidemic attacked the children of Leeds with such vehemence that the press refused to comment on it for fear of causing a public panic. In 1893–4 it returned to the poorer areas with equally devastating effect, leaving 630 fatalities in its wake. But as one Leeds medical officer of health (MOH) remarked 'it was a disease from which children of the well-to-do never die'. To an extent the same could be said about cholera and typhus for these were also diseases that hit hardest in working-class areas. Cholera broke out in 1832 and 1848–9 when some two thousand people died. Typhus appeared in 1847 and 1865–6. All these outbreaks erupted with catastrophic consequences for the most squalid streets of Victorian Leeds.

That same year of 1847 saw the influenza epidemic that was raging in London spread to Leeds with very serious consequences. In 1889 it was back. In December that year the *Leeds Daily News* carried a report which noted that an epidemic of 'La Grippe', a common name for influenza, had struck in Russia. By the end of the month it was raging in London. Yet in Leeds, the paper was able to comment that the only cases of flu reported there – 'typhoid influenza' or 'pink eye' as it referred to the disease – were among the railway horses at the station yard!

By January 1890, however, it had infected large areas of the country. Lord Salisbury, the prime minister, was confined to bed while every document sent from the Foreign Office to Queen Victoria was disinfected. It appeared that Leeds had escaped relatively lightly with E. W. Beckett, who was one of the MPs for Nottinghamshire, laid low at his Kirkstall Grange home at Headingley one of the few in the city taken ill. But that false sense of security may have been created because notification of the disease was not compulsory in Leeds. The authorities therefore had no real idea about its impact.

They soon became aware. Numerous cases were reported in Farnley, Stanningley, Bramley, Holbeck and Roundhay Road. At Headingley the disease took the turn it usually did when a woman there, suffering originally from flu, died of pneumonia, which in those days was virtually incurable. In fact, most of the deaths in the city were caused by pneumonia precipitated by the influenza virus. The vicar at Wortley, himself prostrated by flu, noted in his parish magazine that it had 'carried off many of all ranks and classes'.

Confusion reigned. No cases were recorded at the Infirmary, the Dispensary or the other Leeds hospitals and yet it took a strong hold in the army barracks off Chapeltown Road. The managers of warehouses in Leeds claimed that a few people were suffering from colds but none from influenza. Many Leeds doctors claimed that some of those who said they were suffering from La Grippe were experiencing no more than a common cold. But in 1918 it was to be a very different story.

The source and virulence of the 1918 outbreak are still in dispute. It appears to have struck first at the holiday resort of San Sebastian in northern Spain, hence its name 'Spanish flu'. More recently, historians have suggested that the virus first appeared at an Army camp at Etaples in northern France sometime in 1916.

Attempts by the public health authorities to combat disease had been relatively successful in the latter years of the nineteenth century. But even in 1918 poorer people in Leeds – suffering from cancers, hernias and tumours – could be kept waiting up to two years for a hospital appointment. The *Yorkshire Post* reported on the pitiful queues of hopeless women and children at the city's hospitals and the 'heavy sickly smell' that hung in the air.

There were other health problems. A Mrs Gotto, speaking in October 1918 to the Leeds Branch of the National Council for Combating Venereal Disease, pointed out that laying the blame on the armed forces for the spread of the affliction was unfair; only 2 per cent of the Army and Navy were so affected whereas between 15 and 20 per cent of the civilian population were. The poor standard of food hygiene was also a cause for concern. Despite attempts to impose controls in Leeds, 1919 saw 224,620 lbs of beef and 176,955 lbs of fish – considered unfit for human consumption – being destroyed. Even as late as the 1950s anyone travelling along Wellington Road by tramcar would pass the self-styled 'Max, the working man's butcher'. It was not uncommon to see Max, Woodbine drooping out of the corner of his mouth, cutting-up meat while his pet cat lay asleep in the window amid the joints of beef and pork.

It is against this background of limited public health provision and the debilitating effect of war, that the 'Spanish flu' epidemics of 1918 and 1919 have to be seen. There were three epidemics: the first a relatively mild one in June and July 1918; the second, and most devastating, from October to December; the third, not quite as severe, in February and March 1919.

The first epidemic struck Leeds about the third week in June. Only two deaths were recorded. The following week the number rose to twenty-two and by the second week in July the death toll had reached fifty-six. From then the numbers declined but, in all, 161 people died. Lloyd George, the prime minister, was reported to be recovering from the virus and all seemed well. In August, Sydney Walton of the *Yorkshire Evening News* even offered a potential remedy should flu reappear – whortleberries! The people of the town breathed a sigh of relief that the danger was over. It proved a vain hope.

Influenza was at its most virulent in cold, wet years. From September 1918 – when the West Riding experienced its highest-ever rainfall – to the end of the year the weather was both cold and damp. It was claimed by some that the poorer diet of the war years had weakened resistance. One medical officer of health went so far as to say that for three years running the consumption of fatty foods had been considerably reduced and urged the population to eat more 'fat bacon'. Others argued that calorie intake had changed little from pre-war days but, that said, the nutrition of working-class people was generally poor. Another factor in lowering resistance was that many found it difficult to keep warm due to sporadic reductions in coal stocks.

By October 1918 the Leeds press reported that a new wave of influenza had appeared in South Africa where Johannesburg was described as a 'plague stricken city'. But there were deaths much nearer home to record. By the end of the month the *Yorkshire Post* recognised the alarming trend. It reported the number of fatalities in Leeds soaring from 14 for the week ending 19 October to 256 for the week ending 23 November. It was estimated that 12,000 schoolchildren, mainly between four and eight years of age, were suffering from the epidemic and Leeds found itself an unenviable fourth behind Nottingham, Sheffield and Hull in the list of the most vulnerable cities. At its peak it was estimated that a family was bereaved every fifty minutes.

It is true that on 11 November 1918, as peace was announced, most factories and mills closed down for the afternoon. Crowds congregated in the city centre, girls sang 'Oh It's a Lovely War', and 'Goodbyee!' The young women from the munitions' factories were the most exuberant of all as they waved flags and wore Union Jack helmets. Shops were illuminated and bonfires lit, fireworks set off and bunting decorated the streets. But another conflict was being waged through the streets of Leeds that took no cognisance of class, sex or age, though it does appear to have been particularly prevalent among children and young adults. It was estimated that for every adult fatality, two children died.

It was a battle fought most of all in poorer homes. Here the virus found a perfect breeding ground in the closely compacted back-to-backs, where overcrowding added to the problem. Some houses with a living-room, two small bedrooms and an attic were known to accommodate a family of nine; five adults, three teenage girls and a young boy. It was little wonder infection spread so rapidly. An additional problem was that when a member of the family died, for the period until the funeral, the body was laid in a coffin in an upstairs bedroom or kept in the living room, the only place the family could take their meals.

One Leeds home had three bodies to bury at the same time as demand for undertaker's services reached breaking point. In another case a body was left in a house for ten days awaiting burial. On Thursday, 31 October one soldier arrived home on leave in Leeds to find his wife had died of influenza on the previous Monday having just given birth. The other children were suffering from the virus and there was no prospect of their mother's burial for some days.

Undertakers were under tremendous pressure, as were

carpenters to make coffins. Gravediggers were so overworked that soldiers were enlisted to help and the city engineers department seconded several staff to help out. Understandably, the demand on doctors was also considerable. One Leeds general practitioner reported making 104 calls in one day; two other doctors complained they had at least fifty cases of pneumonia each to care for. Although some doctors were able to use cars they were still busy from morning until night and the fact that the petrol allowance was not increased did little to help.

Nursing was also in trouble as nurses succumbed. At the township infirmary (which catered for the Leeds workhouse on Beckett Street and should not be confused with Leeds General Infirmary and was later renamed St James's Hospital) twenty nurses were smitten and one died. At Seacroft Hospital, thirty staff were laid low. In the poorer areas only the goodwill of neighbours, who were prepared to call on infected households up to three times a day, helped to alleviate the situation. Doctor after doctor raised the issue that nursing provision was totally inadequate. Dr Woodcock, reporting on the death of a child, remarked that the house was 'full of influenza'; the mother was unconscious and the rest of the children were ill.

Letters appeared in the press. Florence Broadhead argued that: 'Many women who have had some experience in nursing . . . would be glad to be of use in an emergency as at present. . . . If this were done promptly many valuable lives will, without doubt, be saved.' Another correspondent railed, 'If anything can be done, it should be done at once.'

A practical solution was raised by a correspondent to the *Yorkshire Post* under the sobriquet 'Medical Practitioner': 'We hear a great deal about the "housing of the poor", is it not time we took up the question about the "housing of the dead"?' The writer graphically pointed out the 'harrowing details of our cottage houses down with influenza' and concluded: 'Can nothing be done in a great city like Leeds to prevent such an unnecessary addition to the sum of human misery?' Another wrote recommending cremation, although the public tended to be antagonistic to the idea until the 1950s. Eileen Purdon drew attention to the fact that people in the wealthier areas of the city had little idea of the enormous difficulties being experienced in the poorer districts, 'especially East Leeds'. Her letter to the *Yorkshire Post* stressed the impossibility of achieving any form of adequate isolation in the small and crowded homes of the working classes. And the call for action was also echoed by 'L. D. R.' who introduced religion into the argument: 'We do talk a lot about Him in Leeds. Perhaps it would be better if we did something more' the writer observed.

To be fair, the authorities did do more. People were advised that all catarrhal infections and any associated illnesses accompanied by a rise in temperature should be regarded as possible influenza attacks. Some thirty thousand handbills explaining how to treat the disease were produced by the local authority and distributed by Scout troops. Large posters were displayed in trams, public toilets, waiting rooms and public offices, while disinfectants and sprays were made available by the medical officer of health to factories, workshops and private dwellings.

Treatments varied. One suggested cure was to gargle with a solution of a spoonful of salt in half a glass of water, coloured purple with permanganate of potash. Another was to use a douche of eucalyptus and menthol. Some cures proved fatal. Four-year-old Ernest Jackson, who lived off Wellington Road, was suffering from influenza and bronchitis. A well-meaning neighbour arrived at his home and in an effort to relieve his suffering applied a hot poultice to his body. Unfortunately the heat was so scorching that the boy went into shock and died. Dr Exley, at the coroner's court, declared that death had been accelerated by the application.

Proprietary brands offered remedies. The manufacturers claimed that Oxo fortified the system against infection, that Milton was 'the real safeguard' while Peter's 'Neumonia'(sic) was described as the 'great lung healer'. But possibly the most popular preventive was suggested by Mr Perham of Albion Place in a letter to the *Yorkshire Post*. He pointed out that, although 1,500 members of the Metropolitan Police had been infected, only one person of the wine trade in London had. He called for the immediate removal of restrictions on alcohol. By December, the Ministry of Food had seen the merit of this argument but announced that, although spirits would be made available, the bottles would 'bear distinctive labels' and could only be purchased with a certificate from a doctor.

The hopes of using the city's hospitals was only partially successful as the Infirmary, Seacroft Hospital and the various Poor Law infirmaries at Beckett Street, Hunslet and Bramley found their own staffs so depleted by the disease that the remaining doctors and nurses found it difficult to cope. The Red House Settlement in East Street arranged for Weetwood Hall to be loaned from Cookridge Convalescent Home to provide beds for the sick and get them quickly out of infected households. They also appealed to the public for bed linen, towels and blankets. The temporary hospital was to be made available to the patients of any general practitioner. The infants' hospital at Wyther near the top of Hough Lane was opened for children under ten and, because many pregnant women were found to be particularly vulnerable, beds were reserved for them at the Leeds Maternity Hospital.

The use of public mortuaries also presented difficulties. The Church was asked to provide temporary accommodation and from mid-November put three mission chapels at the disposal of the local authority. Dr John Johnston Jervis – taking over as medical officer of health from Angus Wilson – planned to use existing mortuaries though at the beginning of November did not feel the demand was great enough. One reason was that people were loath to allow their loved ones to be removed from the family home. It was contrary to their experience of family bereavement.

It had become plain that places where crowds congregated were breeding grounds for the disease. Schools where infection was reported were closed. By the last week of October the entire infants' departments in some districts were shut while Brownhill Board School at Harehills, and Victoria Board School on York Road, were closed completely. On 30 October the Education Committee announced an even more drastic measure. On the recommendation of the medical officer of health, all elementary schools in the city were to be closed from noon that day; they stayed shut for three weeks.

That night a meeting was held at the Church Institute on Albion Place to discuss the situation of Sunday schools. After consultation with the authorities, the vicar of Leeds announced that all Sunday schools would also shut their doors. Evening schools were still allowed to function but in reality the numbers attending were considerably reduced.

Licensed places of entertainment were also breeding grounds for the infection. The Education Committee, following the closure of its schools, pressed for the Watch Committee to respond by imposing severe restrictions on theatres and cinemas. With the backing of the lady mayoress, it urged a ban on children from places of entertainment. Cinema owners pointed out that in the newer picture palaces the air was constantly being changed and filtered but they accepted the imposition as long as theatres also had to comply. The regulation was imposed with the provisos that no performance for adults could last longer than three hours, at least thirty minutes had to elapse between shows and the proprietors had to give an undertaking that their buildings could be effectively ventilated.

But the restriction that caused the most controversy related to the armed forces. All places of entertainment in Leeds were placed out of bounds to British troops. One Leeds serviceman, on leave from the front, was incensed by this constraint imposed by 'cantankerous officials'. 'Disgusted' poured out his bitterness to the *Armley and Wortley News*: 'We are not allowed in any places of amusement of any description, whereas the brave men who are too good for the Army could walk in at their leisure.'

It was an understandable reaction. And stripped of its public health implications the flu epidemic of 1918 has also to be seen in terms of human tragedies. Although it was deadliest in working-class communities it struck the homes of every social group. Some who perished were well-known in the city. Sixty-one-year-old Arthur Thewlis, who was a cashier at J. & C. Croysdale's mill, president of the Bramley carnival committee and an executive member of the Leeds Workpeople's Hospital Fund, died of acute pneumonia. Lady Hepton, lady mayoress of Leeds when Edward VII made his royal visit in 1908, died from influenza. Marian Lapish was accorded a funeral with full military honours – having served at the headquarters of the Royal Air Force – after succumbing to influenza with complications. The home of J. W. Smith, the assistant food controller of Leeds, saw a double bereavement as he lost both his wife and daughter.

And there were those whose names appeared only once in the local press – to record their deaths. Bessie Smith of Greenhill Road, who died from influenza and convulsions, was aged five. Influenza and bronchitis ended the life of Sarah Pickles at her home in Venerable Street; she was seventy-five. Fifteen-year-old Harry Priest was taken ill on Monday night at the lodging house where he lived and was found dead next morning. Mrs Eyres of Pickles Yard, Armley, had a particularly tragic experience. She and her three children were all suffering acutely from the disease. In desperation, to settle her 6-week-old baby, she took the child into her bed. The baby suffocated.

From October 1918 to the end of the year 1,132 people had perished, but by then the contagion had subsided and life began to return to normal. Around six thousand people turned up at Elland Road to grumble about their team's 'ineffective attack' as Leeds City lost 1–0 to Coventry in their first home defeat of the season. At Headingley, Leeds lost to Batley in the traditional Christmas Day fixture. And no doubt people discussed the local press reports about the formation of the Professional Football Player's Union, which was to campaign for a weekly wage of £6.

But by the beginning of February 1919 the epidemic had resurfaced. Jervis, the new medical officer of health, issued handbills and the public were once again assailed with advice in the press. The pattern developed as before but with less vehemence and by the end of March the worst was over. This time the sombre tally of those who perished in Leeds was 623. In the years that followed smaller outbreaks struck the city. But the outbreaks of 1957 and 1968 were much less serious, and certainly nothing like 1918–19, when a total of 1,916 Leeds men, women and children died.

By the beginning of the twenty-first century more treatment options had become available and a global surveillance system had been developed. It is to be hoped they will ensure that never again will such a scourge sweep across the world and inflict on the people of Leeds the suffering their forebears experienced.

15

THE SULTAN OF LEEDS

In Shakespeare's *Julius Caesar*, Cassius says about Julius Caesar: 'Why man, he doth bestride the narrow world like a Colossus.' Two thousand years later, provincial Leeds produced its own colossus, a political leviathan, whose charismatic personality bestrode the politics of the city for over two decades. As leader of the council from 1907 to 1928, with the exception only of 1911 to 1912, it was his beliefs that determined corporation policies and yet in only three of those years did he enjoy an outright majority. His name was Charles Henry Wilson.

He was a twenty-stone giant of a man who, as a dedicated Anglican, read the lesson each Sunday in church and yet, for fun, was capable of wrestling stark naked with the mayor of a French town in a Parisian hotel. A teetotaller, and non-smoking poker player, he was equally at home presiding over a mothers' meeting or dominating the hustings. He was a bibliophile who could read a book and memorise its salient passages; and it was said he had forgotten more about council standing orders than most other people knew. But he also loved nothing better than tramping the fields of his estate at North Duffield in an old suit with his dog by his side and a gun under his arm.

A deeply religious man with a passion for his country and his city, he believed profoundly in the freedom of the individual and opposed both strikes and lockouts. He was also a man who commanded respect from his political enemies as well as his political allies. Here was a man whose life was dedicated to two ideals. He gave unstinting loyalty to a Conservative Party which, he believed, was guided by commonsense principles and for him was 'the only party working for *all* the nation'. And he devoted virtually all his life to the welfare of Leeds. When testifying at a local enquiry on the Leeds and Bradford Extension Bill he was asked what the people of Leeds thought about the proposal. He drily responded, 'I am Leeds'. He was unabashed by his arrogance, stating categorically 'I claim to represent Leeds – the spirit of Leeds, the spirit that will not be beaten by anything or anybody.'

Yet Wilson, for all his love of Leeds, was not born in the city. He was born on 13 January 1859 in the family home, Thorn Hill Grange at Brandsby-cum-Stearsby, some ten miles or so from Borough-bridge. His first post was with the North-Eastern Railway in York but he trained as an incorporated accountant, becoming a Fellow of the Society in 1891. He eventually became president and chairman of its parliamentary committee; vice consul for France in Leeds; a director on the boards of various companies, an active participant in numerous city institutions and, from 1900, a magistrate. But it is as a politician that Charles Henry Wilson is best remembered.

He was working as a young accountant in South Parade during 1890 when the Conservatives asked him to stand in the local elections as a candidate for North ward. He fought a gruelling campaign and the result was close. Nevertheless, Wilson found himself elected by a margin of seventy votes. In 1904, John Gordon, the Conservative leader resigned and Wilson was the obvious successor. By 1906 he had become an alderman and the following year took up his place as leader of the council, a position he would vacate for only one year during the next quarter of a century.

The complexity of running services for a growing city of 430,000 souls – particularly when for the most part he had no overall majority – posed problems enough for Wilson. But bread-and-butter issues were overshadowed by a greater danger, as Wilson saw it, and it was one he believed that threatened the British way of life. Socialism was on the march nationally. In the past the working class in Leeds had turned to the Liberal Party.

Two Leeds socialists, Tom Maguire and John Mahon, had determined to seize power from the Liberals. The Liberals realised that the newly created Independent Labour Party in Leeds was a threat and to combat it they wanted to establish an alliance with the Tories. For Wilson a pact enabled him to erect a bulwark against the socialists, whose growing electoral strength soon had practical consequences. When, in November 1913, Labour increased its seats on the council to sixteen, only two less than the Liberals, council workers saw this as an opportunity to pursue a two shillings a week pay rise. Wilson was determined to enforce his policy of economic prudence claiming, into the bargain, that the corporation employed many inefficient workers. He was adamant; the corporation should not be 'a home for lost dogs'.

The strike began on 11 December. Some three thousand workers joined the protest. The city was paralysed. Leeds was plunged into darkness as electricity and gas supplies failed. Factories and mills ground to a halt. Two days later tram services ceased operating. Stagnant refuse piled up in the streets. Nevertheless, Wilson was determined that the strikers would not succeed.

The people of Leeds were divided. The vice-chancellor at the university, Michael Sadler, encouraged students to help break the strike by working for nothing 'as a public duty'. The Liberals joined with Wilson and his Conservatives to form a strike committee – the 'five intolerant Pharoes (sic)', as the Labour *Leeds Weekly Citizen* bitterly described them. Clashes with police and strike-breakers followed. Gas street-lamps and plant were damaged. Wilson and others were provided with police bodyguards and bombs were even detonated. However, the violence was not all one-sided. Men marching to protest at the gas offices were clubbed to the ground by mounted police.

On 13 January 1914 the workers were finally forced to accept defeat. They had won no concessions. Wilson was victorious. He determined to ensure such a situation would never happen again. Around seven hundred of the strikers were sacked and those managers who had shown sympathy for the workers were also dismissed. Wilson argued they had betrayed the city's trust. The Liberals were also losers. They had made it abundantly clear to organised labour where their sympathies lay, as the *Weekly Citizen* observed, 'They have lost touch with the working class.' Never again would the Liberals control the city. But in less than a year council strikes and the decline of Liberalism in Leeds would pale into insignificance.

In August 1914 Britain declared war on Germany, George V issued a proclamation and both the Conservative and Liberal parties in Leeds supported the king's call for help. Labour, with a large number of pacifists among its supporters, left it to individuals to make their own decision. Wilson, along with the lord mayor, Sir Edward Allen Brotherton and Colonel J. W. Stead, played an active part in forming the Leeds Pals, the 15th battalion of the West Yorkshire Regiment.

It was while training at Ripon with the Pals, in June 1915, that 56-year-old Wilson was thrown from his horse. He was seriously injured and invalided out of the army with the honorary rank of captain. It took him some months to recover but, ebullient as ever, he was not prepared to sit back. Once fit, he assumed command of the Leeds Group of Motor Transport Volunteers.

They were responsible for aiding troops who were guarding the north-east coast. Wilson built up his small force into a unit of 700 men with about 600 vehicles. But no doubt his thoughts were drifting across the Channel to where his Leeds Pals were engaged in the bloodiest conflict in history. He had no time for conscientious objectors whom, as he saw it, were 'peace cranks' and cared nothing for their country. How much more bitter would his comments have been had he known the extent of the butchery on 1 July 1916, the first day of the Battle of the Somme, when it was estimated that every street in Leeds lost at least one man.

Like many of his fellow citizens Wilson experienced personal tragedy during the war. In 1918 his only son, Percy, an airman, was killed when his plane crashed. Wilson himself visited the troops to boost morale, was appointed a major and was mentioned in despatches on the instigation of the secretary of state for war.

He may have been the great nationalist but his patriotism was tempered where public finance was concerned. In 1917 Leeds head teachers proposed that every school in the city should be issued with a Union flag that the children would all be able to salute on 24 May, Empire Day. Wilson asked how much it would cost. Fred Kinder – the Liberal leader on the council – announced, '£850'. The *Weekly Citizen* reported the verbatim exchange which followed.

> Wilson, 'That rules it out.'
> Kinder, 'I thought you were a great Empire man.'
> Wilson, 'I am; but not at that price!'

It was not that Wilson was parsimonious. He saw himself as the guardian of the public purse and spent his days in office ensuring that the citizens of Leeds received value for money. To this end he chaired the parliamentary and finance committees of the council and also the committee set up to negotiate the purchase of Temple Newsam – the 'Hampton Court of the North' – along with its 1,200 acre estate.

The council was responsible for the education service in the city as well as libraries, parks, roads, housing, water, gas, electricity, swimming baths, housing and trams and buses. The Labour Party, in opposition, frequently mounted strenuous objections to his demands for 'stringent economy' in running them but the Liberals tended to support him. Two areas where he was prepared to see money spent were on better water provision and a new teacher-training college. Many opposed Wilson's advocacy of a new reservoir and Alderman Armstrong, the Labour leader, claimed that his opponent had water on the brain. But the council agreed that something had to be done to improve the quality of teachers in the city. In 1907 Leeds opened a new college for teachers in temporary premises before students moved to a new campus at Beckett Park in 1912.

It would be easy to see Wilson as a reactionary, always suspicious of new ideas that made demands on the public purse but he was also a visionary. As the *Yorkshire Post* noted: 'He was an idealist, a dreamer of dreams of a great future for the city.' He envisaged a Leeds where great buildings would rise up from tree-lined streets. No longer would the city be blighted by pollution, thanks to the advent of universal electricity. He saw a citizenry relaxed and contented, literally flying to work. When the government, in 1928, urged local authorities to consider the provision of aerodromes, Wilson proposed Soldiers' Field at Roundhay. But perhaps his most imaginative – and accurate – prophecy was that people would be able to 'see face to face friends and relatives who may be thousands of miles away'. He was also correct in his forecast that the river Aire – with its 'stink guaranteed to kill at a thousand yards' – would become a delightful spot for young couples 'sweet-hearting along its banks'.

Wilson was a municipal imperialist. His dream was to see Leeds extended across the North; a city sweeping eastwards from the Pennines to the sea. To this end the Sultan of Leeds, as his enemies called him, worked tirelessly. The *Leeds Weekly Citizen* believed his policy was 'to make Leeds the hub of the universe'. By 1928, unabashed, Wilson still pursued those dreams and in October that year the *Citizen* again railed against such outlandish schemes: 'He is still after more 'extensions' and frankly we are not. . . . There is plenty to do in the area which is at present inside the city boundaries.'

He launched his first campaign for municipal extension as early as 1904 and over the years slowly saw his city grow as districts as far apart as Shadwell and Seacroft, Middleton and Adel, Eccup and Austhorpe were added to his empire. But his motives rankled with neighbouring local authorities fearing that they too would be soon devoured by the Leeds leviathan. Opposition reached a peak in the dispute over the Leeds and Bradford Extension Bill of 1922 and it was during one of the hearings that Wilson made his most famous remark: 'I am Leeds'.

Opponents to the proposition classed Leeds as a 'cruel and tyrannical city' hell-bent on annexing neighbouring councils. Mr Barrand, the MP for Pudsey, declared that none of his constituents wanted to be part of Leeds. Lane Fox, the MP for Barkton Ash, argued that the bill was 'a pure case of aggrandisement of great boroughs at the expense of weaker neighbours'. Their colleagues in the Commons agreed and threw out the bill.

But Wilson was undaunted. The following year was a memorable one for him. In 1923, Charlie, as he was popularly known, was knighted in the birthday honours list. Then at a joint ceremony in the town hall, he was made an honorary LLD by the University of Leeds and Freeman of the City by his council contemporaries. That same year Arthur Wiley, the MP for Leeds Central, died and Wilson was asked to stand in the by-election. It was a mixed constituency drawing on a working-class electorate, but the votes of businessmen, and of two long established ethnic minorities in the city, the Jews and the Irish Catholics, were also important.

Wilson, now sixty-four, published a manifesto that proposed the establishment of courts to replace the reliance on strikes and lockouts in solving industrial disputes. He condemned the Labour Party's commitment to nationalization, urged a reduction in rates and taxes and declared that strikes and lockouts should be treasonable offences. Wilson may have lost the battle to extend the city but he won the battle for Westminster as his constituents presented him with a 1,700 majority. However, the political situation in the country was so volatile that there were three general elections in two years. Wilson was re-elected each time but he insisted on retaining his position as leader of Leeds City Council.

With no television and very limited radio coverage, public meetings were the only way that candidates could canvass their constituents. However, with meetings being open, would-be MPs had to face not only the cheers of their supporters but also the heckling of their opponents. Campaigns were boisterous affairs that frequently ended in fisticuffs. At Wilson's gatherings left-wingers waved red handkerchiefs, sang the 'Red Flag' and 'Tell Me the Old, Old Story' and yelled abuse. Wilson, sharp-witted and vociferous, was more than a match ridiculing them as 'lunatics' and 'silly boys'. He thrived on the cut and thrust of politics: when driving through

Holbeck with a Liberal alderman a socialist workman yelled out to the watching crowd, 'Look at the swines!' Wilson turned to his companion and smiled: 'Splendid citizen' he remarked.

In October 1924 the third of those general elections saw the country even more bitterly divided as the minority Labour government sought a stronger mandate. As he waged his campaign against E. J. C. Neep, his new opponent in Central Leeds, Wilson's meetings became unseemly battlegrounds. Chaotic scenes marred the gatherings as hooligans ran amok. Wilson thundered that the audience should 'behave like men' and all twenty stone of him threatened to take action personally.

At the polls the first-ever Labour government was heavily defeated. Wilson was returned with an increased majority and a Conservative government under Stanley Baldwin was formed. In 1926 his government would be plunged into one of the greatest emergencies the country had ever faced. It was a crisis that would see Charles Wilson once again taking the leading role locally, this time in the General Strike. The dispute originated in the mining industry where mine owners believed that a reduction in pay and an increase in hours were necessary. Trade unionists feared that an attack on miners' wages would be the first salvo in an all-out attack on workers' wages and so, at midnight on 3 May 1926, the General Strike began. Baldwin asked for volunteers to help maintain and run public services.

Wilson spearheaded the Leeds response. He called a special council meeting on 10 May. Drawing on his experiences in the council workers' dispute a decade before, he proposed setting up a committee – three Conservatives and two Liberals – with similar delegated powers to the one that had successfully seen off the workers' challenge in 1913. This time the Liberals were divided. Wilson realised there was a real danger of a pact being drawn up between Labour and the disenchanted Liberals. He adjourned the meeting for a week.

Meanwhile the Leeds Volunteer Services committee was established with 10,000 volunteers offering their services. Leeds City

Police was supplemented by reserves. Though the *Yorkshire Post* reported that the pickets were 'by and large peaceful' violence did erupt on the city's streets. Some trams driven by strike-breakers were attacked and serious rioting was reported in central Leeds around Duncan Street, Vicar Lane and Swinegate.

The General Strike petered out after only nine days saving Wilson the embarrassment of reconvening his meeting. However, he had long recognised that the Labour Party was no longer simply a minority party hell-bent on destroying everything he valued in British society. In 1924 he had witnessed the unthinkable when Ramsay MacDonald had formed his minority Labour government. He had seen the party flex its local government muscles as it gained more and more council seats. Now he realised that Labour could even assume control of his beloved Leeds.

During the summer of 1926, he engineered a move that he hoped would ensure the Tories remained the governing party. By now the Liberals were deeply divided. Many senior figures had joined the Conservatives while the more radical had gone across to Labour. In the 1926 council elections in Leeds the Liberal Party's share of the vote tumbled by a third in just one year. Its number of seats was reduced from eighteen to eight. Previously Wilson had held the reins of power thanks to an informal alliance with the Liberals but now he saw this as his opportunity. He induced five Liberals to join the Conservatives to give him an overall majority but failed to realise the bitter reaction this would provoke. In November the infuriated Liberals, in retaliation for Wilson's scheming, decided to contest thirteen of the seventeen seats in the elections. They split the anti-Labour vote and the unthinkable occurred: Labour took control of Leeds.

That October Wilson had just gained an extremely valuable and time-consuming business contract. It was an appropriate moment to go. The same day that Labour assumed power he resigned from the council and even the *Leeds Weekly Citizen* mourned his departure from the local scene as 'a serious loss'. It would be wrong, however, to think that Wilson's resignation was regretted by everyone. Even some members of his own party were relieved at his departure, glad to be rid of his autocratic methods and brusque manner.

In Parliament, however, his vast knowledge of local government was invaluable. True to his reactionary soul he opposed giving women equal rights in guardianship over their children, arguing that 'ladies rule the house every time'. Time and again he raised the issues of unemployment, particularly as it affected Leeds and the West Riding. To ease the problem he spoke out strongly in support of local industries. He put pressure on the government to include black beer, a locally produced sweetened cordial, on a list of non-alcoholic drinks scheduled for tax reductions. When the kitchen committee of the Palace of Westminster served French fish, he was incensed that British-caught sardines were being ignored. He was all too aware that Leeds canners produced four-fifths of the nation's consumption of brisling and sardines.

In February 1928 he captivated the House over the Rabbits Bill, a scheme to eliminate the pest and its destruction of so many crops. Wilson spoke against it, arguing that rabbits provided work for 60,000 people and captivated the House with a description of how silk and bowler hats were made – not a difficult task for he was closely involved in the trade. The Rabbits Bill perished. But the tide was running against the Conservatives. In May 1929 Baldwin went to the country on a policy of 'Safety First.' Though his party polled more votes than Labour the country rejected Baldwin, and Central Leeds rejected Wilson.

However, that November, the Tories were back in power in Leeds. A vacant aldermanic seat became available and Wilson once again returned as Tory leader. It was not to last. Ten months later he left the chamber for the last time. Terminal cancer had struck. Just before the municipal elections he had been invited to the lord mayor's rooms to receive his portrait by R. G. Eves. He joked about how much it made him look like Henry VIII. In his heyday it may well have been the case, now nothing was farther from the truth. He had become a shadow of his former self. He died at 6.30 a.m. on 30 December 1930.

Tributes poured in from all sides. The *Weekly Citizen* acknowledged that he 'always stood up for what he believed was the right thing'. The *Yorkshire Observer* spoke of his 'selfless communal service'. The *Leeds Mercury* reflected that his contribution to Leeds 'can hardly be paralleled in the long and honourable history of the city'. But it was the vice-chancellor of Leeds University, Dr J. B. Baillie, who perhaps came nearest to summing up Charles Henry Wilson's life when he commented: 'There is hardly a part of the life of Leeds for the last generation in which he had not left his enduring impression.' It was a fair observation and a fitting epitaph.

16

THE YORKSHIRE WITCH

Late at night, on Monday 20 March 1809, a large crowd gathered outside Leeds General Infirmary. They were waiting eagerly for the arrival of a hearse and its grisly load. It was near midnight when the wagon finally turned into Infirmary Street. The spectators strained to get a glimpse of its contents: the corpse of a small, neat-looking, 41-year-old woman; the body of Mary Bateman. The most infamous female the town had ever known had paid the price for her crimes on the gallows at York. Now she was back in the place where she had perpetrated much of her villainy for her body to be dissected by surgeons. The journey had taken hours and the *York Herald* described how the York to Leeds road had been congested with pedestrians, horses, carriages and gigs returning from her execution. It was a road lined with ogling spectators hoping to catch a glimpse of the witch's remains.

According to the *Leeds Intelligencer*, the next day 2,400 Leeds folk paid three pence for admittance to the surgeon's room at the hospital to gaze at the body of the woman whose doings as a witch had been surpassed only by her reputation as a poisoner. As they left, many touched the corpse hoping that its magical powers would aid them in some way. Others, fearful that her miraculous potency might have triumphed over death, tried to ensure that Mary's spirit would not return to haunt their dreams by brushing their hands against her corpse.

When William Hey dissected her cadaver in a series of twelve public lectures, the crowds still came to view, and the surgeon raised £80 14s. for Leeds General Infirmary. In a matter of weeks, the *Leeds Mercury* booklet on Mary and her doings sold 10,000 copies at a time when the population of the town and its out-townships was only 60,000. And the fascination has continued right up to the present day. Almost two hundred years after her death people still stand in the Thackray Medical Museum in Leeds and stare at her skeletal remains. Her face, which forensic experts have so effectively recreated, silently gazes back and the viewer is left to ponder on the dark forces at work within her.

What was the source of the charm that duped so many gullible Leeds people and generated such interest? One thing is certain; she was very much a product of her age. Leeds was experiencing the birth of the Industrial Revolution as factories like Gott's and Marshall's transformed the textile industry. Sophisticated society enjoyed balls at the Assembly Rooms, concerts in the elegant Music Hall on Albion Street and borrowed books from the Leeds Library at its new premises on Commercial Street. Most of the wealthy citizens of Leeds lived in splendid homes to the west of the town in places like Park Row and Park Place, while many tradesmen occupied homes in St Peter's Square.

The working classes tended to inhabit the slums east of the parish church, particularly in an area known as the Bank. Poverty was ever-present as war with France created periods of unemployment and reduced many to subsistence levels. This, for a time, was Mary's home. Yet despite her surroundings, she was a clean person who dressed carefully. She showed none of the vulgarity of many of her neighbours and kept a tidy house. When she spoke, her words were soft and sincere. Her husband John, a wheelwright, was a sober, hardworking man. For sixteen years he worked for the same employer and never missed a day unless it was absolutely necessary.

The area was riddled with crime and drunkenness. Murder, assault, disorderly behaviour, rape, theft, burglary, forgery and vandalism were dealt with by the magistrates in the Rotation Office in Kirkgate. The culprits were then sent either to the House of Correction at Wakefield or, for more serious crimes, to the assizes at

York. Prostitution and illegitimacy were major problems and abortions were regularly carried out in the back streets. But sometimes suicide seemed to be the only solution for the distraught mother-to-be. Sarah Furnish, a young Leeds servant girl, was typical: finding herself pregnant, and with no one to turn to, she took herself down to Leeds Bridge early one morning in June 1800. There she threw herself into the river and perished in the murky waters.

Most people, living out their bleak lives, found no comfort in religion. Some saw atheism as the only reality in a pitiless world. Others, more simple-minded, turned to superstition and magic. Particularly vulnerable were servant girls who believed that magic potions and the hidden secrets of the stars could lead to happiness or at least to a husband. It was these gullible people that Mary Bateman so shrewdly exploited. In 1806, the *Leeds Mercury* reported a strange phenomenon. It claimed that an anonymous prophetess living on the Bank had a wondrous hen which, on payment of a penny, laid an egg with the words, 'CrisT is coming' clearly visible on it. The hen, of course, belonged to Mary.

On one occasion she went to York where she worked her charms on an old widow who offered Mary a bed for a time and made her welcome. However, when the hostess refused to drink some mutton broth her new lodger had prepared, Mary decided to leave. Only later did the old woman discover that her money and many of her clothes had left at the same time! In the light of subsequent events, however, the widow was fortunate; far more fortunate then Rebecca Perigo of Bramley.

It was Rebecca Perigo's untimely end that finally brought about Mary's downfall. It began with the innocent visit of a relative on a peaceful Whit Sunday morning in June 1806. When Sarah Stead, a young servant girl, walked up from Leeds to Bramley to see her aunt, 48-year-old Rebecca Perigo, she little realised that she was about to set in motion a series of events that would lead to murder and bring to light a series of crimes that shocked the whole country.

Sarah found her aunt Rebecca in poor health, complaining of a fluttering in her side which a country doctor had said was the result of an 'evil wish' being laid on her. The young girl listened sympathetically and then announced that she had heard of a woman, though she did not know her name, who lived in Black Dog Yard on the Bank and who could cure her. Sarah immediately made her way to Mary Bateman's house. Mary said she knew of someone who could help but the lady would need a flannel petticoat, or any garment worn next to the skin by Rebecca, if a cure was to be found.

Naturally, William Perigo, a local clothier, was concerned about his wife's health. In their twenty years of marriage she had never ailed and he was prepared to consider anything that would cure her. He duly took the petticoat to Mary, who said she would send it to the mysterious Miss Blythe in Scarborough. It more probably found its way to a pawnbroker's. Perigo then began to receive letters from Miss Blythe and these enabled Mary systematically to fleece the gullible couple of almost everything they owned.

In April 1807, the Perigos received a letter to say that they would be taken ill in May. However, they were to add six powders sent by Miss Blythe into a pudding mixture. These were to be added at the rate of one per day and the pudding eaten for six consecutive days. On no account should the boy who ate with them have any and their door must be kept locked for fear an enemy would come and overpower them. Should they feel ill, they should take some honey from a jar Mary Bateman would provide. Unknown to them it contained the deadly poison, corrosive sublimate (mercuric chloride).

On Monday 11 May they began to eat the pudding. For five days nothing untoward happened but on the Saturday, having mixed in the sixth powder, they were both overcome with nausea and, as instructed, turned to the honey jar. William took two spoonfuls, his wife six or seven. For twenty-four hours she continued vomiting violently but refused to call a doctor as this was contrary to Miss Blythe's instructions. Rose Howgate, a neighbour, came to help and by Wednesday William was beginning to recover and managed to ride to see Mr Chorley, a Leeds surgeon. He concluded that the symptoms suggested poisoning. Rebecca, however, still refused medical help and her condition deteriorated. Her tongue swelled, her mouth became black, she developed a raging thirst, lost her strength and just after noon on 24 May 1807, she died.

Perigo confronted Mary with the doctor's comments, but Mary vehemently denied any impropriety. She was so convincing that Perigo believed her. Miss Blythe was not to be put off. Further letters continued to arrive from Scarborough over the next year. By September 1808 Perigo had lost virtually everything. Beset by creditors, he told his friends John Rogerson and Joshua Stockdale what had happened.

On 20 October, Perigo arranged to meet Mary near a bridge on the Leeds and Liverpool Canal to have the matter out. When she met him, William Duffield, the chief constable of Leeds, was there too. She was found to have a bottle containing arsenic in her possession. Mary was arrested and sent to the House of Correction in Wakefield and then to the castle at York to await trial at the assizes. A search of her house produced many articles that had belonged to the Perigos.

The public was horrified. Joseph Rogerson, John's brother and a Bramley fulling miller, reflected local sentiment in his diary. 'She is the deepest monster of a woman I ever heard of' he wrote and then made his home available to two magistrates, Thomas Tennant, the mayor of Leeds, and Benjamin Gott, in order that they could examine various witnesses from the township.

The press leapt on the story. According to the *Leeds Intelligencer* Mary Bateman was a 'rogue and a vagabond' guilty of the 'grossest villainy' and described how the eggs from her miraculous hen had been 'most cruelly forced back into the hen's body'. By 7 November she had become 'Bateman the Witch' who for years had exploited the 'lower classes' and in particular 'female servants'. The *Leeds Mercury* was equally scathing about the 'the diabolical arts' practised by Mary Bateman and went on to describe 'the Witch and the Dupes'; the cases in which Mary had been involved. Only now did these come to light as dozens of people came forward with stories of her misdeeds. In view of the publicity, it is difficult to see how any Yorkshire jury could not have been influenced by the press reports.

Mary did not hail from Leeds. She was born Mary Harker in 1768. Her birthplace was the small North Riding village of Aisenby in the parish of Topcliffe five miles north of Boroughbridge. Like many in the area her parents were livestock farmers. They were hardworking, respectable souls with little idea that the child they had reared would become one of the most infamous women featured in the *Newgate Calendar* or, as Edward Baines's booklet, published by the *Leeds Mercury* claimed, the perpetrator of actions, 'almost unrivalled in the annals of British atrocities'.

At about twelve years of age Mary moved to the market town of Thirsk. Among its population of 2,000 was a considerable smattering of professional gentlemen and independent ladies. Here she found employment for seven years as a servant. However, she moved from one employer to another and around 1787 found herself again in service, but this time in York. Here she began living with a dressmaker and had the aptitude to learn the trade. But in 1788 she suddenly left the city, leaving behind both her clothes and her wages and made her way to Leeds. Popular gossip had it that she had left in disgrace having been discovered pilfering but there is no evidence of this.

When she arrived in Leeds she found employment making dresses and supplemented her income by 'witchcraft', as the press later described it, though in all probability it was no more than fortune-telling. In 1792 Mary met John Bateman, a Thirsk wheelwright, who was by now working in Leeds and, following a whirlwind courtship of three weeks, they married. They took lodgings in High Court Lane off the Calls but shortly after her first foray into crime the Bateman family moved. Between 1792 and 1808 they had six or seven homes. From High Court Lane she and her husband went to a Mr Wells's yard, and from there to Marsh Lane near Timble Bridge. By 1806 they were renting a house in Black Dog Yard on the Bank, home of the divinely inspired hen. It was here that William

Perigo originally met her. But press publicity about her exploits with the egg forced the next move to Meadow Lane and finally to Camp Field off Water Lane, where she was living when arrested.

Once the press released the details of her apprehension more of her doings became known. Many of her crimes were ineptly executed. Her first theft in Leeds was from a lodger named Dixon. It resulted in her giving back the two guineas she had taken. Her trick to swindle a butcher boy out of a leg of mutton ended with her being traced and forced to pay for the meat. By using the services of the mysterious (and wholly fictitious) 'Mrs Moore' she claimed she could prevent a Mrs Greenwood from committing suicide. As Mrs Greenwood had no intention of doing any such thing, Mary's attempt at fraud ended in failure. On another occasion, for a sum of two guineas, she was employed to divert paternity away from a natural father by witchcraft. The child was born, the man was named and Mary was forced to return the fee. It was yet another fiasco in a litany of criminal failures.

Some of her crimes were bizarre. She forged a letter purporting to come from Thirsk stating that her husband's father – the local sexton and town crier – was dangerously ill. She knew John Bateman would immediately down tools and go to comfort the dying man. She knew, too, that he would find the old man in perfect health. When Bateman got back to Leeds he discovered that their home had been stripped. Mary had sold everything, and kept the money but what she did with it is not clear. Yet despite this John Bateman continued to live with his wife.

Mary was aware that her apparent openness and sincerity appealed to people eager to hear the things she was saying. But her soothsaying skills soon gave way to sorcery and the legend of the Yorkshire Witch was born. She wove her web imaginatively, often involving Mrs Moore and later the similarly mysterious, and equally fictitious, Miss Blythe.

Some of her crimes were simple thefts, usually things that could be easily pawned: a watch taken from the Anchor Inn; clothes off a hedge; even the clothes of her husband and relatives.

Twice she worked the same confidence trick on two unsuspecting milliners. She went to their shops asking for a sample of different materials for two women who existed only in Mary's imagination; a Miss Stephenson and a Mrs Smith. Yet the gullible shopkeepers obliged her.

Some of her crimes, however, were heartless. In February 1796, the *Leeds Intelligencer* reported that Marshall's new mill on Water Lane had been engulfed by fire, a wall had collapsed and seven people were killed. Several others were injured. Among the dead was Robert Oastler's son, also called Robert, whose brother was the more famous Richard, later to become known as the 'Factory King'. Mary approached a well-known local benefactress, a Miss Maude, with the sad tale that the mother of a child who had been killed in the accident did not even have a pair of sheets in which to lay the youngster. Miss Maude obliged and Mary went straight to a local pawnbroker with the sheets. She then walked around the town claiming to be a nurse from Leeds Infirmary and begged people to contribute sheets for dressing the wounds of the injured.

Her manipulation of the wife of Barzillai Stead, a failed Leeds businessman, was particularly callous. First Mary spread rumours that Stead was having an affair with a woman from Vicar Lane. She then warned him that the bailiffs were on his track and so, to escape, he left his pregnant wife and sought refuge in the militia. Mary then proceeded to induce the simple-minded wife gradually to sell everything in the house including furniture and clothes. Even the money granted to the now nearly destitute woman by the Leeds Benevolent Society was purloined in the name of the fictitious Mrs Moore. Mary assured Barzillai Stead that Mrs Moore would prevent further disasters. But a disaster did occur. When a pregnant unmarried relative arrived at the Stead house, Mary undertook the abortion and prescribed certain medicines. The abortion was successful but the girl herself was taken ill, wasted away and died.

In 1803, she inveigled herself into the confidence of two young sisters; the Misses Kitchen, Quaker linen-drapers of St Peter's

Square. In early September, one of the sisters became ill. Mary took on the responsibility of feeding her and providing her with medicine from a 'country doctor'. The young woman's condition deteriorated. Her mother came from Wakefield to nurse her daughter but by the time she arrived the young woman was dead. Then both the mother and the remaining daughter developed similar symptoms. Mary quickly spread the rumour that they had been stricken by plague, knowing that people would give the house a wide berth. Within ten days mother and both daughters had succumbed. A doctor was called and, although he recognised that cholera was a possible cause of death, he suspected poison. But having no authority to conduct an autopsy, the bodies were interred and their secret buried with them. Of course, Mary stripped the house and the drapery of everything of value.

In April 1807, Judith Cryer, an old washerwoman, became concerned about the behaviour of her 11-year-old grandson. A friend, Winifred Bond, recommended Mary Bateman. Mary said she would contact Miss Blythe in Scarborough for guidance. Miss Blythe warned that the youngster was doomed to end his days on the gallows unless four guineas were secreted in a leather bag to remain untouched until the boy was fourteen. Needless to say when the bag was finally opened the money had long since been spirited away.

A year later, the wife of John Snowden, Mary's neighbour on Water Lane, developed an irrational fear that one of her children would be drowned. Once again Mary was consulted and the mysterious Miss Blythe contacted. This time the advice was that Mary should sew up Snowden's silver watch in his bed along with several magic charms. On Saturday 22 October, Snowden was enjoying a drink in a Bradford public house and listening to one customer read out loud the report in the *Leeds Mercury* of the arrest of Mary Bateman. As he listened to the catalogue of frauds she had committed Snowden became alarmed. He raced home, ripped the bed apart and, as he feared, found that his watch had disappeared. It was discovered later in Bateman's house.

The trial of Mary Bateman began at York Assizes on Friday 17 March 1809 before Sir Simon le Blanc. The court was so crowded that the judge himself had difficulty in making his way to the bench. John Hardy, the Recorder of Leeds, laid out the case against Mary and then a string of witnesses followed. Sarah Stead, the young niece of the Perigos, testified about Mary's role in her aunt's death. Willliam Perigo, the second witness, gave a meticulous account of the subsequent events. He claimed he was able to quote, virtually verbatim, a series of letters he had received both by post and by hand delivery from Miss Blythe. Most had been destroyed.

Winifred Bond said she worked for Bateman, delivering letters for her, but then Mary had ordered her to go and live at Haworth, which she did. The bemused judge asked why, to be told that Winifred was afraid of Mary's supernatural powers. Rose Howgate and Mary Perigo described the symptoms Rebecca Perigo had exhibited. John Rogerson and Joshua Stockdale confirmed the tale about the empty bags. William Duffield took the jury through the arrest and the discovery of so many of Perigo's articles at the Bateman home. Mr Clough, a druggist from Kirkgate, remembered refusing to sell 4d. of arsenic to two boys, Thomas Gristy and Jack Bateman, Mary's son. Thomas Chorley, a local surgeon, testified that the poisons found were in all probability 'metallic or mineral poison'.

Mary offered no defence other than to claim she was not guilty. Mr Hemingway, a local solicitor, read out the statement she had made before Edward Markland, a Leeds magistrate, in January. In it she categorically denied the charges. The judge summed up the case and the jury decided not to retire but to make up its mind in the jury box. It was by now nine o'clock at night. The foreman, John Ellerby, announced the verdict of guilty and the judge then passed sentence. She was to be hanged and her body given to the surgeons for dissection. There were those in society who believed that that was a fate even worse than hanging.

In an attempt to delay the inevitable Mary, who was still suckling a child in prison, contended that she was pregnant again. The judge immediately ordered married women in the court to be empanelled to discover the truth. Several women quickly made for the exits rather than be involved but the judge ordered the doors locked. The panel found Mary was not 'with quick child'. She was conveyed to the castle prison to await execution.

John Talbot, the *Leeds Mercury* reporter who had pioneered court reporting in Yorkshire, dashed off to Leeds with his deadline only a couple of hours away. The *Mercury* was published on a Saturday morning but he managed to get his furiously scribbled report of about a hundred and seventy words to the office in time for the presses. The next day people in Leeds were reading about the verdict. The following week Baines, the editor, devoted three and a half columns to a full report of the case.

Mary spent the weekend in peaceful meditation, joined the ordinary (the prison chaplain), Revd George Brown, in his devotions, but refused to admit murder. Her husband failed to visit her once the verdict had been announced but Mary wrote him a letter apologising for the disgrace she had brought on her family by her confidence tricks, enclosed her wedding ring to be given to their daughter but emphatically denied murdering Rebecca Perigo. She then continued to suckle her baby and touched the hearts of the guards with her caring manner. But Mary continued to be Mary. One young female prisoner was desperate to see her boyfriend and Mary produced a suitable charm. Needless to say, the young woman found herself out of pocket.

They woke Mary at five o'clock on the Monday morning and from then she prayed devotedly in preparation for what was to come. At eleven o'clock she was taken outside the walls of York castle to the New Drop where a crowd of 5,000 had gathered. The more credulous wondered if she might, as the *Intelligencer* reported, 'fly off the scaffold in a cloud'. The crowd fell silent as Mary and Joseph Brown – a soldier convicted of the murder of Elizabeth Fletcher of Hensal near Ferrybridge – were taken onto the platform. Mary's last act on earth was to declare her innocence.

Thus died Mary Bateman, the Yorkshire Witch; a warning to the gullible and a gold mine for newspapers. Her story had everything: magic, scandal and murder. On 1 April Edward Baines of the *Leeds Mercury* went into partnership with John Davies to publish a booklet entitled *Extraordinary Life and Character of MARY BATEMAN, the Yorkshire Witch, traced from the earliest thefts of her infancy, through a most awful course of crimes and murders, till her execution at the New Drop, near the Castle of York, on Monday the Twentieth of March, 1809.*

The cost was a shilling, but Baines claimed to have the public's interest at heart. His reason was clear: 'to hold her up as a Beacon both to the present and future ages; to deter some from treading in her footsteps'. To this end he offered employers, wishing to place bulk orders for their workforces, copies at 9*d.* a dozen. It was a masterstroke. In four days some 1,000 copies were sold. In two months 7,000 copies had been bought and eventually sales of 10,000 were recorded. Such was the demand that in 1811 Davies decided to publish a twelfth edition on his own while two other publishers, Webb and Millington of Briggate and J. Johnson of Kirkgate, produced similar booklets. Publishers in both Birmingham and Easingwold also became involved.

The story of Mary Bateman has captivated the people of Leeds for two centuries. It showed the press and public at their worst, and their best. Both were horrified by her crimes. But at the same time the people of Leeds were prepared to be titillated as they watched her hang, stroked her corpse and read of her nefarious activities. The Leeds press was quick to exploit that ghoulish obsession, ostensibly in the name of public service, but in reality to make a considerable profit.

17

ARNOLD ZIFF: MAN OF LEEDS

Leeds today is wealthy and diverse, a diversity enriched by the various groups who have settled there. No group has made a greater impact than the Jews. Men like Herman Friend, Montague Burton and Michael Marks are beacons of progress and, through their endeavours, they have left Leeds a far better place than they found it. No man deserves to stand alongside them more than Arnold Ziff, whose benevolence over the years has touched virtually every citizen in the city.

During the 1880s Polish and Russian Jews fled their homelands as pogroms swept Eastern Europe following the murder of Tsar Alexander II. Jews from a cluster of villages in Lithuania were part of that diaspora. They made their way from the Baltic ports and finally arrived at Hull and Goole. From there they travelled west, some intending to make for Liverpool and then the United States. Others reached Leeds and decided to settle in the slum area known as the Leylands. By 1891 there were some eight thousand Jews in the town, most of them employed in tailoring.

Over the years others followed, often heading for the places where their relatives had settled. At the beginning of the twentieth century the young Max Ziff left his home in Russia and also headed west. His destination was Leeds, for there his great-uncle had a clothing business. Max worked in the clothes shop until 1914 when an assassin's bullet in far-off Sarajevo heralded the start of the First World War. He quickly joined up.

At this time the manufacture of boots and shoes was a major industry in Leeds. The industry had been established about 1860 and as the population increased, production of boots and shoes amounted to 40,000 pairs a week; by 1890 some eight thousand people were employed in the trade. Although the bulk of the Jewish population of working age was employed in tailoring half of the rest found work in the footwear industry.

This may have been the link that had encouraged Max Ziff's aunt to open a shoe shop in the working-class district of Holbeck in 1917. It was a fortuitous choice. Domestic Street was some miles from the Leylands where that year an outbreak of anti-Semitism blighted the city. A violent riot ensued and Jewish properties in the area were vandalised and looted. However, the shoe shop in Domestic Street was unscathed and by the end of the war was so busy that she was able to employ her three brothers. It would become one of the most famous shoe retailing companies in Britain. Max's aunt sought a suitable name for her company and found it on a fountain pen! Stylo was born.

With the end of hostilities Max returned to the family firm. The company prospered and the family prospered too. In 1927 Max became the proud father of a son, Israel Arnold. Jews have always set great store by education and Arnold was sent to primary school and then moved up to Roundhay School, a grammar school in the north of Leeds run by the council. It had only just opened but offered a wide-ranging curriculum. Just what its impact on young Arnold Ziff was is hard to say. He regularly boasted that whilst he was there he was one of the most consistent of its scholars – consistently bottom of the class! In the school holidays he was expected to help in the growing family firm. He did so, unpacking shoe cartons. But the firm certainly was growing and with Max Ziff now in charge it was floated on the Stock Exchange in 1935.

However, Arnold's academic achievements at Roundhay cannot have been as bad as he made out. When he left school he was accepted by Leeds University where he read economics. But events beyond his control intervened. In 1939 Hitler invaded Poland and Britain declared war on Germany. From June 1941 Stylo, like all British manufacturers, was affected by rationing.

Clothing coupons were needed to buy a pair of boots or shoes – seven coupons for adults and three for children. Arnold, however, felt his responsibilities lay elsewhere. Like his father before him he joined the armed forces.

He was posted to the Royal Army Ordnance Corps and in many ways it provided him with invaluable experience for a career in business. The main responsibility of the regiment was the supply of equipment; anything from ammunition to laundries, vehicles to clothing factories. His natural abilities were soon recognised and by the end of the Second World War he had reached the rank of staff sergeant. It was a position he enjoyed, not least because he found himself in charge of postings, including his own. With a touch of humour he decided to post himself to Europe, to Paris in fact, where he developed a wide-ranging knowledge of fine wines.

When he was demobilised he returned to Leeds. In 1948 he joined his father in the family business. Like all successful companies Stylo needed to expand. These were difficult years for retailers because of rationing and the effects of six years of war on the British economy. It was decided to develop new outlets and Arnold Ziff was given the responsibility of finding them. It was a decision that would have a significant impact on his life and on the lives of thousands of others. A quietly spoken man – he never shouted – he was a shrewd analyst of real estate with a great ability to identify profitable sites. Thus it was that in 1959 he decided to set up Town Centre Securities with capital of £1,000. Eighteen months later he floated it on the Stock Exchange, at which time the company was valued at £250,000.

Then Ziff's new company decided upon a bold new venture. Leeds had been famous as a shopping centre from its earliest days. For centuries people from the surrounding townships had flocked to its twice-weekly market and by 1900 the town was looked on as the shopping Mecca of the North. It was popular not only for its numerous shopping arcades but also because its shops were concentrated into a surprisingly small area. It stretched no more than a mile from Vicar Lane to City Square and no more than half a mile from Boar Lane to the Headrow. In this compact area the great department stores and shops of Leeds flourished.

The council drew up its development plan for the area north of the Headrow in 1951 and contemplated building a new bus station and a multi-storey car park on Merrion Street. The plan fell through and in the early 1960s Arnold Ziff had a vision. His Town Centre Securities would create a huge, covered shopping-complex on the Merrion Street site. It would be the biggest in the country. Local people shook their heads and prophesied doom. It was too far out. People would never use it, they argued.

Nevertheless he went ahead. By 1963 most of the building had been completed and on 26 May 1964 his wife, Marjorie, officially opened the Merrion Centre. Apart from its wide range of stores it included the Merrion Hotel and, from 1968, the studios of BBC Radio Leeds. However, it was not a success at first. People did find it too far out and winds often whipped through the malls. However, Arnold Ziff persisted. Then with the building a little later of the St John's Centre immediately on the north side of the Headrow, a shopping link was created between the Merrion Centre and the rest of the city's stores. Since then it has become one of the major shopping centres of Leeds.

Meanwhile Stylo, under Ziff's chairmanship, has continued to grow. Today the Bradford-based company has over six hundred stores nationwide, partly due to a shrewd acquisition. Stylo had a strong base in the North. The Northampton-based Barratt's was a southern-based shoe company with a good reputation. During the war its adverts, 'Walk the Barratt way' became as famous as 'My Goodness my Guinness' and 'Did you MacLean your teeth today?' However, in 1964 Barratts was threatened with a hostile takeover when Charles Clore and his British Shoe Corporation tried to take control. Stylo stepped in and battle was joined and, eventually, Arnold Ziff prevailed and Barratt's became part of the Stylo group. It was decided to use the Barratt name for retailing and Stylo for wholesaling. The company continued to expand. On top of the 225 Barratt's stores, it now operates 250 concessions in Dorothy Perkins and 125 discount-footwear outlets. In 2003 Shelly's chain of footwear outlets was added to the company's portfolio, taking its assets to £60 million with a turnover of £200 million and 5,799 staff. It had come along way from a small shop on Domestic Street.

Although chairman of Stylo until 2003, the bulk of Arnold Ziff's fortune came from Town Centre Securities, which was involved in imaginative projects like the development of Manchester's Rochdale canal basin. In 2004 the *Sunday Times* rich list placed Arnold Ziff as the 377th richest person in Britain, and among the ten richest in Yorkshire. If that had been the whole story it would still have been worth telling. But success in business, admirable as it is, was not the main reason the citizens of Leeds came to respect and admire Ziff. His life was one of selfless dedication to the people of the city and owed much to the support he received from his wife Marjorie.

In 1888 the city celebrated the opening of the Leeds Art Gallery. A hundred years later it was in a sorry state and urgently needed refurbishment. Leeds had played a significant part in the development of modern art. Both Jacob Kramer, the artist, and Henry Moore, the sculptor, studied at the Leeds School of Art and by the 1950s it was said that this institution was to the post-war art world what the Bauhaus had been in Weimar Germany between the wars. Arnold and Marjorie Ziff decided to help finance the refurbishment and to build an extension to the sculpture gallery. The Henry Moore Sculpture Gallery now houses works by Moore, Epstein and Barbara Hepworth, among others, and was opened by the Queen in 1982.

If the people of Leeds could be proud of the city's art, they were less enamoured of Yorkshire's performances on the cricket field in the 1980s. Once synonymous with success, the county now languished in the doldrums. To reverse the decline it decided to open a cricket school at Headingley. Arnold Ziff saw the need, sold the key building to the county at a reduced price and then paid for much of the conversion.

He was a regular at charity functions and one day he was present at one held by the lord mayor. He heard of a dramatic proposal being discussed to establish a tropical world, a Kew Gardens of the North, at Canal Gardens at Roundhay. It would also include tropical creatures: there would be a butterfly house with thirty to forty species of butterflies flitting through the citrus trees and exotic plants. In the aquariums, there would be angelfish and red-tailed sharks. In the Amazonian zone, golden lion tamarins would share the environment with screeching macaws. In the desert zone, canaries and finches would fly about freely while arachnids, lizards and snakes shared the insect zone. One of the most imaginative ideas was the nocturnal zone where, through the dim twilight, owl monkeys, Egyptian fruit bats and giant jumping rats would be spotted by the eagle-eyed. Ziff listened with interest to the proposal. The very next day the parks department received a cheque for £30,000. The overall cost was estimated at £1 million and it was reached in no small measure because of a further contribution of £250,000 from Arnold and Marjorie Ziff. When a plaque was put up at the opening acknowledging their contribution, Ziff appeared quite put out: 'Why did you do that?' he asked. Tropical World is still one of the most popular of all the attractions in the city.

Another project he was involved in was raising funds for a body scanner for St James's Hospital. At the time very few existed in the country and it was radiologist Hans Herlinger who persuaded Ziff to come to Israel with him to see the new device. The projected cost of £1 million was no deterrent to the great man. Working with the *Yorkshire Post* and a group of like-minded friends he raised the sum in just six months. He had one proviso, however. As the people of Leeds had raised the money, the people of Leeds should be able to use it free of charge.

Arnold Ziff was a Leeds man and never forgot his roots. He was a keen supporter of both universities in the city. He endowed a chair in retailing at Leeds Metropolitan University and always maintained a close contact with his Alma Mater, the University of Leeds, helping to set up its new business school on the site of the former Leeds Grammar School. He remained one of the university's staunchest supporters, presenting it with an £80,000 Steinway only months before he died. He was a member of the university council and frequently chaired fundraising committees. 'My involvement with Leeds University has given me more pleasure than anything' he once remarked.

But his support for Leeds extended far beyond the university. He was active in the campaign to bring the Royal Armouries Museum to the city and his ongoing support for the Leeds International Pianoforte Competition was described by the organiser, Fanny Waterman, as 'legendary'. To that end the Marjorie and Arnold Ziff Charitable Trust provided the second-prize medal and £6,000.

The Chief Rabbi, Dr Jonathan Sachs described him as 'One of Anglo-Jewry's most outstanding figures . . . His life was marked by pride in his Jewish identity, love of Judaism and the Jewish people.' But Arnold Ziff was a man who tolerated people of all faiths and none. In 1994, when the Leeds Parish Church launched a restoration appeal, he became a trustee of the fund. Perhaps his toleration was best exemplified on a drive through London with a friend. On their way the car passed an infamous gay club. His friend passed a comment on how distasteful it was. Ziff simply responded, 'I just don't know why you can't live and let live.'

People mattered to Arnold Ziff. That was apparent at the Queen's Hotel, which he used frequently. He knew the first names of almost all the waiters and waitresses. But he also cared deeply for those less fortunate than himself. To that end he supported charities like the NSPCC and both the Lionheart and Variety Club of Great Britain. He also championed the Leeds Jewish Welfare Board by helping to redevelop its Queenshill day centre, which catered for people with disabilities.

This 'no-nonsense and gritty Yorkshire style' businessman, as *The Times* described him, did not have a lavish lifestyle. It is true he enjoyed being chauffer-driven in his Rolls Royce but he also liked driving himself in a small family car. He enjoyed art, collecting silver buckles and had a passion for automata; he particularly liked those of his friend Rowland Emmett whose whimsical mechanical devices he often displayed in the Merrion Centre. He sat on the boards of both the Leeds Permanent and Halifax Building Societies and, as one of the city's leading entrepreneurs, played a significant role in turning Leeds into a major financial centre. He sat as a magistrate for thirty years and was a patron of the Civic Trust. For his services to the community, he was awarded an OBE in the Queen's Birthday honours list in 1981 and for his contribution to education he received honorary doctorates from the University of Leeds in 1993 and from Leeds Metropolitan University in 2003. In 2000 he was presented with a special lifetime achievement at the Yorkshire Awards Ceremony in recognition of his success, his support for the arts and his major contribution to charities in the city.

His success was, in no small way, a result of the support he received from Marjorie, his wife of fifty-two years. He was proud of his family and was close to his three children and thirteen grandchildren. He died on 14 July 2004.

It is difficult to assess the contribution of Arnold Ziff to Leeds. He is remembered there not just as a successful businessman but also as a great philanthropist. The people of the city recognised him as a man with a keen sense of humour and one who showed integrity in his dealings. But he was also a man who cared, a man who used his own success to benefit others. He touched the lives of so many people in so many ways. Whether it be studying at the university or undergoing a body scan, whether it be enjoying the artistic excellence of the Leeds Piano Competition, sauntering round the art gallery or Royal Armouries, watching the flitting butterflies in the tropical gardens at Roundhay or scuttling around the Merrion Centre, Arnold Ziff's presence is unavoidable. As Mark Harris, leader of Leeds City Council said, 'Arnold Ziff's death is a great loss to this city.' Indeed it was and perhaps a memorial should be erected in his memory.

But in some ways that is unnecessary. The memorial already exists and will last far longer than any stone sculpture. It exists in the institutions he supported, the projects he masterminded and the rich legacy he bestowed upon the city, a legacy that generations yet unborn will go on enjoying. As long as Leeds can produce men of the quality of Arnold Ziff, the city need have no fears for its future.

18

THE GAMES WE PLAYED

The modern world has brought great change to the lives of our children. The fear of paedophiles means that children today are carefully watched by their parents. Much of their time is spent watching television, playing on computers and with manufactured toys. During the first half of the twentieth century, however, it was normal for children to play outside, go to school on their own and make up games. In Leeds there were those lucky enough to have gardens in which to play, or who lived close to the open spaces of Roundhay Park, Temple Newsam or Golden Acre. For thousands of others the back-to-backs were their playground.

In sport, football and cricket tended to dominate. They were often played in the street. Wickets were chalked on lavatory walls or on the gable ends of houses and boundaries were agreed: the lamp post by the fish-and-chip shop was the offside boundary; the old church wall the onside boundary. One-handed catches were needed if the ball bounced off a wall; hit it into Mrs So-and-So's lavatory yard and it was six and out. Umpiring disputes were settled simply; the batsman had to score three runs off the next two balls. If he did he stayed in, if not he was out. Football goals would be drawn on two opposite walls.

There was much improvisation on open ground. Something would be provided to use as a set of wickets but a brick or coat marked the bowler's end. Pads were a luxury and, if worn, were usually worn on the left leg only. The wicket keeper had to use a coat to stop the ball speeding past. He needed it. Playing on these open spaces a hard 'corkie' ball would be used. A tennis ball was preferred in the streets. It was less likely to break a window!

Football played on waste ground saw old coats used for goalposts. Any size of ball was used but the bigger the better. Whoever provided it became captain of one of the teams. Old Arthur Tate reminisced over sixty years later how he had never achieved that distinction. He had never had a ball good enough to be played with until one Christmas. Then he was given a large rubber ball, which was ideal. Triumphantly he took it to show his pals but what a disappointment was in store. Another boy in the gang had been given a brand-new leather football. Of course the boys opted to play with that and Arthur's ball became no more than the goalpost.

Rugby, always rugby league, was played less often but was popular in parts of North Leeds and south of the river, both in Holbeck and at that hotbed of the game, Hunslet. When played over the cobbles the game became touch-and-pass. In the place of scrums two boys faced each other, the ball was placed between them and they scrambled for it with their hands. These scrums were known as biskets.

Another game often played on patches of waste ground was piggy. A small piece of wood, shaped to a point at each end, was used. This was hit with a stick to make it jump into the air and the striker then hit the piggy as far he could. The opponents then gave a number to the striker who had to reach the piggy in the number of steps he had been given. Rounders, pizeball (when the hand was used instead of a rounder's bat) and French cricket were also popular and could be played either in the streets or on an open area.

Girls joined in at times but they specialised in skipping. Sometimes they skipped individually but at other times the boys would join them. Two people twirled a long rope and the rest would skip together. 'Pitch, patch, pepper' was chanted and the speed of the rope increased as each word was called out. 'All in, all out' was a variant. When 'All in' was called the waiting children all had to begin skipping. When 'All out' was called they leapt out of the rope and stopped. Anyone fouling the rope in the process had to twirl the rope next. As they skipped they chanted rhymes such as:

> Two, four, six, eight, Mary at the cottage gate,
> Eating cherries off a plate, two, four, six, eight.

One of the most popular rhymes was:

> The moon shines bright on Charlie Chaplin
> His boots are cracking for want of blacking,
> His old baggy trousers they want mending,
> Before they send him to the Dardanelles.

Some were historically inaccurate: 'Nelson lost his eye at the Battle of Waterloo'.

Others made a propaganda point:

> Whistle while you work; Hitler is a twerp.
> Goering's balmy, so's his army
> Whistle while you work.

If skipping was a traditional girl's game, so was playing doctors and nurses, and again the boys might join in. A particular girls' activity was asking the mothers of newborns if they could wheel them out in their prams. Meanwhile boys enjoyed playing soldiers. Clambering over the outbuildings of disused factories or hiding in ambush near local mills, two armies would fire endlessly at each other. When shot, a wounded soldier had to count to ten before firing again. In winter they might play in the snow at the siege of Stalingrad; in summer, as often as not, they became the Seventh Cavalry confronting Sitting Bull's Sioux. Much would depend on what was showing at the cinema. Wooden sticks made excellent swords for playing Robin Hood and a raincoat buttoned only at the neck produced a flowing cloak for a swashbuckling Zorro.

Boys and girls often played together, bounding hoops through the streets, although the girls used wooden hoops and the boys iron ones. Later, old car tyres were used. Marbles, known locally as taws, and whip and top were seasonal games. Coloured chalk-rings were drawn on the tops and when they spun they turned into a kaleidoscope of colour. Nothing was ever said yet one day a child would arrive with her whip and top and half an hour later the road was filled with children furiously doing the same thing. Conkers was another seasonal game though those who pickled them in vinegar, or baked them in the oven, were frowned upon.

Roller skating on tarmacked roads was also popular and, with few cars about, relatively safe. Bicycles too were commonly used. A piece of card stuck into the back wheel made the sound of a rasping motorbike. The ups and downs at Beeston was a favourite location for cyclists; piles of grey clay had been dumped and formed a series of humps, ideal for cycling up and over.

Hopscotch was very popular and grids were chalked on any convenient pavement, though paving stones in Leeds were always known as flags. For some reason the box at the end of the grid was labelled OXO. For the game 'Monday, Tuesday, Wednesday' a flight of steps was needed – Silver Royd Methodist Chapel was ideal as it had six steps. The top step was called Sunday and each step was named after a different day right down to Saturday at ground level. Whoever was chosen to be 'it' called out the day of the week and everyone had to jump from where they were to the step named.

Selecting who was 'it' was required for a large number of games. Dips were chanted to determine who was to be selected. A typical dip went as follows:

> One potato, two potato, three potato, four,
> Five potato, six potato, seven potato more.
> With a rotten cotton dishcloth torn in two, out goes you.

Hot rice was different. Here the children stood in a circle with their feet apart. A ball was dropped in the middle and if it rolled between your legs you were 'it'. The player dropping the ball would often apply spin, if they could get away with it, ensuring that it went through someone else's legs. That player then had to throw the ball and try to hit someone. If he succeeded the player who had been hit joined him and the two worked as a team, adding to their numbers as more people were hit. There were strict limits imposed on how far people could run and the throwers were not allowed to run with the ball.

No such limits were imposed for kick-out-ball. In this game the ball was placed on a grate, or stone, in the middle of the street. Whoever was 'it' called out a name and that child kicked the ball as far as he could. While it was being retrieved the others sped off to hide. Lavatory yards, ginnels and old walls all provided ideal spots. 'It' placed the ball back on the grate and then began searching. Once he spotted someone, he called out their name and raced to touch the ball. However, if the one whose name had been called reached the spot first, kicked the ball and shouted, 'Kick out ball!' he was free again and anyone who had been caught was also free to escape. Kick-can-and-hook-it was a variant, only with this game an old tin can was used instead of a ball. Another variation on these games was relievo. Here whoever had it had to grab hold of an individual and count ten in order to catch him. The prisoner then had to stay in the den until either some free spirit dashed in and shouted 'Relievo!' or all were caught and the first person captured then became 'it'.

Whereas kick-out-ball and relievo required people to be agile in order to escape – often swarming over lavatory roofs – other games were simply played across the street. Tig was popular but glue man, or statues, was a variation where the person tigged had to stand still with their arms outstretched. The first one caught was 'it' next time. Hopping Tommy was quite a physical game. Whoever was 'it' had to place their hands on one wall. The rest placed theirs on the wall opposite. On a given signal they had to hop across the road and reach the opposite wall. However, 'it' with his arms folded had the right to attack them, bumping into anyone and trying to force them to put both feet on the ground. Donkey was equally violent. One team bent down against a wall, the other leapt on their backs. The winner was the team that held the most people for the longest time before collapsing under the weight.

The seasons dictated many of the games played. Sledging and

sliding were obviously winter pursuits but a candle rubbed on smooth flagstones and then on the soles of the shoes enabled sliding to be enjoyed all year round. Winter provided the chance to earn some extra money. Carol singing was always popular. More energetic was snow shifting. People took a pride in the flags outside their houses. They were swilled at least once a week and when snow fell they wanted their pavements cleared. Children would go round in gangs sweeping the snow onto the roads and for their trouble were given anything from a penny to three pence.

November meant Bonfire Night. The gathering of wood, old settees or anything that would burn was known as chumping and this was carried on for a few weeks before 5 November. The chumps were often stored in a nearby yard and care had to be taken to prevent them from being stolen by rival gangs as raiding was common. The bonfire was finally assembled on the cobbles of the street but away from manhole covers and never on anything that resembled a tarmacked area. One boy, nicknamed Biggo, showed extraordinary devotion to duty. It began raining before the bonfire could be lit so he borrowed all the family's raincoats to protect it. The problem was that the raincoats were all white!

The night before Bonfire Night in Leeds was known as Mischief Night. On that night children would go round knocking on doors and running away, pushing caterpillars through letter boxes or tapping mysteriously on windows with a button rigged up on a piece of cotton. However, by the 1960s and 1970s, the pranks became outright vandalism. Garden gates were stolen, car tyres were slashed and by the beginning of the twenty-first century, it was a relief to many that Mischief Night had been replaced by the American custom of trick or treat.

Mischief, however, was part of everyday life. Throwing fireworks, though dangerous, was considered fun as Little Demons were tossed here and there. Lamp-posts were kicked to make the gas lights come on in daylight. By the 1960s some had worked out that with a magnet the newly installed electric lights could also be turned on during the day.

At times secret smoking would be arranged. Taking empty pop bottles back to the shop would realise a penny a bottle. With the proceeds five Woodbines and a box of matches could be bought. Then, hidden away in their den and away from the prying eyes of adults, the culprits smoked their illicit cigarettes.

Some activities were just cheeky. Occasionally someone would go into a fish shop and ask if they had any fish left. If the answer was 'yes' the response was, 'It's your fault for frying so many!' Another prank was to change the indicators on the trams. Tong Road was a good place to do this for at Whingate Junction the road split in two. One road, Whingate, led to the tram terminus at Charley Cake Park, the other continued as Tong Road up to the terminus at the New Inn. It was quite easy to change the indicator from '15 Whingate' to '16 New Inn'. The unsuspecting passengers wanting to go to the New Inn, and seeing the indicator, would climb aboard. The unsuspecting driver, however, knowing he was due for Whingate, would carry them off to Charley Cake Park. The uproar that followed was always a source of great amusement. Another antic involving trams was placing a penny on the line and listening for the crack as the tram ran over it.

Some pranks were dangerous but the children concerned were usually oblivious to the fact. Playing duffs and dares meant setting dangerous targets and anyone who failed was deemed a 'cowardy, cowardy custard'. At Sheepscar, for example, the duff would be to go through the tunnel that carried Sheepscar beck under the streets to the city centre. Chasing rats was just part of the game.

Other parts of Leeds would have their own duffs. Children near Heights Lane would duff to walk the railway bridge. That meant walking along the parapet of the bridge some forty to fifty feet above the ground. On other occasions it meant negotiating disused tunnels, running across railway lines, swinging over the local beck on a rope or jumping off a roof. Some boys in West Leeds walked what they dramatically termed the Death Path. This was a steep path high up the side of a local quarry that sloped at an angle of forty-five degrees. To pass along it in dry weather was difficult, in wet weather virtually impossible. When parents discovered these activities stern warnings were issued but did not prove effective for long.

Some subjects were strictly taboo and referred to in hushed tones. Sex was the main one though no-one knew exactly what it entailed. Occasionally a boy would get hold of a copy of *Men Only* and the group would gather round to look at the nudes. Smutty jokes were told, and often not understood, though everyone laughed so as not to feel out of it. Some boys swore but swearing was not common. However, when the mood took them both boys and girls chanted such rhymes as:

> Bugger, bugger, bugger; damn, damn, damn.
> Who stole my bloody new pram?
> I don't care a bugger, I'll soon buy another,
> Bugger, bugger, bugger; damn, damn, damn!

Some activities were disgusting. Boys enjoyed both spitting competitions and seeing who could urinate highest up a wall. But these activities were only part of that way of life. There were other more civilised pursuits. Blackberrying in September was popular and it was amazing how many patches of waste land, railway cuttings or open spaces sprouted brambles.

Swimming at the local baths was also a favourite pursuit. Some over-cautious mothers, however, always insisted their children could not go to the baths until they could swim! At the beginning of the twentieth century, when baths were not as readily available, many learned to swim in the polluted becks or in the canal. Old Walt Smith recalled how, as a boy, he was swimming in the canal at Rodley about the year 1900, when a barge carrying a supply of sugar sank. The water tasted sweet!

Children were willing to help others and were often given a penny for going to the shop for an adult neighbour. They helped at school by collecting waste paper or jam jars thus raising funds for the school or the war effort. Some, perhaps, were a little too enthusiastic. Moorhouse's jam factory on Old Lane at Beeston was happy to buy empty jam jars back from a local school. However, they took exception when they found that two boys were climbing into their yard on an evening, removing their own jam jars which the school, in all innocence, sold back to them!

Children were also remarkably adept at making things. An old pram could easily be turned into a bogey, while two long pieces of wood with a wooden block fastened to each became a pair of stilts. The building of rafts for use on stretches of water, such as flooded local quarries, was also tried. But every so often the drowning of a youngster deterred others, at least for a time. Simpler, but still dangerous, objects were arrows with a piece of string acting as a sling, and gas-tar bombs. The latter were made by taking a piece of stick then digging the tar from between the cobbled setts of the road. The tar added weight to the bomb when it was thrown. The problem was that gas tar, as it was always called, was difficult to get off the fingers once it was on. Lard was the only remedy!

Leeds has moved on from the days of jam-jar collections. Some things have changed for the better, others not so. A packet of five Woodbines smoked in secret was a far less dangerous activity than the drug menace facing the youth of today. Comparisons can be misleading, and the memory can play tricks, giving a much rosier glow to the past. The world of children has dramatically changed but in many ways children have not. At heart theirs is still a world of excitement and fun, a world of magic and wonder. It is a world where cynicism has not yet soured their view of life.